SYNAGOGUE OF THE SUBURBAN TORAH CENTER

CURRICULUM, COMMUNITY, COMMITMENT

*Views on the American
Jewish Day School
in Memory of Bennett I. Solomon*

CURRICULUM, COMMUNITY, COMMITMENT

*Views on the American
Jewish Day School
in Memory of Bennett I. Solomon*

edited by
**Dr. Daniel J. Margolis
Rabbi Elliot Salo Schoenberg**

BEHRMAN HOUSE, INC.
West Orange, New Jersey

© Copyright 1992 by Daniel J. Margolis
and Elliot Salo Schoenberg

Library of Congress Cataloging-in-Publication Data

Curriculum, community, commitment : views on the American Jewish day
    school in memory of Bennett I. Solomon / edited by Daniel J. Margolis
    & Elliot Salo Schoenberg.
          p.   cm.
    ISBN 0-87441-545-4
        1. Jewish day schools--United States. 2. Jewish day schools--
United States--Curricula. I. Solomon, Bennett I. II. Margolis, Daniel J.
III. Schoenberg, Elliot Salo.
LC741.C87 1993   93-2812
377'.96--dc20   CIP

CONTENTS

Acknowledgements	ix
Contributors	x
Authors	xiii
Introduction	
Daniel J. Margolis & Elliot Salo Schoenberg	xv
A Note on Bennett's Writings	xxi

I. COMMITMENTS AND PHILOSOPHY

FROM BENNETT—Prologue
Why Jewish Education for Me	3
The Challenge for the Day School	5
Judaism's Philosophy of Education:	
An Interpretation of Classical Sources	
Israel Scheffler	7
Jewish Education: Purposes, Problems	
and Possibilities	
Israel Scheffler	20

FROM BENNETT
On Rationality, Math and Moral Education	29
On Teaching Towards Cognitive Emotions:	
Joy, Surprise, Awe	30
On Creativity	33
The Elements of Education: Coincidence and	
Differences in General and Jewish	
Education	
Perry London	34

FROM BENNETT
On Success in Hebrew School and Public	
School	43
On Goals and Objectives	44
On Loyalty as our Goal	45
To Begin with Belief or Caring?	
Louis Newman	46

What Makes a Reform Day School Distinctive?
A Question of Practice and Purpose
Michael Zeldin 67

FROM BENNETT
On American and Jewish Values 78

Utilizing Research in Jewish Education and
Community Organizations:
Bridging a Cultural Gap
Susan L. Shevitz 79

II. CURRICULUM

FROM BENNETT
On Curriculum: The Sacred/Secular Dilemma ... 95
On Curriculum: Religious Symbolism in
the Curriculum 97
On Curriculum: Curriculum Innovation 99

Teaching Rabbinics in the Day School
Mark Smiley 101

Teaching Midrash in the Day School
Alvan H. Kaunfer 110

Footsteps on the Ceiling and Idols on the Floor:
Integrated Study of History and Story in the
Conservative Jewish Day School
Benjamin Edidin Scolnic 122

FROM BENNETT
On Integration 132
On Honesty in Teaching 136

Starting With Yourself: A Model for
Understanding the Jewish Holidays and
Teaching Them
Joseph Lukinsky & Lifsa Schachter 137

Integration—Doing It
Lifsa Schachter 153

FROM BENNETT
On Curriculum Implementation: Change 160
On Curriculum Implementation: Process 163

Kedushah as an Integrative Focus:
The Implementation of a Vision
Robert Abramson 164

FROM BENNETT
Examples of Integration in the Classroom 177
Moral Education 178

III. COMMUNITY

Obstacles to the Development of the Day School as the Normative Mode of Jewish Education in the Conservative Movement
Burton I. Cohen — 181

Synagogue, Rabbi, and the Day School
Charles A. Klein — 188

The Day School Principal and Reflective Practice
Alvin Mars — 195

FROM BENNETT
On Effective Principals — 207

Lay and Professional Relationships in the Day School
Joshua Elkin — 208

The Leader of the Team
Walter I. Ackerman — 219

IV. BENNETT I. SOLOMON: REFLECTIONS AND WRITINGS

FROM BENNETT
Personal Beliefs — 227

A Colleague Reflects
Joshua Elkin — 229

Our Mentor, Our Colleague, Our Friend
Pearl Brenman Greenspan, Leah Pearl Summers, Laura German Samuels, Marcie Greenfield Simons — 232

FROM BENNETT
On Teachers — 240
On Students — 242
On the Home — 243

The Cookie Jar
Susan Solomon Stibel — 244

FROM BENNETT—Epilogue
The Task is Not Finished — 248

Bennett I. Solomon (1951–1987)

Acknowledgements

We are grateful to those listed below who contributed out of love, respect, and concern to this project. Those who donated their labor, their finances, and their intellect, each in their own way helped make this dream into a reality. Jan Zidle, secretary and administrator of Temple Aliyah, and the office staff of the Bureau of Jewish Education of Greater Boston handled the burdens of administration.

We acknowledge with much thanks the major financial gifts received from the Solomon family and Lucius N. Littauer Foundation. It was the initial support from Bennett's parents and William Lee Frost, President of the Littauer Foundation, that put the project on solid ground.

Many pulpit rabbis, both Reform and Conservative, listed elsewhere, gave financial support. Several Solomon Schechter Day Schools from around the country, also listed, assisted in funding the project. Individuals who knew Bennett, studied with him, or whose children learned from him are among the many private people who contributed towards the publication of this volume.

Finally, we want to thank all the authors who wrote for this *festschrift*. We appreciate the time, energy and knowledge you shared with us. Though the reader is the ultimate judge of the quality and usefulness of these essays, it is our sense that they, collectively and individually, indeed make a substantial contribution to the literature of the field and, as such, a lasting tribute to Bennett Solomon.

Postscript

As we put the finishing touches on the manuscript, we suffered yet another loss in the Solomon family. On February 9th, 1990, the 14th of Shevat 5750, Sidney Solomon, Bennett's father, succumbed to the same disease which claimed his son. In many ways, this volume is a tribute to Sid, too.

Contributors to the Bennett I. Solomon Memorial Book Fund

Akiba Hebrew Academy
   Merion, PA
   Rabbi Marc S. Rosenstein, Principal

Alperin Schechter Day School
   Providence, RI
   Dr. Alvan Kaunfer, Headmaster

ANONYMOUS

Bet Shraga Hebrew Academy of the Capital District
   Albany, NY
   Devorah Heckelman, Principal

Rabbi Herman Blumberg
   Temple Shir Tikva
   Wayland, MA

Rabbi Jonathan M. Case
   Temple Shaare Tefilah
   Norwood, MA

Rabbi Samuel Chiel
   Temple Emanuel
   Newton, MA

Rabbi Neil Cooper
   Temple Beth Am
   Aberdeen, NJ

Rabbi Robert Dobrusin
   Beth Israel Congregation
   Ann Arbor, MI

Henry A. & Judith L. Feldman, M.D.
   Newtonville, MA

Rabbi Lyle Fishman
   Ohr Kodesh Congregation
   Chevy Chase, MD

Rabbi Marc Boone Fitzerman
   Congregation B'nai Emunah
   Tulsa, OK

Rabbi Wayne Franklin
   Temple Emanuel
   Providence, RI

Donald & Ruth Freedman
   Newton, MA

Rabbi Mark Friedman
   Beth Jacob Synagogue
   Norwich, CT

Michael Gardener & Diane Levine
   Newton, MA

Rabbi Myron Geller
   Congregation Ahavath Achim
   Gloucester, MA

Rabbi Elliot B. Gertel
   Congregation Rodfei Zedek
   Chicago, IL

Rabbi Michael Gold
   Beth El Congregation
   Pittsburgh, PA

Jonathan & Mary Ellen Gould
   Newton, MA

Dr. Sidney Greenberg
Temple Sinai
Dresher, PA

Dr. Sidney P. and Helen Kadish
Waban, MA

Rabbi Samuel and Melinda Kieffer
Congregation Agudat Achim
Schenectady, NY

Rabbi Charles Klein
Merrick Jewish Center
Merrick, NY

Rabbi Judah Kogan
Rosh Pina Congregation
Winnipeg, Manitoba, Canada

Rabbi Harold Kravitz
and Ms. Cindy Reich
Minneapolis, MN

Rabbi Harold and Suzette Kushner
Natick, MA

Rabbi Lawrence Kushner
Congregation Beth El of the
Sudbury River Valley
Sudbury, MA

Rabbi Murray Levine
Temple Beth Shalom
Framingham, MA

Rabbi Steven Lindemann
Rodef Shalom Temple
Newport News, VA

Rabbi Chaim Listfield
Temple Emanu-El
Englewood, NJ

Lucius N. Littauer Foundation
William Frost, Esq., President
New York City, NY

Dr. Daniel & Patricia H. Margolis
Brookline, MA

Dr. & Mrs. Daniel Marwil
Providence, RI

Rabbi Bernard Mehlman
Temple Israel
Boston, MA

Michael & Grace Miller
Philadelphia, PA

David E. Moeser Trust
Mr. Michael J. Bohnen, Trustee
c/o Nutter, McClennan & Fish
Boston, MA

Rabbi Abraham Morhaim
Temple Ner Tamid
Peabody, MA

Rabbi Burton Padoll
Beth Shalom
Peabody, Ma

Rabbi Robert Pilavin
Jewish Community Center
Spring Valley, NY

Rabbi Charles Popky
Beth Shalom Congregation
Kansas City, MO

Rabbi Jay Rosenbaum
Congregation Beth Israel
Worcester, MA

Rabbi Scott Rosenberg
Temple Reyim
Newton, MA

Rabbi Gershon Schwartz
Bayshore Jewish Center
Bayshore, NY

Rabbi Sanford Shanblatt
Temple Israel
Swampscott, MA

Rabbi Alexander Shapiro
Congregation Oheb Shalom
South Orange, NJ

Elliot Salo Schoenberg
and Cathy Felix
Needham, MA

Rabbi Alan Silverstein
Agudath Israel
Caldwell, NJ

Sidney and Flossie Solomon
Elkins Park, PA

Solomon Schechter Day Schools
  Northbrook and Skokie, IL
  Jay Leberman, Principal
  Charlotte Glass, Principal
Solomon Schechter Day School
  Bala Cynwyd, PA
  Dr. Steven Brown, Headmaster
Solomon Schechter Day School
  of Greater Boston
  Newton, MA
  Rabbi Joshua Elkin, Headmaster
Solomon Schechter Day School of
  the Merrimack Valley
  Haverhill, MA
  Deborah N. Margolis, Principal
Solomon Schechter Day School of
  Suffolk County
  Commack, NY
  Rabbi Stuart Saposh, Headmaster
Charles E. Smith Jewish Day School
  Rockville, MD
  Shulamith R. Elster, Headmaster
Rabbi Barry Starr
  Temple Israel
  Sharon, MA

Gerald P. & Elizabeth S. Tishler
  West Newton, MA
Rabbi Alan Turetz
  Temple Emeth
  Chestnut Hill, MA
United Synagogue School
  Willowdale, Ontario
  Dr. Aaron Nussbaum, Principal
Rabbi Edgar Weinsberg
  Temple Beth El
  Swampscott, MA
Rabbi H. David Werb
  Temple Beth Emunah
  Brockton, MA
Rabbi Richard Yellin
  Congregation Mishkan Tefila
  Chestnut Hill, MA
Rabbi Gerald B. Zelermyer
  Emanuel Synagogue
  West Hartford, CT
Rabbi Henry A. Zoob
  Temple Beth David
  Westwood, MA

List of Authors

Dr. Robert Abramson
　Director, Dept. of Education,
　United Synagogue of America
　New York, NY

Dr. Walter Ackerman
　Shane Family Professor
　of Education,
　Ben Gurion University
　Beer Sheva, Israel

Dr. Burton Cohen
　Assistant Professor of
　Jewish Education,
　Jewish Theological Seminary
　New York, NY

Dr. Joshua Elkin
　Headmaster, Solomon
　Schechter Day School of
　Greater Boston
　Newton, MA

Pearl Brenman Greenspan
　Senior Division Coordinator,
　Bialik Hebrew Day School
　Toronto, Ontario, Canada

Dr. Alvan Kaunfer
　Director, Alperin Schechter
　Day School
　Providence, RI

Rabbi Charles Klein
　Merrick Jewish Center
　Merrick, NY

Dr. Perry London, ז״ל
　Dean, Graduate School of Applied & Professional Psychology,
　Rutgers University
　New Brunswick, NJ

Dr. Joseph Lukinsky
　Theodore & Florence Baumritter
　Professor of Jewish Education,
　Jewish Theological Seminary
　New York, NY

Dr. Daniel J. Margolis
　Executive Director,
　Bureau of Jewish Education
　of Greater Boston
　Newton, MA

Dr. Alvin Mars
　Executive Vice President,
　Brandeis Bardin Institute
　Simi Valley, CA

Louis Newman
　Executive Director Emeritus,
　Bureau of Jewish Education of
　Greater Boston
　Newton, MA

Laura German Samuels
　Former teacher,
　Cohen-Hillel Academy
　Marblehead, MA
　currently Wexner Foundation
　Fellow in Jewish Education
　Cincinnati, OH

Dr. Lifsa Schachter
    Associate Professor of Education and Dean,
    Cleveland College of Jewish Studies
    Cleveland, OH

Rabbi Elliot Salo Schoenberg
    Temple Aliyah
    Needham, MA

Dr. Israel Scheffler
    Victor S. Thomas Professor of Education and Philosophy,
    Harvard University
    Cambridge, MA

Rabbi Benjamin Edidin Scolnic
    Temple Beth Sholom
    Hamden, CT

Dr. Susan L. Shevitz
    Assistant Professor of Jewish Education,
    The Benjamin Hornstein Graduate Program in Jewish Communal Service
    Brandeis University
    Waltham, MA

Marcie Greenfield Simons
    Former teacher,
    Cohen-Hillel Academy
    Marblehead, Mass
    currently Jewish Educator in Pittsfield, MA

Dr. Mark Smiley
    Headmaster,
    Hillel Day School
    Detroit, MI

Susan Solomon Stibel
    Marblehead, MA

Leah Pearl Summers
    Assistant Principal,
    Cohen-Hillel Academy
    Marblehead, MA

Dr. Michael Zeldin
    Professor of Jewish Education,
    Rhea Hirsch School of Education
    Hebrew Union College
    Los Angeles, CA

INTRODUCTION

Bennett I. Solomon died on December 24, 1987 at the age of thirty-six. His death obviously brought an end to his career, his achievements, and the relationships he had with his colleagues, friends and family. But like the intense love for his family, like the powerful influence he had on his faculty and students, his professional impact will continue to be felt for many years.

Though his accomplishments in many ways speak for themselves—in the institution he helped shape and the powerful educational ideas he pioneered—Bennett had much to say ... and not enough time to say it to a wide audience. Since he regretted that he had not been able to reflect properly on what he *did* or write "his" conceptual framework of Jewish day school education, we undertook the task of producing this *festschrift* as the book he wanted to write, but never did.

A *festschrift* is a volume of learned essays in celebration of a special occasion or in memory of a scholar, teacher, or rabbi, written by his students, colleagues, and admirers. The custom of publishing *festschriften* became popular in academic circles in the nineteenth century when formal recognition of Jewish studies was denied.

However, we had several goals in mind when we decided to undertake this tribute. On one hand, this volume continues the tradition of publishing a *festschrift* as an appreciation of the past. On the other, this book is intended to be a projection into the future.

Several of the volume's essays expand on ideas that up until now have only been informally expressed. Other articles articulate some preliminary thoughts, while still others are more complete versions of new directions in thinking about Jewish education in America today, with a particular emphasis on the non-Orthodox day school. Taken as a whole, it is our intention that the book provide a wider forum for some concepts which have already achieved a certain level of recognition or successful implementation.

Moreover, we feel the volume will fill some major gaps in the literature on day schools, ethnic and Jewish education. We hope it will make a significant contribution to the field and serve as an important addition to school and university libraries; appropriate for presentation to faculty and/or lay leadership, and useful as a text for graduate study and training.

Structure

Among the many elements of educational theory, three of the most critical are educational philosophy, curriculum and the design and support of a social context. Bennett had much to say and much interest in the articulation of ideas in these three fundamental areas. Therefore, the first three sections of the book reflect these basic educational concerns. A fourth section includes some personal reflections about Bennett from colleagues and family.

Throughout the book, we have inserted excerpts from Bennett's few published and mostly unpublished writings. These are intended to serve as a "commentary" on the ideas expressed by Bennett's colleagues, teachers, and friends who have contributed to the *festschrift*. We feel that this somewhat innovative approach will serve to amplify some of Bennett's pioneering thoughts on Jewish day school education in general and curricular integration in particular.

Commitment

Rarely did Bennett ever *do* anything—as a parent, educator, or much else for that matter—without struggling to understand and articulate his philosophy about it. He was deeply committed to *being committed* and could not understand those who acted seemingly without an ideational or value framework. Israel Scheffler, in the first of two essays, analyzes and transforms classical rabbinic sources into a *Jewish* philosophy of education—an effort long overdue. His second essay presents points of distinction and departure between secular and Jewish education.

Where Jewish and general education coincide and share issues and where Jewish education *must* differ because its ultimate aims are different are explored in the essay by Perry London, which continues his seminal work on Jewish identity and the paradigm shifts in education. London wonders why the same Jewish student that does not do well in religious school is an excellent student in public school. He hypothesizes that this is due to the absence of *integration* or *contextualization* in many settings where Jewish learning takes place—thus exploring in a systematic way two of Bennett's constant themes.

Newman and Zeldin follow with explorations of the distinctions between normative—read "Orthodox"—day schools in America and the recent strengthening and expansion of non-Orthodox institutions. Louis Newman, himself a pioneer in non-Orthodox day schooling in America, challenges those schools and their sponsors to develop unique ideologies, contents and strategies, compatible with their particular "theology" or religious values. He suggests a series of questions and models focusing on the core values of "human worth" and "aspirations for goodness" that these schools must consider, so they will neither imitate their parallel Orthodox institutions, nor escape confronting the tension between educating for autonomy versus educating for indoctrination. Zeldin's emphasis is on those characteristics which distinguish the Reform day school in particular from those under the auspices of other religious movements.

We are mindful that much of this volume adds to what Ackerman has called elsewhere the "hortatory" literature on Jewish education. However, many of these essays go well beyond what he calls "informed opinion" about the field and raise questions which beg further research. Shevitz calls for greater symbiosis between educational practice and research, particularly where there is enough time for the responsible use of research findings in heretofore "research-poor" settings.

Curriculum

Whether it was making it possible for fourth graders to empathize with the mythic qualities of Abraham by linking the Biblical nomad with the more "concrete" world of the Bedouins; or designing a daily camp schedule such that campers would sense a natural, organic flow to the day filled with classes, sports, *tefillot*, and bunk projects, Bennett was committed to the principles of curricular integration.

At Cohen-Hillel Academy, integration efforts went far beyond the thoughtful blending of appropriate subject matters in individual classrooms. The entire school would "become" Jerusalem with children of every age group interacting, learning by themselves and from each other, and multiple arts and disciplines brought to bear to effect the educational goals and institutional transformation. On other occasions, Hillel "became" a kibbutz or a Constitutional Convention debating the yet to be finished American Constitution. Clearly, Cohen-Hillel became Bennett's "laboratory" where his many early experiments in integration could be more fully realized.

The essays in this section apply the principles of integration to some of the subject areas common to the day school curriculum. Mark Smiley suggests that rabbinic studies—taught from a distinctly Conservative perspective—might form the core of the Solomon Schechter day school program. Kaunfer contends that *midrash* ought to be taught in the modern day school to expose students to the wealth of its ideas and values. Further, Kaunfer suggests that midrashic method enables youngsters to develop their skills of interpretation, creative expression, and critical thinking.

Scolnic explores the distinction between, and the relationship of, history and story, in Conservative Jewish study of the Torah. Lukinsky and Schachter, in their paradigm for curriculum design on Jewish holidays, confront the complexity of the curricular process, using a phenomenological approach. Lifsa Schachter, in her essay, describes the implementation of a curriculum review and integration process in a school. Abramson provides a record of the staff development process he conducted which led to a new integrative, "generative" focus—*kedushah*—for his school's curriculum.

Although clearly not a complete curriculum design, these essays can serve as a beginning. It is in this area that much more work in curriculum development must be done for the non-Orthodox day schools to realize their unique potential.

Community

In this section we attempt to focus on two parallel dimensions of Bennett's work, which he felt were critical to his own sense of self as a Jewish educational professional. Within the larger Jewish community, he was committed to being an active, *enfranchised* participant and a thoroughly respected *professional*, and he urged his colleagues to do so as well. He made sure that his school was prominently seen as a "centerpiece" institution for the community and its Jewish federation, taking pride in its public roles on *Yom Ha'atzmaut*, for example, or opening its fledgling resource center and library to other schools and groups.

Within the school itself—and in his work and discussions about camps, afternoon schools, and youth groups—he worked to *create a community*, the intellectual and Jewish-based social context within which all learning should take place. Cohen-Hillel *was* a community—of children, educators, and families, inter-generational and multi-faceted. And it was an intensely *Jewish* community, caring for the less fortunate, taking action on environmental matters, teaching about Soviet Jewry and embracing new Americans upon their arrival, and committed to the creation of a Jewish aesthetic in both school and home. Bennett used his leadership skills and charismatic personality to make significant contributions to his community and to create a community of his institution.

Burton Cohen's essay describes the challenges facing the Conservative movement should it wish to make its day schools normative for its membership. Klein explores the relationships—currently and in potential—among the congregational rabbi, synagogue, and day school. Mars, drawing upon recent research on the principalship, reflects on what the professional day school principal needs to know to be effective and reflective.

Joshua Elkin and Walter Ackerman describe aspects of the day school principal as institutional leader. Elkin concentrates on the importance of nurturing effective relationships with lay leadership. Ackerman focuses on the role the principal plays as instructional leader and the necessity for the community to embark on a major effort to recruit quality educators for those positions.

On Bennett: Personal Reflections

Like his physical presence—even in illness—Bennett's *persona* dominated his environment. Children, quite obviously, and adults, very much equally, looked up to him. Engaging, virtually indefatigable when driven, Bennett commanded your attention with his ideas, his wit, or his multiple interests. (It is important to remember that perhaps his basic interests—after his beloved Sue, Jordie, Noah and his extended family; followed by his school and colleagues—were the Phillies, the "Sixers" and, begrudgingly, the Celtics.)

Joshua Elkin, not content to submit only an academic essay or to arrange for his Schechter principal colleagues to pay tribute to Bennett with a lecture, provides us with a personal reflection on the meaning of their professional and personal relationship. These two strands of his life—the personal and the professional—were inextricably interwoven in virtually everything Bennett did, as evidenced in the loving memoir written by four of his most devoted faculty members.

A few words about Sue. Susan Ettinger Solomon was part of Bennett for over twenty years. Rarely did one say "Bennett" without adding "and Sue," whether in talking about Cohen-Hillel, their home and children, or their tennis matches. An accomplished educator on her own, and an expert on children's language and literature, Susan is recognized as a major contributor and designer of day school curriculum and environment.

An indispensable partner and helpmeet to Bennett, to whom he turned for advice as well as comfort, love and support, Sue desperately wanted to write an essay which would have provided some insights into Bennett's (and their) *unfulfilled dreams*: what he(they) really hoped to accomplish; what he really meant when he talked about integration and community ... a *perush* (commentary) on the plain text of his life.

Ultimately, the effort proved too painful and intense for now. It is another task left to be completed at a later time. However, her metaphorical reminiscence, "The Cookie Jar," is perhaps an even more eloquent testament, in all its understatement, to their unique relationship—and the meaning of Bennett's work than any other essay in this volume.

On a personal level, Bennett was part of *our* support group. Through college, the early working years, and later in our personal and professional lives, Bennett played an intensely personal role.

For Elliot, he was roommate, friend, mentor, cajoling but loving guide, and loyal supporter.

For Danny, whether in the bright sunlight, full of hope, of a Ramah afternoon, or in the dimly lit and even more darkly ominous hospital room, Bennett was "there" to argue, provide intellectual stimulation, caring and concern, and criticize demeanor and dress.

We miss him.

Daniel J. Margolis
Elliot Salo Schoenberg
February, 1990
Shevat 5750

A Note on Bennett's Writings

Under the heading "From Bennett," we have excerpted selections from Bennett's papers—published and unpublished. The full list appears below. The citations in the text are identified by the abbreviations in parentheses.

"A Critical Review of the Term 'Integration' in the Literature of the Jewish Day School in America." *Jewish Education*, Volume 46, Number 4. Winter, 1978 ("Critical Review").

"Curriculum Innovation: What Jewish Education Must Learn from Education Research" [unpublished paper] presented at the International Research Conference on Jewish Education. The Hebrew University of Jerusalem, The Samuel Mendel Melton Centre for Jewish Education in the Diaspora, June 24-27, 1984 ("Curriculum Innovation").

"Curricular Integration in the Jewish All-Day School in the United States" [unpublished paper presented to the Melton Centre for Jewish Education in the Diaspora at the Dushkin Conference on Jewish Education in the Diaspora, August, 1980]. Subsequently published in Michael Rosenak, ed. *Studies in Jewish Education, Vol. 1* (Jerusalem: Magnes Press, The Hebrew University, 1984) ("Curricular Integration").

"Curricular Integration in the Jewish All-day School in the United States." Ed.D. Dissertation, Harvard University, 1979 ("Dissertation").

"Goals and Objectives of American Jewish Education" [unpublished paper] Brandeis University, January, 1971 ("Goals and Objectives").

"Reflections upon Jewish Education-I: A Philosophical Investigation of Goals and Objectives." [unpublished paper] Harvard University, January, 1974 ("Reflections I").

"Reflections upon Jewish Education-II: A Philosophical Investigation of a General Curricular Approach." [unpublished paper] Harvard University, February, 1974 ("Reflections II").

I. COMMITMENTS AND PHILOSOPHY

FROM BENNETT
PROLOGUE

WHY JEWISH EDUCATION FOR ME

I believe in Judaism and I believe in Jewish education ...

In the last four months I have decided that my future occupation must be within the realm of Jewish education ... I hope that some day I will look back upon this paper as the springboard to my dedication, my efforts, my results in alleviating the crisis in Jewish education and contributing to a new generation of richly educated, deeply concerned, and sensitively committed American Jews.

Judaism had always been a part of my home. My Bubby was Judaism for me. And when my Bubby left us, my mother and father continued the traditions—continued that Jewish life that was so much a part of them. And most importantly, my parents sent me to Camp Ramah.

The beauty of Camp Ramah was, and is, that 400 kids get together who had or have Bubbys and parents who feel close enough to Judaism to want their children to leave home and live Judaism completely—totally—for two months. I met rabbis' sons who were not fairies, but who rather could beat me in basketball. I met kids who liked Hebrew school, and even knew more than me, and they could also play baseball. So we lived together—Hebrew, kashrut, services, Israelis, bible classes, sports, friends—we lived together for two months, and after that, nothing could separate me from my Jewishness ...

Jewish education in America is wavering today more tenuously than ever before. Intense Jewish environments are needed to overcome the greatest problem with American Jews—their ambivalence to what being Jewish means. American Jews are confused as to what they are—human, American or Jews —and only a rich, fully integrated Jewish existence can overcome that problem.

Camp Ramah was the most vital component to my Jewish growth. Rabbi David Mogilner, the late national director of the Ramah Camps, presented a number of alternatives for Conservative education. ... He felt that camp situations and day schools were the preferred models for Jewish education.

Further, Mogilner wrote that to be meaningful, "Jewish education must allow for the creation of a new 'market place' and must free the person being educated from the competition of the old 'market place.' Also, since Judaism is a rational tradition it requires the development of a series of rational skills pertinent to the pursuit of that tradition. The more formal schooling possible, the more the pursuit is possible. So the best model is one that involves combinations of informal situations and formal schooling."[1] And the single most detrimental factor to the success of Jewish education is the lack of competent people who can become accessible models to lead that Jewish education.

Even after all of my research and recent thought, I still remain perplexed today as to my goals and reasons for Jewish education. Do we want to teach, and even inculcate Judaism just so it will survive for another generation? Should we associate and live as Jews simply because our ancestors did, and they had to persevere with far more than we do today? But now I want to live as a Jew because Judaism offers me a way of living—of confronting life in my world today. I'm beginning to see the ethical, moral and human alternatives that Judaism offers—and now I can't get enough of Judaic studies. And today I do feel that I have been unduly deprived!

I think I could have accepted a few philosophical concepts four years ago. I think I could have thought deeply about what Judaism says concerning war and peace and conscience. I think I could have appreciated considering a Torah that wasn't necessarily written by God or prayer as something other than asking favors of the guy in the sky with the white beard. But none of these alternatives was offered to me. I didn't hear of Martin Buber until I came to Brandeis. That is sad, and I'm terribly disappointed about it now! Maybe that is why I want so fervently to work with Jewish education as soon as I can ...

Goals and Objectives, Introduction, pp. 21-23, 31-33.

---

1 Personal correspondence from Rabbi David Mogliner, December, 1970.

THE CHALLENGE FOR THE DAY SCHOOL

The Jewish day school in America, in attempting to offer an integrated and integrative educational program, faces a significant challenge. It could continue to assume the more easily organized "subject-centered" approach to curriculum planning, but doing so would virtually eliminate its ability to pursue the integrative ideal which is its unique potential and purpose. This opportunity to forge unity and wholeness must not be lost!

The day school must develop within its students the ability to relate all the various aspects of these educational and general life experiences within an overall philosophy of life. The day school must enable its students to participate within a rich and authentic Jewish-American civilization, in which each cultural heritage enhances the appreciation of the other. The day school must convey to its students a knowledge of Judaism which recognizes that Jewish values and personalities have helped shape mores and customs throughout time and can continue to guide Jews as they interact with modern society and culture.

The day school is committed to more than the survival of the Jewish people. The number of hours it provides for study of Judaica and the [commitment] of most of its community [to Judaism] provide the student with the time and support which can engender a knowledgeable, positive, secure and active Jewish identification. The day school student will have gained the wherewithal to move beyond mere rote learning and inculcated religious and moral behavior to autonomous religious interpretation and action based upon a personal and educated understanding and association with the Jewish and American heritages. Only such an individual will contribute to the dynamic growth of Judaism and America.

[However,] the education of such Jewish-Americans cannot follow one pattern. The input of specific teachers, the special concerns and contingencies of local communities and the individual interests, needs and capabilities of each student rule out the feasibility and desirability of a normative curriculum for all day schools.

We can suggest outlines for the structure and content of the day school program. We can urge the employment of full-time teachers who personify the integrated ideal of the school, and demand that Hebrew teachers' colleges begin programs for their education. We can list those facts, concepts, skills and dispositions which can be integrated and correlated throughout the school and suggest procedures for teacher in-service training. We can recommend structures which will help avoid the creation of artificially dichotomized educational experiences. But in the end, the process of curriculum planning and implementation must take place in each school and classroom!

... [E]ducation does not occur in a vacuum. An integrative educational milieu will convey an image different from a bifurcated or fractionalized environment. It will lead to a particular understanding of the facts, concepts, skills and values being taught. The content cannot be divorced from the context! The educational context must reflect the educational purposes of the school if those goals are to be achieved. As day schools seek unifying capabilities within their students, their curricula must be structured to pursue this worthy ideal in the most advantageous manner.

Curricular Integration, pp. 25-27

JUDAISM'S PHILOSOPHY OF EDUCATION

AN INTERPRETATION OF CLASSICAL SOURCES

Israel Scheffler

Introduction

It is impossible to overestimate the importance of education in traditional Jewish thought. Learning is central to Judaism, a religious duty, a source of ultimate meaning, a form of worship. The motivation assigned to education is quite different from that which is prevalent in modern systems: It is not to be pursued for the sake of career, or vocation, or self-development, or society or national glory. Rather all else that Jews do is to be thought of as pursued for the sake of *it*. "Torah" indeed, is wrongly translated as "law." It means *teaching*, and represents an ultimate value in Judaism, inextricably bound both to Israel and the Almighty, according to the maxim "Israel, the Torah, and the Holy One, Blessed be He, are one."

So pervasive is education in Jewish thought that it is impossible to separate it from the complex of religion and culture as a distinguishable component. A recent writer remarks that "education was so much a part of Jewish thought and way of living that it was taken for granted; Jewish Sages considered it hardly necessary to set down an articulated plan of its principles and practices. In a similar sense, the advanced conceptions of social ethics, abundant in Jewish classical writings, were not preserved as an organized system but rather as dynamic expressions of how to live."[1]

---

1 Julius B. Maller, "The Role of Education in Jewish History," in L. Finkelstein, ed. *The Jews: Their History, Culture, and Religion*, Vol. II (New York: Harper, 1949), p. 897.

There is thus no explicit philosophy of education, in the contemporary sense, to be recounted.

However, certain fundamental emphases, distilled from the classical writings, provide a thread of educational continuity from the earliest times to the contemporary period. Among such emphases the following have been suggested: 1) that study is essential, 2) that "human character is ... improvable" through education, 3) that "learning and doing must be integrated," 4) that "education is a continual process ... from cradle to grave," 5) that education is social, 6) that "education ... must start with the very young," 7) that "individual differences among pupils must be recognized," 8) that "responsibility for education rests with the parents and the community," 9) that "training for work is ... both essential and honorable."[2]

These emphases provide a general sense of the direction of Jewish thought on educational matters. But they are too broad, in themselves, to be very informative. What I propose to do here is to illustrate some of the main conceptions of postbiblical Jewish thought on education, by drawing on Talmudic or Midrashic passages relating to the following four rubrics: 1) The Conduct of the Scholar; 2) Teachers and Students; 3) The Learning Process; and 4) the Content of Learning. In these passages we may begin to discern the outlines of a Rabbinic philosophy of education embodied in lore and practice, which has not only been enormously important historically, but which is, I believe, of great interest for present thought as well.

The Conduct of the Scholar

I begin with this topic for it presents, in a concrete way, the ideal outcome of learning as embodied in character and conduct. The basic point is this: *religion, morality* and *good manners* are to be combined in the everyday "conduct of life, in order to win both Divine and human approval. The greatest responsibility rests upon the scholars, as representatives of the Torah."[3]

The picture of the scholar is drawn in terms that may seem to the modern ear not homogeneous, including moral and religious aspects as well as those pertaining to social tact and etiquette. To the Rabbis, these elements formed indeed an indissoluble whole comprising character: Mind, soul and conduct are all integral parts of such character. Thus, the modern concept of *moral education* as distinct from *cognitive educa-*

---

2   *Ibid.*
3   Michael Higger, ed., *The Treatises Derek Erez: Edited from Manuscripts with an Introduction, Notes, Variants and Translation* (Brooklyn, New York: Moinester Publishing Co., 1935), editor's introduction, p. 12.

tion is alien to the Rabbinic conception. The scholar is to be humble, truthful, and tactful. He is characterized by the Rabbis as

> meek, humble, diligent, intelligent, submissive, beloved by all, humble of spirit before members of the household, and sin fearing. He inquires after everyone's welfare in terms of his vocation. He sits at the feet of the wise; no one finds displeasing traits in him; he questions according to the subject matter and answers to the point. The scholar loves the Torah and honors it. He keeps aloof from everything hideous and from whatever seems hideous; he does not slander his neighbor. He performs his daily acts in accordance with good manners. ...
>
> A scholar does not eat or drink while standing, nor does he wipe off his plate or lick his fingers, or belch in front of his neighbor. He is moderate in conversation, laughter, sleep and pleasure. ... A scholar reveals his character in five ways: 1) by his purse, 2) by his wine-cup, 3) by his anger, 4) by his attire, and 5) by his speech. ... No scholar should seat himself before his elders are seated. He should be decorous in eating, drinking, bathing, anointing, putting on shoes, walking, dressing, speaking, and in performing his duties. ... When his needy and poor neighbor appeals to him for help, he does not refuse him. If his colleagues have insulted him, he makes peace with them, for peace is noble and strife is despicable.[4]

The particular virtues are also integral; they are not to be thought of as belonging just to a single department of life but as radiating into every area. Thus, humility is described as an *intellectual* virtue, not simply as a *general moral* trait:

> Be pliable like the reed which the wind blows hither and thither, for the Torah is preserved only by him who is humble in spirit. And why is the Torah likened to water?: to indicate that just as the course of the water is not towards high places but rather towards low places, similarly the Torah is preserved only by him who is humble in spirit.[5]

Arrogance, it seems, is not merely a moral deficiency. It is also an *intellectual* fault, an educational obstacle. It produces rashness, impulsiveness, lack of respect for the opinions of others, and even untruthfulness. Thus, we are told that there are seven marks of the uncultured:

> He speaks before him who is greater than he in wisdom; he interrupts the speech of his fellowman; he is hasty to answer; he does not question according to the subject matter, and does not answer to the point; he speaks upon the last subject first and upon the first last; he says, "I understand" when he does not understand; and he does not acknowledge the truth.[6]

---

4   *Ibid.*, pp. 13-15.
5   *Ibid.*, "Masseket Derek Erez," Ch. VII, p. 50.
6   *Ibid.*, Ch. VI, p. 48.

By contrast, the student is advised:

> Sit at the feet of scholars and hearken unto their words. Do not be hasty to answer, and plan your answer according to the subject matter. Answer the first point first and the last point last. Acknowledge the truth, and do not speak before him who is greater in wisdom than you.[7]

Acknowledging the truth means also avoiding false claims to its possession. The scholar is not to deem himself a source of absolutely certain knowledge; he is not a dogmatist. He is advised, on the contrary:

> Accustom yourself to say "I do not know," lest you be led to tell a falsehood and be apprehended.[8]

The scholar is, moreover, to be scrupulous with himself as to his own level of understanding:

> If you desire to understand the Torah, do not say regarding that which you do not understand, I do understand; when you are taught and you do not understand, be not ashamed to say, I do not understand. If someone inquires of you about something in which you are not well versed, be not ashamed to say, I do not know.[9]

The scholarly ideal is, then, that of a *seeker* of understanding and wisdom rather than that of a *seer* who claims the certain possession of it. There is in principle no difference between scholar and student. The very term for scholar, i.e. תלמיד חכם, means "wise student." Teaching another person is not separable from teaching oneself. Knowledge is conceived not as a matter of possession but rather a matter of quest. The rejection of dogmatism is succinctly expressed as follows:

> Love the "perhaps," but hate the "and if so?" Rabbi Hidka states it differently: Love the "perhaps"; but hate the "what of it?"[10]

אהוב את השמא ושנא את הכי מה. ר' חידקא אומרה
בלשון אחרת, אהוב את השמא ושנא את המה בכך.

Here we have a commitment both to the *importance* of the quest for knowledge and to its *never ending scope*. Even if we never get beyond the "perhaps," we must never despair and say "so what?"

Teachers and Students

We have already seen a very important idea, i.e., that the teacher is not separable from the learner. He is himself a learner. He is more advanced than his student, but he must always retain a helpful and patient attitude toward his student. Thus, we are told:

---

7 *Ibid.*, Ch. I, pp. 36-7.
8 *Ibid.*, Ch. II, p. 40.
9 *Ibid.*, Ch. I, p. 37.
10 *Ibid.*, Ch. I, p. 34, The Hebrew, from Masseket Derek Eretz, Ch. I: 11 is found on p. 63 of the Hebrew section in Higger, *Ibid.*

> Raba said: If you see a student who finds his studies as difficult as iron it is because his teacher does not take a kindly attitude toward him.[11]

Hillel declares that:
> the diffident cannot learn nor can the impatient teach.[12]

The pupil must be able to press his questions, not to be too diffident to express his doubts and lacks. But then the teacher needs to take such expressions seriously and deal with them patiently:

> Rabbi Perida had a pupil with whom he found it necessary to rehearse a lesson four hundred times before he learned it. One day the Rabbi was called away to perform a charitable act. Before he left, however, he repeated the lesson at hand the usual number of times but, on this occasion, his pupil failed to learn it. "Why," asked Rabbi Perida, "is this time different from any other time?"
>
> The pupil replied, "Because, from the moment the master was summoned to discharge another duty, I diverted my attention, and every now and then I said to myself, 'Soon the master will get up, soon the master will get up.'" "Well, then," said the Rabbi, "pay attention and I shall teach it to you again." And he repeated the lesson a second four hundred times and the pupil learned it. Whereupon a Heavenly voice came forth and said to Rabbi Perida: What reward do you want? You may add four hundred years to your life, or you and your generation may merit the world to come. The latter, said R. Perida. Whereupon the Holy One, Blessed Be He, said: Give him both rewards.[13]

The general relation between teacher and pupil must be one of mutual respect. This does not mean that there are no distinctions of educational level and experience to be acknowledged. Thus, R. Jose, son of Judah of Kephar Babli, says:

> He who learns from the young, to what is he like? To one who eats unripe grapes, or drinks wine from the vat. And he who learns from the old, to what is he like? To one who eats ripe grapes, or drinks old wine.[14]

Rabbi Meir, however, disagrees with R. Jose on this matter, saying pointedly:

> Look not at the flask, but at what it contains: there may be a new flask full of old wine, and an old flask that has not even new wine in it.[15]

---

11 *Taanit*, 8a.
12 *Abot* 2, 5.
13 *Erubin*, 54b.
14 *Abot*, 4, 20. Translation of J.H. Hertz, *Sayings of the Fathers* (New York: Behrman House, 1945), p. 81. (Hertz's numbering of verses differs from the traditional numbering I have followed here.) I have used Hertz's translations wherever I refer to him in footnotes.
15 *Ibid.*, (Hertz, *Op. cit.*, 81).

Age is not a decisive criterion of scholarly or educational maturity. One hopes that the older scholar will in general have gained from his greater experience. The ultimate test, however, is not chronological age but intellectual capacity and ripeness. We must all be prepared to learn from whoever can teach us, young or old. As Ben Zoma said: "Who is wise? He who learns from all men, as it is said, 'From all my teachers I have gotten understanding'".[16]

This point is made strikingly in a passage which reads:

> He who learns from his fellow a single chapter, a single rule, a single verse, a single expression, or even a single letter, ought to pay him honor.[17]

Honor and respect are, however, reciprocal:

> Rabbi Elazar, the son of Shammua, said: Let the honor of thy disciple be as dear to thee as thine own.[18]

Both master and disciple are engaged in the common enterprise of study. It is this common effort which confers on *each* a mantle of honor; the teacher's guidance and the pupil's efforts to learn are bound together by the activity of study which is their shared purpose.

The teacher's honored role also implies serious responsibilities. His influence in guiding the understanding of the Torah presupposes the utmost meticulousness and care. Thus, R. Judah, son of Ilai, declares:

> Be cautious in teaching, for an error in teaching may amount to presumptuous sin.[19]

Teaching is not reserved for a special group of people. Everyone who has learned has the duty to teach:

> Rabbi Yochanan said: He who learns Torah and does not teach it is like a myrtle that grows in the desert.[20]

An important theme in the thought of the Rabbis is the relation of study and doing, of theory and practice. One aspect of this theme is the recognition that the study of Torah must take place in the practical world. It follows that the teacher is to enable the student not only to learn the Torah but also to acquire a livelihood. The teacher is both a religious and a practical mentor. Thus, the Rabbis taught that:

> A father is required to teach his son Torah, and also to teach him a trade. R. Judah says: Whoever fails to teach his son a trade, it is as if he has taught him to rob.[21]

---

16 *Ibid.*, 4, 1 (Hertz, *Op. cit.*, 65-6).
17 *Abot*, 6, 3 (Hertz, 109).
18 *Ibid.*, 4, 12 (Hertz, 75).
19 *Ibid.*, 4, 13 (Hertz, 75).
20 *Rosh Hashanah*, 23a.
21 *Kiddushin*, 29a.

And R. Elazar, son of Azariah, tells us that:

> Where there is no flour there is no Torah; where there is no Torah, there is no flour.[22]

The sublimity of learning depends on material sustenance, which is itself fulfilled and ennobled by study.

A further aspect of the theme of theory and practice has to do with the practical application of the Torah *itself*, rather than its relation to the learning of a trade. Torah is no merely theoretical matter, since it is essential to the conduct of the religious life; it is impossible to live such a life properly without the guidance of learning. The teacher in effect offers religious guidance and not only religious doctrine. In this vein, Hillel says:

> An empty-headed man cannot be a sin-fearing man, nor can an ignorant person be truly pious.[23]

From this point of view, *study* might be said to be more important than *doing*. But it would not follow that study could be separated from doing and exalted in itself, apart from its influence on conduct. Thus, the Rabbis asked:

> Which is greater, study or doing? R. Tarfon answered: Doing. R. Akiba Answered: Study. The majority agreed that study is greater, for study leads to doing.[24]

Although proper conduct is impossible without study and although study is valuable in promoting doing, there is an ultimate balance to be struck between the two. In such a balance, conduct outweighs, not only because it affords the final justification for study but because it enables learning itself to endure. Thus, R. Chanina ben Dosa said:

> He whose deeds exceed his wisdom, his wisdom shall endure; but he whose wisdom exceeds his deeds, his wisdom will not endure.[25]

And R. Elazar ben Azaryah likens the one whose wisdom exceeds his deeds to:

> a tree whose branches are many but whose roots are few; and the wind comes and plucks it up and overturns it upon its face,

while he whose deeds exceed his wisdom is like:

> a tree whose branches are few but whose roots are many, so that even if all the winds in the world come and blow upon it, it cannot be stirred from its place.[26]

---

22 *Abot*, 3, 17.
23 *Abot*, 2, 5 (Hertz, 33).
24 *Kiddushin*, 40b.
25 *Abot*, 3, 9 (Hertz, 55).
26 *Abot*, 3, 17 (Hertz, 63, 65).

To this point, we have been concerned with general relations between teacher and student, and with the bearing of learning on conduct. We now note the Rabbis' recognition of individual differences in the capacities and proclivities of students, and their special acknowledgment of critical attitudes on the part of the learner. Thus,

> There are four qualities in disciples: He who quickly understands and quickly forgets, his gain disappears in his loss; he who understands with difficulty and forgets with difficulty, his loss disappears in his gain; he who understands quickly and forgets with difficulty, his is a good portion; he who understands with difficulty and forgets quickly, his is an evil portion.[27]

Mere glibness and facility are not sufficient; it is the durability of learning that is of paramount value. Analogously, mere absorptive capacity is not the highest virtue in a student (such a student is compared to a sponge by the Rabbis), but rather discrimination and selection in what is learned from one's teachers. This is a remarkable valuation of critical thinking by the student even in the course of study at the feet of the wise: Thus,

> There are four qualities among those who sit before the wise: they are like a sponge, a funnel, a strainer or a sieve. A sponge, which sucks up everything, a funnel which lets in at one end and out at the other; a strainer, which lets the wine pass out and retains the lees; a sieve which lets out the bran and retains the fine flour.[28]

One sort of difference among good students is the subject of several discussions, and the Rabbis themselves are divided on the question of relative merit. Which is more valuable, erudition or analytical originality? Rabbi Yohanan ben Zakkai is described as listing the good qualities of his five students, among whom Eliezer ben Hyrcanus is praised as being "a cemented cistern, which loses not a drop," while Elazar ben Arakh is praised as being "like a spring flowing with ever-sustained vigor." R. Yohanan is then the subject of two reports as to his relative estimate of these virtues. One report quotes him as saying:

> If all the sages of Israel were in one scale of the balance and Eliezer ben Hyrcanus in the other, he would outweigh them all.

On the other hand, Abba Saul reports him as holding that:

> If all the sages of Israel, together with Eliezer ben Hyrcanus were in one scale of the balance and Elazar ben Arakh in the other, he would outweigh them all.[29]

---

27 *Ibid.*, 5, 12 (Hertz, 95).
28 *Ibid.*, 5, 15 (Hertz, 97).
29 *Ibid.*, 2, 8 (Hertz, 37).

We find this theme elsewhere as well:

> A vacancy occurred in the position of Head of the Academy and the students found it difficult to decide upon a successor. Some preferred R. Joseph for his remarkable store of knowledge. Others preferred Rabbah for his dialectical ability. The former was called "Sinai," the latter "uprooter of mountains." The students decided to ask the counsel of the Academy in Palestine. The reply came: All must come to the owner of the storehouse for food.[30]

The Learning Process

The process of education is *social*; it can be effective only when it is conducted with others. Thus, it is said:

> Form groups for the purpose of study, for Torah can be acquired only in a group.[31]

And again:

> R. Nehorai [some say this is R. Elazar b. Arakh, the "original" scholar, student of R. Yohanan b. Zakkai referred to earlier] says, Wander forth to a home of the Torah—and say not that the Torah will come after thee—for there thy associates will establish thee in the possession of it; and lean not upon thine own understanding.[32]

The need to seek out a community of teachers and scholars is perhaps to be seen in the words of Jose ben Yoezer, of Zeredah, who said: "Let thy house be a meeting house for the wise, sit amidst the dust of their feet, and drink in their words with thirst."[33] As one of my own teachers, Mr. Zusevitz, interpreted this passage, it does *not* mean "Make your home into a salon for scholarly meetings," for who can do this? Rather, the sense is "Find out where scholars meet to study the Torah, and make your home *there*. Follow the Torah actively, and do not expect it to follow you."

Study is most effective when it is pursued *from an early age*. In a striking simile, R. Elisha ben Abuya says:

> If one learns as a child, what is it like? Like ink written on clean paper. If one learns as an old man, what is it like? Like ink written on blotted paper.[34]

The curriculum is to be *systematically organized in accordance with age*. R. Judah b. Tema said:

---

30 *Horaiyot*, 14a. See also L.I. Newman, *The Talmudic Anthology* (New York: Behrman, 468).
31 *Berakhot*, 63b.
32 *Abot*, 4, 14 (Hertz, 77).
33 *Ibid.*, 1, 4 (Hertz, 16).
34 *Ibid.*, 4, 20 (Hertz, 79, 81).

At five years the age is reached for the study of Scripture, at ten for the study of the Mishnah, at thirteen for the fulfillment of the commandments, at fifteen for the study of the Talmud.[35]

Study is to be made *steady and continuous*. Thus, Shammai says: Fix a period for thy study of the Torah.[36]

And Hillel warns:

Do not say, when I have leisure I will study; perchance thou wilt have no leisure.[37]

The point is *not only* that study is to be *built into* the ordinary schedule of life, and that lack of leisure is to be rejected as an excuse for avoiding study. The point is *also* that any such excuse will breed others, unless a momentum of disciplined study is established. Once the *routine* of study is broken, there will be many pretexts for further neglect. Thus, R. Meir warns:

If thou neglectest the Torah, many causes for neglecting it will present themselves to thee.[38]

Nor should you be despairing over the immense range of things to be learned, for *completeness* in learning is a false ideal; it cannot be achieved. Thus, R. Tarfon says:

It is not thy duty to complete the work, but neither art thou free to desist from it.[39]

The aim of study is not completeness, yet learning is to be pursued with steady devotion. But it does not simply accumulate in a static way; it does not stand still in the mind. Unless it is *added to*, it is *diminished*. This dynamic property is expressed succinctly by Hillel, who says: "He who does not increase his knowledge, decreases it."[40] Here is an ancient statement of the principle of growth in education.

With respect to specific methods of teaching, I will only mention the importance of memory in all traditional education, a particularly valued skill in the age before printing. Literary mnemonics were well developed in Jewish practice. The Talmud tells us that according to R. Hisda, "The Torah cannot be retained except through signs."[41] The "oldest reference to detailed alphabet metaphors, apparently designed for children, appears in B. Talmud Tractate *Shabbat*," where homiletic interpretation is given to "the names of the Hebrew letters, based on their

---

35 *Abot* 5, 20 (Hertz 101, 103).
36 *Ibid.*, 1, 15 (Hertz, 25).
37 *Ibid.*, 2, 4 (Hertz, 33).
38 *Ibid.*, 4, 10 (Hertz, 73).
39 *Ibid.*, 2, 16 (Hertz, 45).
40 *Ibid.*, 1, 13 (Hertz, 23).
41 *Erubin*, 54b. See Diane Roskies, "Alphabet Instruction in the East European Heder: Some Comparative and Historical Notes," *YIVO Annual of Jewish Social Science* XVII, 1978), 21-53, esp. p. 29.

graphic appearance."[42] The shape is associated with something known to the child, who is then to associate it with the name of the letter. (The notion of phonics, which associates a letter directly with its sound, is different.)

> The rabbis told R. Joshua b. Levi: Children have come to the Bet Hamidrash and said things the like of which was not said even in the days of Joshua b. Nun: *Alef beys* means learn wisdom. *Gimel daled*, show kindness to the poor. Why is the foot of the *gimel* stretched toward the *daled*? Because it is fitting for the benevolent to run after the poor. And why is the roof of the *daled* stretched toward the *gimel*? Because he must make himself available to him. And why is the face of the *daled* turned away from the *gimel*? Because he (gimel) must give him (daled) help in secret, lest he shame him.[43]

The Content of Learning

The content of learning is the Torah. But the Torah is not the text. It comprises two parts, *Torah she-bikhtav* and *Torah she-beal peh*, the *written* and the *oral* Torah. It is therefore not limited by the fixed boundaries of the printed word, but is infinite. One pursues the truth of the Torah through the printed word, to begin with, but the oral interpretations are an indispensable vehicle. Moreover, they continue to grow and develop in an endless dialectic.

There is thus no final human authority that can claim complete mastery of the Torah. The evolving Torah itself is independent of any person or historical group of persons; it is autonomous in this sense. A striking Talmudic story illustrates this point in showing that even Moses, our teacher, was no better than any of us in this regard:

> R. Judah said, in the name of Rab: When Moses rose to the heavens, he found the Holy One, Blessed Be He, occupied in tying crowns to the letters (of the Torah). He said to him: Lord of the Universe, who requires you to do this (i.e. to add to your written word of the Torah)? He replied: There is a man who will be born several generations from now and his name will be Akiba the son of Joseph; he will derive from each jot of the Torah's letters mountains of halachic conclusions. Said Moses: Lord of the Universe, show him to me. Replied He: Turn around. Moses then went and sat in the eighth row (of Akiba's lecture hall), but could not understand what was being discussed. He felt faint, disheartened. When the discussion reached a certain point, R. Akiba's students asked him: Rabbi, whence do you derive this? And R. Akiba replied: This is (part of) the halacha given to Moses on Mt. Sinai. Moses then felt better. He returned and came before

---

42 Roskies, *Ibid.*, 29, 32. This whole article by Roskies is of considerable interest.
43 *Shabbat*, 104a. See also Roskies, Ibid., 29.

the Holy One, Blessed Be He, and said: Lord of the Universe, you have a man like that, yet you gave the Torah through me? To which came the reply: Be silent! This was my design.[44]

Moses, who brought us the text of the written Torah, did not understand the depth of the interpretations and inferences built upon it. In some sense all these inferences are embodied in the text, but they are not accessible to anyone at any given time no matter how wise and learned. Only the historical process of continuing dialectic discussion can draw them forth. Such discussion is, in effect, an instrument of perception, revealing what is hidden in the text, in a piecemeal and continuing process in historical time.

If the Torah transcends all human authorities, it is autonomous in a further sense, even from the Almighty. Already in the story just quoted, we saw the Holy One, Blessed Be He, occupying Himself with the Torah, His own creation. Now in the following story, we see the boldest stroke of the Talmudic Masters. For they here tell us that the very process of interpretation which forms an integral part of the Torah is independent of the Divine authority itself—since the written Torah explicitly construes such interpretation as a human process.

> On that day, R. Eliezer brought forward every imaginable argument but they did not accept them. Said he to them. If the *halakhah* agrees with me, let this carob tree prove it. Thereupon the carob tree was torn a hundred cubits out of its place—others affirm four hundred cubits. No proof can be brought from a carob tree, they retorted.
>
> Again, he said to them: If the *halakhah* agrees with me, let the stream of water prove it. Whereupon the stream of water flowed backwards. No proof can be brought from a stream of water, they rejoined. Again he urged: If the *halakhah* agrees with me, let the walls of the schoolhouse (academy) prove it. Whereupon the walls inclined to fall.
>
> But R. Joshua rebuked them (the walls) saying, When scholars are engaged in a *halakhah* dispute, what have you to interfere? Hence they did not fall, out of respect for R. Joshua, but they did not become straight again out of respect for R. Eliezer, and they are still standing thus inclined.
>
> Again, he said to them, if the *halakhah* agrees with me, let it be proved from Heaven. Whereupon a Heavenly voice cried out: Why do ye dispute with R. Eliezer, seeing that in all matters the *halakhah* agrees with him. But R. Joshua arose and exclaimed: It (the Torah) is not in heaven. (Deut. 30:12)
>
> What did he mean by this? —Said R. Jeremiah: That Torah had already been given at Mt. Sinai. We pay no attention to a Heavenly voice, because Thou hast long since written in the Torah at Mt. Sinai: After the majority one must incline (Ex. 23:2)

---

44 *Menahot*, 29b.

R. Nathan met Elijah and asked him: What did the Holy One, Blessed Be He, do then? He laughed with joy, he replied, saying, My sons have defeated Me, my sons have defeated Me.[45]

Not even the Lord has the final word in matters of interpretation of the Word. The world of sacred learning, the Torah, is accessible not through magic, not through visions, not through formulas, not through authority whether human or Divine, but only through the patient and infinite process of human study and learning. No greater tribute to education can be conceived. It is this tribute, I believe, which best symbolizes Judaism's philosophy of education.

This paper was originally given as an adult education lecture at Temple Emanuel, Newton, MA, in February 1984.

45 *Baba Metzia*, 59b.

JEWISH EDUCATION

PURPOSES, PROBLEMS, AND POSSIBILITIES

Israel Scheffler

Purposes

I begin with a caution: If we turn to Jewish education worldwide with the categories of public national systems in mind, we are sure to be misled. Unlike schooling under these systems, Jewish education is not compulsory, it does not derive from national citizenship nor connect with university or professional education. It does not aim to introduce students to the arts and sciences nor does it evaluate them in terms of academic achievement. It provides no vocational, career, or artistic training, nor does it function to select students for adult roles in society. It is, further, neither parallel to, nor a substitute for what may be regarded as *general* education or *universal* culture; it no more frees one from the need for such culture than does an Argentinean or Alaskan or Norwegian education.

The purposes of Jewish education differ wholly from those of public education. These purposes are neither civic, nor individualistic, nor utilitarian. Viewed in relation to the pupil, they are: to initiate the Jewish child into the culture, history, and spiritual heritage of the Jewish people, to help the child to learn and face the truth about Jewish history, identity, and existence, to enhance his or her dignity as a Jewish person, and to enable the child to accept, and to be creative in, the Jewish dimension of its life.

Viewed rather in its relation to the Jewish people, the purposes of Jewish education are: to promote Jewish survival and welfare, to interpret and communicate authentic Jewish experience, to sustain and defend Jewish honor and loyalties, to create living links with the Jewish past, preserving and extending its heritage for future generations. Ideally, Jewish education should be a natural reflection of the inner dignity of the Jewish people, and of its ethical, spiritual and cultural resources, as well as a response to current social and intellectual realities. This means: it should not be merely defensive, or apologetic, or imitative, or archaic, or nostalgic for a past that is no more. Rather, from its own position of inner strength and historical self-awareness, it should have the courage not only to reevaluate its directions, but also to adapt whatever is worthwhile in the environment to its own purposes, thus promoting the creative continuity of its civilization.

Problems

The problems facing Jewish education in modern industrial society stand out sharply by contrast with the pre-modern period, for which education in the Jewish school, home, and community was one continuous entity, embodied concretely in all spheres of life. Insofar as formal Jewish schooling or study was differentiated in the earlier period, it was accorded the highest religious and metaphysical status, regarded as an intrinsic value, a form of worship, but also a practical guide in all spheres of life. Scattered in their diverse and fragile communities, Jews assuredly had no control over the world, but they had the word, and the word gave them access to the highest heavens, to which their religious life was dedicated. What sociologists have remarked as the peculiar mixture of Jewish intellectuality, otherworldliness, and steadfastness in adversity is perhaps illuminated by the special role of classical Jewish education.

The Jew lived a precarious existence, but the philosophical framework of Jew and non-Jew alike was largely the same. The world revealed by faith was created by a personal and omnipotent God, who put mankind at the center of his creation, endowed human beings with free will and made absolute moral and devotional demands of them. Human actions were freighted with significance, supervised by Providence, consequential in the last degree. History, an interplay of God's will and men's wills, was to be read partly as natural, partly as miraculous, but in any case as inviting interpretation by personal, moral, and religious categories, such as loyalty, gratitude, reciprocity, covenant, punishment and reward, reverence, sin, stubbornness, and repentance.

The holiness of the Jewish Scriptures, central to this philosophical world-view, was virtually unquestioned. Although Jews suffered for refusing to accept Christianity or Islam as the higher fulfillment of these Scriptures, the Scriptures themselves were regarded by all as sacred. Jewish education was thus based on systematic beliefs, of which the basic philosophical features were recognized and shared by all. Such education offered a genuine reflection of historical Jewish existence, offering an authentic response to that existence in the doctrines and practices of Judaism.

Now every feature of the pre-modern context has been destroyed or rendered problematic in the modern period. The emancipation and entry of the Jew into the mainstream of Western life broke the tightly knit harmony of home, school and community. The general breakdown of the medieval world view shattered the inherited conception of nature and history shared by Jew and non-Jew alike, undermined traditional attitudes to their religious Scriptures, and destroyed the uniform traditional response to Jewish existence which constituted the basis of education in the past.

The Jewish genius for religious creativity, already severely threatened by these changes, has now, further, been profoundly shocked by the incalculable trauma of the Holocaust. Jewish predilections for intellectual and otherworldly thought have, concomitantly, been secularized, largely diverted into scientific and academic channels—thus reinforcing universalistic ideologies corrosive of Jewish loyalties.

The momentum of the technological society meanwhile proceeds apace, most rapidly in the United States. Mobility destroys communities and dissolves family bonds. Individualism and voluntarism erode the base of religious, and specifically Jewish, values. The pervasive commercialism, the ever more distracting media, the consumerism, the vulgarity, the sheer volume of competing activities and communications salient in contemporary life, all constitute obstacles to a vital Jewish education. Unlike their educational forebears, Jewish educators of today cannot rely on a nearly universal philosophical consensus undergirding religious faith, nor on the support of a devout Jewish home, nor on an authoritative Jewish community and—unlike their public counterparts—they cannot call on political and civic incentives for education, or on those of self-interest or career advancement. It is commonly said that education is a reflection of its society. Contemporary Jewish education has the task of creating the very society of which it should be the reflection.

There is no use bemoaning these facts, or looking back fondly to the memory of circumstances more favorable to Jewish education. If such education is to succeed, it must do so here and now. If it fails, fond memories will afford no consolation. To grasp the possibility of success, educators need to realize the magnitude of the problem and then to mobilize their efforts to address it. Concerted action on several fronts is needed. I shall here offer some suggestions, divided into two rough categories: organizational and philosophical.

Possibilities

Organizational Suggestions

The problems of Jewish education, arising from a shared commitment to Jewish survival, nevertheless vary qualitatively with the communities into which the Jewish people is divided. Seen in the worldwide perspective of its overriding purpose, Jewish education must, however, take as a primary task to strengthen the bonds among these communities, to build and reinforce lines of communication among them, developing morale, understanding, and mutual support. The problems they severally face differ in various respects, and they must find correspondingly varying ways of meeting them. But in shared purpose and fate, each has a stake in the success of the rest. Each must therefore foster an awareness of all, seeing itself not merely in local and current terms, but as part of a continuous people, stewards-in-common of a precious heritage of culture.

Among the several Jewish communities, the one in Israel occupies a central place, as the only one in which the historic language of Jews lives, in which the self-consciousness of Jews as a people is public and explicit, in which the possibility of continuous cultural development is maximal. The love of the land and the deep bond between diaspora and Israeli Jewish communities are basic to Jewish educational goals and, consequently, so also is a profound concern for the welfare of the Jewish community of Israel.

Yet Jewishness is not to be confused with Israelism. Israeli citizens include non-Jews, while most Jews are not Israeli citizens. Nor can Jewish education be reduced to pro-Israelism. It must take into account the rich content of Jewish experience throughout the centuries, reckon with the diverse characteristics and needs of diaspora Jewish communities, and take as its fundamental goal the strengthening of informed Jewish loyalties in diverse spheres of life. It must educate each Jewish community to take a role in the worldwide deliberations of the Jewish people, for each such community has a role to play and a point of view to represent.

Jewish education, in this conception, is inevitably pluralistic. Within the framework of its common purposes, it is to be realized in different ways, every such realization based on an authentic relation to the Jewish past and an effort to make some portion of that past usable in the present. But is bound, at the same time, to respect the differing interpretations of Jewish life which strive, in their various ways, to preserve and promote Jewish values.

Jewish education ought, in every one of its realizations, to promote an inclusive *sense of time*—an awareness of, and affiliation with, the history of the Jewish people; a comprehensive *sense of space*—an awareness of, and association with, the Jewish communities scattered across the globe, and a cultivated *sense of self*—a knowledge of the Hebrew language and other languages of Jews, and an acquaintance with the treasured achievements and literatures of Jewish thought, feeling, striving, and expression throughout the ages.

Some suggestions of a curricular and institutional sort are these:

A rethinking of *real educational time* should be undertaken, both as regards the annual *calendar*, to emphasize learning time outside traditional school hours, and as regards the *life span*, to emphasize adult education, family education, education in university settings, and projects linking older and younger generations.

Analogously, a rethinking of *real educational space* is needed, to emphasize local learning sites outside the traditional school, e.g. Judaica collections in university libraries, Jewish institutions such as hospitals, museums, newspapers, presses, bookstores, homes for the aged, community councils, studios, educational and service bureaus; as well, exchanges and visits to Jewish communities elsewhere.

In addition, a rethinking of the educational development of Jewish *selfhood* is needed, to prepare and revise learning materials for children of various ages, and for adults, emphasizing not only history, language and literature, but also experiences and practices, arts and music, and the analysis of social problems confronting contemporary Jewish communities.

Finally, institutions for the worldwide coordination of educational efforts should be developed. These would facilitate research, comparative studies and evaluations, preparation and dissemination of educational materials, and exchanges amongst Jewish educators in the various communities. Centers for research, development, training, field studies and planning should be formed.

Philosophical Suggestions

The problems of Jewish education are not, in any event, primarily organizational. Nor are they wholly soluble by exhortation, inspiration, funding, or research. All of these have their place but none can substitute for a philosophical rethinking of the bases of Jewish life in our times.

By philosophy, I intend nothing technical or abstruse, but an engagement with such basic questions as: How can the purposes of Jewish education best be realized in the present? What is the justification for such education? What is our positive vision of an ideal Jewish life in this century? What ought we to expect of Jewish youth under the actual constraints of their life conditions? How help them, and ourselves, to an authentic appreciation of Jewish values? How enable them to go beyond us to develop the latent intimations of Jewish traditions and insights? How shall we introduce them to Jewish materials so that these materials may germinate and grow in their minds and hearts and flourish in the world they will inhabit rather than the worlds we can remember? A reflective answer to this last question requires a fresh perception of the materials themselves, without which they will remain educationally inert. I offer no complete answers here, but only some suggestions on two basic sorts of materials: Jewish texts and religious rituals.

Texts   Jewish education is said to be traditionally text-centered. The attribution is misleading, for the study of sacred texts in classical Judaism was not self-sufficient, but supported by constant educative influences flowing from the life of the family and the practice of the community. Nevertheless, these texts and their interpretive literatures did constitute the basic focus of formal study.

This traditional role of textual materials, incidentally, offers another, and a positive, dissimilarity with general public schooling. For where such schooling has often come to rely on scattered and artificial items of the "See Spot Run" variety in early education, Jewish education can draw on the rich and momentous texts that have shaped both Jewish and non-Jewish consciousness throughout the centuries.

But magnificent as these texts may be, they must be seen from an educational point of view, as providing only raw materials for learning. In themselves lifeless, they cannot speak to our pupils until these pupils have learned to hear, come within range, acquired the needed meanings, and been prompted to ask the appropriate questions. If these texts seem so obviously meaningful to us—that is, to adult educators—it is only because we have already gone through the processes of learning to hear them. The obviousness of their meaning is an artifact of *our* early training, and cannot be generated in our youth by mere exposure. They need themselves to learn how to hear the message, to grasp it in a way that will be effective for them, whether or not it was our way in the past.

A reflective or philosophical approach to this task requires us to rethink the texts ourselves; unlearning our habitual perceptions, we need to look at the texts again with fresh eyes and from new angles. The teaching of the young ought to be an occasion for the re-teaching of ourselves—their teachers. Such re-teaching is a matter, not merely of recalling our own half-remembered learnings, or of relating the text to past context and commentary, but also it is an occasion for exploration and discovery—for finding those new meanings in the text which can only be revealed by the serious effort to make it available in the present. A philosophical approach to teaching the text should, in short, renew the text itself, as well as teach both teacher and pupil.

Religious Rituals   Religion is a closed book to large numbers of Jews and non-Jews alike. To open this book, at least partially, through reinterpretation in contemporary intellectual terms is a philosophical task of the first importance. For Jewish education it is crucial in view of the intimate historical dependence of Jewish civilization upon its religious core. I do not pretend to do more here than make some suggestions on the topic of ritual as educational matter.

To begin with, it is worth emphasizing the fact that religion has a history, despite common denials by religionists themselves. Every doctrine and rite preserves echoes of earlier beliefs no longer accepted reflectively today. The continuity of religion is in substantial part a product of reinterpretation, acknowledged or not. Thus, the effort at contemporary reinterpretation has ample precedent.

Attitudes toward ritual have clearly undergone enormous changes, the details of which can here be left to the scholars. But a brief sketch, following Yehezkel Kaufmann, will make the point.[1] Primitive pre-Biblical culture conceived of ritual as magic, a technique for manipulating nature. The rites, properly performed, guaranteed the fertility of flocks and fields, protection against drought, freedom from sickness, victory in war, control over one's enemies, success in enterprise. This conception did not give the gods or spirits a privileged position. These spirits themselves used ritual and magic to gain their ends, and were in turn subject to manipulation by ritual and magic employed by other spirits and by man. These characteristics are amply exhibited in pagan mythology and stories of the gods.

A more humanistic but still primitive view which overlay the magical conception was that of ritual as propitiation of the gods or spirits in control of some natural resource. Pleasing the god in control of rainfall would, it was hoped, guarantee rainfall—not automatically—but through the mediation of the will of the god, who could be dealt with on the basis of pleas and gifts, but not coerced through a mechanical technique. This was the world view of polytheism—nature as a set of different regions or forces, each under the rule of an independent local will that could be bargained with, as one would bargain with a human being.

Biblical religion wrought a radical transformation in these beliefs, propounding the doctrine of a transcendent, single God, who was not part of nature but who stood wholly beyond it, having created it and all that it contains, and whose will was the source of absolute moral commands laid upon human beings generally and the children of Israel in particular. Such a being had no need of magical devices to attain his goals. He could not be manipulated by the techniques of men nor bargained with like a local landowner or petty politician. The Bible contains the record of this transformation in its rejection of all mythology and its strong polemic against magic, idolatry, and divination. Yet elements of earlier beliefs as to the magical efficacy of rites can be still discerned in the Pentateuch.

Prophetic attitudes toward the rites as conditional and subordinate to the moral commands prevailed in later, Rabbinic Judaism. What,

---

1 Yehezkel Kaufmann, *The Religion of Israel* [translated and abridged by Moshe Greenberg], (Chicago: The University of Chicago Press, 1960), esp. pp. 53-59, 101-103.

however, was the purpose of rites for which no rational meaning could be found? Kaufmann says, "The ultimate sanction of the rite became the divine will. Judaism thus created a noble symbol for its basic idea that everything is a divine command; fulfilling the command is an acknowledgement of the supremacy of God's will. A cult of commands evolved; the system of commands sanctified all of life to the service of the One. To laws for which no rational explanation could be found, the Rabbis applied the general principle, 'The commandments were given only for the purpose of purifying human beings' (Gen. Rabbah 44.1)."[2]

רב אמר: לא נתנו המצוות אלא לצרף בהן את הבריות. וכי מה איכפת ליה להקב"ה למי ששוחט מן הצוואר או מי ששוחט מן העורף. הוי לא נתנו המצוות אלא לצרף בהם את הבריות.

This humanistic attitude of the Rabbis views the rites as, in effect, educative through their symbolic value. Ritual "purifies human beings" not through magical force or propitiatory effect but through its reflexive symbolic impact which helps to relate its participants to higher values and more exalted purposes.

This historical attitude is available to reinterpretive efforts today, and can indeed be considerably extended. A ritual system can be viewed as an elaborate symbolic apparatus, a complex language which profoundly alters the perceptions and sensibilities of those who learn to interpret and apply it in living practice. I mention here three, out of several, cardinal symbolic functions performed by ritual: denotation, expression, and reenactment.[3]

a) *Denotation*: Jewish rites pick out or portray various events and aspects of life associated with Jewish history and with the distinctive values distilled in that history. By repeated occurrence though the year and at major junctures of personal life, rites bring participants into continual contact with these values. Judaism as a historical religion has rites that are largely commemorative. The seasonal rhythms of agricultural rites were historicized as well and thus reflected in ritual after the land was lost. Thus, the ritual calendar became the denotative cement holding the whole system together. Beyond the day-to-day practical tasks of their lives, Jews had in the scheme of ritual observance referential access to a dramatic world of history and purpose in which they found meaning.

b) *Expression*: Ritual actions have a second symbolic function, beyond denotation, i.e. expression. Just as a painting may express joy or nostalgia while denoting a landscape, a rite may express a feeling or

2 *Ibid.*, p. 102.
3 Much of what follows derives from my studies of symbolic aspects of ritual, included in my *Inquiries: Philosophical Studies of Language, Science, and Learning* (Indianapolis: Hackett Publishing Co., 1986) Part I, Chs. 6, 7, 8.

attitude while portraying a historical event. Jewish rituals thus indeed express a whole range of feelings and moods, fear and deliverance (Purim), the bitterness of slavery and the joy of redemption (Passover), contrition and exultation (Rosh Hashanah and Yom Kippur), wonder, trust and peace (Sabbath). The rites carrying these expressive values do not uniformly evoke the respective emotions in performance. Yet, the repeated exposure to such symbolized values shapes the character and sensibility of its participants, over time.

c) *Reenactment*: Ritual performances allude indirectly to previous performances. Each new Seder calls to mind Sedarim past, i.e. reenacts them while at the same time *portraying* the exodus, and *expressing* the joy of liberation from bondage. The repetition of rites thus serves another purpose beyond the shaping of individual perceptions—that is, the development of tradition—the sense, with each repetition of a rite, that it *is* a repetition. And tradition further structures time; beyond the commemoration of historical events, and beyond the ordering of rhythms of the calendar year, tradition offers a sense of the lengthening duration of ritual performance, hence a sense of stability in a world of change and danger, a *rootedness in time*. All participants are, further, linked indirectly—by the same ritual-reenactments—to one another, thus sharing a *linkage in space* as well, the sense of a historical community with members bound to one another in the present, wherever they may be. "More than the Jews have kept the Sabbath, the Sabbath has kept the Jews." (It is understandable that the yearning of Soviet Jews for linkage with their brethren should have found expression in rediscovery of the joyful celebration of Simhat Torah.)

The symbol system of Jewish ritual can, I suggest, be treated in these terms in contemporary education. This system is not a piece of magic, superstition, rational theory, cosmic technology or outmoded theology. It constitutes a language which organizes a world, structuring time and space, orienting us in history, binding us in community, and sensitizing us to those features of life in which our forebears have found the highest value and deepest meanings—freedom, responsibility, sincerity, humility, care, loyalty, righteousness, compassion. The specific interpretations given to this symbolic system have changed throughout our history more frequently than the system itself. It is the system itself we need, however to treat seriously again, recovering it as a potent resource for Jewish education.

This paper was originally given at a Commencement of the Jerusalem Fellows, in June, 1985.

FROM BENNETT

ON RATIONALITY, MATH AND MORAL EDUCATION

Stephen Brown and Joseph Lukinsky suggest a role for mathematics in the development of moral decision making skills. Citing the overlap which exists between these two realms they insist that the intellectual and affective skills and inclinations crucial to morality can be reinforced within a mathematics curriculum. They emphasize that rigorous analysis is a crucial component of morality as well as mathematics.

> The task both in mathematics and morality would seem to be to encourage students to view both intuition and rigorous analysis as important; and to attempt to utilize both or either where they are appropriate.[1]

In this section we have described the important role of rationality within every subject area of the Jewish day school curriculum. We have emphasized not only that the use of reason is compatible with these subjects but that a rational approach to them is the path most conducive to a deep and authentic appreciation of their content and message. Rationality has therefore been stressed as a unifying methodology within the day school—a means of approaching study which can be consciously reinforced by all teachers. By doing so, the child will gain the ability and the propensity to employ this skill which will ultimately enable him to consistently and sensitively integrate the various facts and experiences before him.

Dissertation, pp. 84-85.

---

1 Stephen Brown and Joseph Lukinsky, "Morality and the Teaching of Mathematics," *Ethical Education* I:2 (Summer, 1970) 4.

ON TEACHING TOWARDS COGNITIVE EMOTIONS: JOY, SURPRISE, AWE

Scheffler introduces two specific cognitive emotions which are of considerable importance to the day school: the "joy of verification" and the "feeling of surprise." As both suppositions are based in the cognitive realm, they are accessible throughout all realms of knowledge.

The "joy of verification" is the joy which accompanies the fulfillment of an expectation, "a triumphant feeling of having guessed correctly."[1] Awareness of this special feeling of joy can play a vital reinforcing role in the educational process. The religious studies as well as the natural and social sciences must be open to critical study and investigation so that the student can become a part of the learning process. Study of the Bible, prayers and Jewish history through the method of inquiry characterized by an openness to discovery—and the opportunities to predict outcomes or attempt interpretations based on historical precedent or prior commentary—are types of educational experiences which must be available to the day school student. A closed, tradition/authority centered religious program would never provide opportunities for students to enjoy the invigorating joy of verification for they would never have been personally initiated into the study of the material. If the religious education as well as general education make these experiences possible, an important unifying emotion will be developed by the school.

Scheffler's second cognitive emotion—the "feeling of surprise"—is intrinsically linked to the religious domain. Surprise results when events conflict with prior expectations. But in order to be surprised, one must be open to it. Contrary facts must be acknowledged for this feeling of surprise to occur and for the unexpected events to be reconciled. Within classical religious education, however, surprises would not occur. Every event—every doubt—would be explained with traditional responses. Questions which might lead to surprising answers would eventually fade away, for the repetitive replies would ultimately stifle those thoughts which led to the original perplexity. The Conservative Movement (and, therefore, its day schools) are ideologically open to such questions and should encourage that inquiry and personal involvement which might lead to surprises. The school, therefore, must be prepared to deal with these feelings when they arise, for, as Scheffler describes,

---

1 Israel Scheffler, "In Praise of the Cognitive Emotions," *Teachers College Record*, 79:2 (December, 1977), p. 183.

receptivity to surprise involves ... a certain vulnerability; it means accepting the risk of a possibly painful unsettlement of one's beliefs, with the attendant need to rework one's expectations and redirect one's conduct ... This risk may, to varying degrees, become palatable, even exciting; certainly accepting it is one of the normal requirements of rational character. Yet it *is* a risk of possibly painful disorientation, and it requires emotional strength to face and to master.[2]

A school dedicated to forging integrative individuals will not seek to avoid surprise through dogmatic instruction. Rather, it will prepare teachers to respond to surprise when it arises, e.g., during science class when Biblical stories seem to contradict scientific explanations; when moral decisions seem to demand contradicting God's commandments; when historical perspectives run counter to those expected; when theological questions arise after shattering emotional traumas. The teacher must react in consistent manners to these instances of surprise.

> Surprise may be dissipated and evaporate into lethargy. It may culminate in confusion or panic. It may be swiftly overcome by a redoubled dogmatism. Or it may be transformed into wonder and curiosity, and so become an educative occasion. Curiosity replaces the impact of surprise with the demand for explanation; it turns confusion into question ... critical inquiry in pursuit of explanation is a constructive outcome of surprise.[3]

The ability to doubt and still retain religious commitment is tantamount to an appropriate response to the feeling of surprise.

A "sense of wonder" is another "cognitive emotion" which the day school must develop. Greenberg stresses this attitude as one which should permeate the entire learning environment. He refers to an appreciation of Heschel's idea of "radical amazement."

> To sense wonder involves a profound intuitive conviction that there are realms beyond one's intellectual comprehension and immediate emotional experience ... it inevitably involves a simultaneous awareness of one's personal inadequacies...[4]

The child's sense of wonder can be developed in relation to the phenomena of the physical world as well as the historic experiences of the Jewish people. It would entail the use of empirical facts as well as an openness to questions and reasons which

> at the same time, would not rob (the child) of the sense of wonder and even radical amazement as he contemplates the universe ... and events in Jewish history.[5]

2 *Ibid.*, pp. 185-186.
3 *Ibid.*
4 Simon Greenberg, "The Religious Policy of the Solomon Schechter Day School," *The Synagogue School*, 24:3 (Spring, 1966) 5.
5 *Ibid.*, p. 6.

The development of this appreciation of awe qualifies as a cognitive emotion because it dwells in the cognitive domain but is appreciated as an emotion. If every teacher in the school is sensitive to this sense of wonder it could help develop a vital religious appreciation within the children's perception of all knowledge and experience. This will reinforce the Jewish rituals which are performed for very similar reasons—to help remind the Jew that he is forever in awe and grateful to God for the bounty which is his.

Dissertation, pp.87-90.

ON CREATIVITY

Creative imagination has been and remains a vital component to full appreciation of the Jewish heritage, both religious and historical. The most fundamental and extensive example is its role in the understanding of the Biblical text. Maimonides wrote his *Guide to the Perplexed* for those individuals who through literal interpretation of the text had run into unsettling, irreconcilable conflicts with reason. He offered a philosophical interpretation in his *Guide* based upon an allegorical interpretation of the text. Understanding of God (not the "notion of God" or the "idea of God" but God Himself) demands a creative insight capable of lifting one beyond the anthropomorphic representation of Him in the Bible. Attempts to conceptualize the events of the Bible also demand keen creative talents.

Understanding the nature of revelation demands creative insight as well. If one accepts the literal text as an accurate account of God's revelation then comprehension of the majestic glory of that encounter between God and the children of Israel demands a finely tuned and highly developed imagination; not a fanciful imagination but rather one whose mental pictures can evince emotional commitment and affiliation. If one cannot accept the veracity of the literal depiction of the theophany at Sinai, efforts to formulate a compelling alternative view demand creativity and sensitivity. Is revelation similar to the feelings of inspiration often described by creative persons? Or is revelation substantially different from this phenomenon? Both views have been articulated by contemporary Jewish thinkers, each necessitating the creative encouragement of creative thinking—the active and purposeful development of this skill and propensity within every aspect of the school curriculum must be pursued—from scientific theories to mathematic formulas to poetic license to Midrashim (religious legends) to historical role playing activities. Creative interpretation will only be possible by the mind which is prepared for it, so a unified approach to the development of this talent will serve the interests of the total day school.

Creativity can be encouraged through an openness to new ideas, and respect for individual contribution. Once the child is comfortable he will be able to freely express himself in all areas. Activities such as role playing, puppet shows, dramatic readings and recreations, creative writing and creative dance and movement are specific means through which the child can express himself. These activities can help foster the necessary emotions which accompany the free display of creative ideas and insights.

Dissertation, pp. 92-94.

THE ELEMENTS OF EDUCATION

COINCIDENCE AND DIFFERENCES IN GENERAL AND JEWISH EDUCATION

Perry London

This essay has a minor and a major aim: Its minor aim is to disabuse Jewish educators of the idea that general educators have an easier life than they do. Its major aim is to argue for the importance of reconceptualizing and promoting Jewish education in terms of two dimensions which I call, respectively, *integrity* and *content*. My hypothesis is that their pertinence to the general education of Jewish children helps to explain why these youngsters perform better in secular than in Jewish schools.

Coincidences in General and Jewish Education

The complaint lists and recommendations that emerge from recent evaluations of general and of Jewish education in the United States convince me that we lack clear-headed vision for guiding what educators should do, what the means of doing it are, and what the overall goals of educational systems ought to be. It is easier to address the elements of education, as I have been asked to do, than it is to elaborate such a vision, but looking at the elements of education alone may overlook more fundamental questions of what business are we in and why we are in it.

Education's many conceptual and administrative elements are labelled by a substantial number of theme words and buzz words, including some which are unique to Jewish education: Conceptual terms, for instance, include *learning, curriculum, subject matter, information, facts, skills, literacy, cultural literacy, computer literacy, Jewish literacy, Torah, Bible, Hebrew, life cycle, ritual, customs, ceremonies, Israel, identity, creativity, adjustment, growth, socialization, citizenship, character, involvement, attitude, intermarriage,* and *survival.* Administrative terms include such items as: *organization, centralization, voluntarism, responsibility, accountability, standards, outreach* (e.g. to *parents, community, business, synagogue, center*), *schools, formal, informal, teacher, recruitment, retention, training, professionalization, restructuring.*

Such varied themes preoccupy educators not only for whatever topical importance they have, but also, for the general educator, because the nation does not quite know what it means by education or just what role schools and the whole formal teaching and training apparatus ought to play in education, whatever it means. Nor does the nation know what resources it should assign to education or how to divide those resources among its divisions.

The questions are timely, I think, and Americans are fretting about how to define educational goals and how to assess whether the system is meeting them chiefly because they sensibly, if vaguely, fear that the United States is a declining society. This fear also sensibly lends urgency to some of our current preoccupations with budget deficits, with Japanese culture and foreign economic competition, and with social disorganization and dislocation at home. Fears of economic decline fuel one of the main thrusts of public concern with general education—the hope to invigorate economic reform by improvement in teaching of the three R's and in computer "literacy" (note the apparent shift within the past generation or so from computer "skill" to "literacy"). E.D. Hirsch leads a growing movement that promotes "cultural" rather than "computer literacy," but I fancy that many of its supporters will judge its efficacy more by increases in automobile sales than in Shakespeare recitals. The public's "third ear" is tuned to businesses which are crying for employees who can read and write the English language.

Another emergent goal of general education is that of reducing social disorganization and dislocation among the young—teenage pregnancy, substance abuse, crime, and school dropouts—and of increasing outreach to parents as one means of doing so. The full impact of these problems is still little recognized and sometimes barely admitted by the moguls of national education and by prestigious university schools of education and psychology programs, despite the fact that some demographers claim that up to 40% of all American school children are at moderate to great risk. Economic and social goals, in any case, increasingly compete for attention at all levels of general education.

Jewish Education

The Jewish community, despite its special needs, is not so different from the rest of the country in the character of its educational problems. The

United States Jewish community has no well-defined view of exactly what it means by Jewish education or just what role schooling should play in it or what resources to allocate to it or how to divide them up among educational agencies. I am told that the Council of Jewish Federations was hardly aware of such problems until 1969, when student demonstrations at its General Assembly awakened it to the educational needs of the Jewish community.

All the Federations are plenty worried now about Jewish education, I think for reasons paralleling those which concern the general community. American Jews are not overly concerned about their economic welfare, nor perhaps that their children are wholesale victims of social disorganization. But the Jewish community is nonetheless worried that we may not be an eternal people after all, especially in face of the relentless temptations which America extends to our children for affluence and assimilation. This kind of fear motivates and funds discussion and research (including mine) on Jewish identity. It also sponsored outreach efforts to converts and mixed marriages and, in part, things like the patrilineality decision of the reform movement, one of those motives was to reduce population attrition of the Jewish community. Fears about intermarriage and disaffiliation may be the two most prominent motives governing today's institutional urgency concerning Jewish education.

There are other similarities between the problems of general and of Jewish education: Jewish kids have little motivation to succeed at Jewish schooling, and the motivation of many kids in the general education system is likewise low. Achievement standards are low in Jewish supplementary schools, and so are they in most of the country's public schools. General knowledge seems to be at a low level everywhere in this country: As Russell Baker said, "You probably don't know who Louis B. Mayer was unless you're one of those few people who also know what Belgium is or who Abraham Lincoln was." Also, Jewish and general educators have similar kinds of problems allocating time, involving parents, and accommodating boards and bureaus and legislatures.

But there is one very conspicuous difference which ought to unnerve Jewish educators in particular: The same Jewish kids who do not learn very much in Jewish supplementary schools do very well indeed in general education, far better than most other children do. Far from leading beleaguered lives and being at risk when they later enter the labor force, Peterson and Zill's study of American Jewish high school students finds them doing better than any other group. Their families and home environments encourage educational achievement; their parents have high expectations and provide material support for learning.

The kids themselves have high self-esteem and an internal locus of control—they plan to take charge of their own destiny. Somewhat unlike their parents, on the other hand, they may not be committed to social causes: they endorse many of the goals of the "me" generation—they want to "have time for my own interests" and "have lots of money." But they are also committed to marriage, to a happy family life, and to having children (three or more, not so popular in middle-class America today), though they also want graduate degrees and their careers. Finally, their religious involvement is lower than that of any other religiously affiliated group in the United States, which may be related to their low achievements in Jewish education.

Why have so many of these kids performed poorly in the Jewish educational system and, indeed, dropped out of it early on? Most of these splendid kids will be good citizens, contributors to this society (in respects where they will personally benefit from it), and lead successful material lives. Maybe dropping out of Jewish school has some psychological parallels to abandoning public high school, even though many high school dropouts have hard lives in and out of school, while most of the Jewish school drop-outs lead lives which, in conspicuous respects, are just fine. Yet both groups do poorly in these respective schools, probably worse than they would have done a generation or two ago, and probably worse than school kids in poorer countries (though data are lacking).

Fractionation, Fragmentation and Educational Context

This brings me to my major argument, which for lack of a better term I shall call a *fractionation* or *fragmentation* hypothesis. It says that our implicit model of what an educational system is about—what it is for, what it ought to do, and how it ought to do it—is based on *an organizational paradigm* which cannot "work" in the present social context of American life. There has been such an extreme development of social anonymity and personal alienation in American society that the community necessary to give children a psychological infrastructure which supports schooling no longer thrives and can no longer provide what it has to. Under the circumstances, a paradigm shift in secular and in Jewish schools is needed to reinvigorate education. I shall focus here only on Jewish education.

This hypothesis has two parts. The first says that experience and knowledge—education—needs a quality of integrity, a unity of self-perception, and a cohesiveness of action, which encourages us from childhood on to connect all aspects of our consciousness and experience. That striving for connection leads children to be aware, and to be conscientious, to try to integrate the topics they learn, are involved with, and are interested in. Whatever promotes the disposition towards integration, or synthesis, promotes the learning process.

The more the educational system splits and dissociates intellect and affect, cognitive and experiential, skills and attitudes, knowledge and citizenship, craft and character—the more it (inadvertently) tends to reduce a person's ability to learn things in any of those domains, because it reduces the degree of attention one would otherwise give to harmonizing them. Modern schools create such disfunction in many ways: By dividing things up into time periods (especially in high schools: Have you ever learned much in 45 minutes?); into subject matter topics rigidly separated from one another; and by dividing topics among teachers who routinely *do not* refer any of the material they teach to what any of their colleagues teach or collaborate with colleagues in co-teaching.

So there is a *dis-integrity* in the system which facilitates *dis-integration* in the learning process such that kids simply learn less of everything or learn it less well than they otherwise would. I do not think that decreased learning nationwide over the past thirty years can be blamed simply on influences like television, though TV is perhaps hazardous to learning because of the time it takes. Nor do I believe that diminished learning in our schools overall is a function of bad teaching, though there is plenty of bad teaching, and it certainly interferes with many children's learning. I think broad declines have resulted largely from the effects of our tendency to accept naively a paradigm of work and performance which has dominated our society since the Industrial Revolution.

The "production paradigm" of the Industrial Revolution that worked so well *de-contextualized* manufacturing. The "breakthrough" discovery of the industrial Revolution, so to speak, was that it was possible to make a great number of a product of good quality by reducing the product to identical component parts that could be constructed and assembled with a minimum of skill by the people doing the work. The de-contextualization of manufacturing "worked"—an interesting term, as Daniel Margolis pointed out to me, which may not have been used in our society in this way before the Industrial Revolution's paradigms had seized our minds far beyond our consciousness.

The essence of the paradigm—a good one for manufacturing, but with questionable effects on other aspects of the human condition—is that it de-contextualized what people did. It moved most labor out of the home and out of the family's sight into large factories where acquaintance with other workers and interdependence with them for a quality product were diminished. At the same time, it further reduced the meaningfulness of labor by minimizing the contribution each worker made to the whole product. (One need not subscribe to the political philosophy of Karl Marx to accept his social analysis of the Industrial Revolution.) It also de-contextualized people's lives by moving them off the land and into the cities. The increase in mobility alone—a pattern that has continued inexorably for two centuries to reach its peak in our time—further depleted the context of community and family stability. In addition, the cultural heterogeneity of large-scale immigration and a liberal political philosophy which supported this heterogeneity, helped to create an overall condition which undid the rhythms, the seasons, the expectations, and the backgrounds of most subcultures. This condition arose everywhere in the industrial world, but nowhere as much as in the United States.

Now the point, with respect to learning, is that one cannot learn much of anything without having a context in which to put it. My prior argument, about the integrity of knowledge, concerns the connections among its elements. This second part concerns their absorption and application to other parts of life. Content does not get absorbed without context, and an insidious split of content and context weakens learning greatly.

Context has at least two broad dimensions: One provides a *background* in which things are learned, and the other provides a *foreground* to which learning can be applied. The foreground means an area of contemporary interest, or approval, or aspiration.

To put this in plainer language—given something to learn, the first reason a youngster learns it is because school and its subject matter are presented in a context (i.e., against a background) where the child "knows" (indeed, takes for granted) that other people expect him or her to learn; for Jews, "You as a Jewish child need to know this, because Jews—with thousands of years of continuous history of which you are this moment's expression—have to know this." That is what I mean by background.

Foreground means you learn this because it is of interest to you, which in turn means that you like it, or you think you will get some reward from it, or you think you can apply it to something—or because you gain the approval of someone who will like *you* if you master it, even if you don't like *it*, so liking it becomes secondary to learning it. Or you learn it because learning it fits an aspiration, ambition, or vision you have of yourself in a future context, and that vision is reason enough for you to absorb what might otherwise be boring material in the context of your present experience. All those things are what we mean by context.

The main context for general education has always been the community. Where a sense of community does not exist, perhaps no other context can replace it. For 15% to 40% of the kids I worry most about, moveover—not the Jewish kids who are going to be doctors instead of rabbis, but the underclass mostly of black and Hispanic kids who are going to be "stoned," pregnant, or dead—the lack of community is a shatteringly difficult situation which may make it impossible for them to live their lives effectively.

Thus my hypothesis, in short: If you do not have integrity, at least of educational material, your have a very difficult learning situation. If, in addition, you do not have a context in which to put your knowledge, you have a hopeless learning problem.

Traditionally, Jewish religious education was completely contextualized and thus integral. It had no purpose in and of itself. The purpose of Jewish education—largely religious education—was to facilitate Jewish living, that is, to serve God, through all the media of experience, of community, of family, of ritual and rhythm and season. That context was so much the substratum of all specific educational experience that the form, the content, and the mode of presentation of the educational material itself may have made relatively little difference. The psychological context of contemporary American Jewish life has been drastically weakened as the Jewish community, with respect to this context, has been diminished in many ways.

For one thing, increased mobility and suburbanization have reduced the population density and therefore reduced the visibility of the Jewish community. There has also been some diminution or attenuation of affiliative activity which would make children aware of the satisfactions of being Jewish within a Jewish community. There is, finally, the strong tendency towards assimilation in the warm and accepting society from which Jews have benefited so much in America.

This acceptance tempts Jewish children with rich and rewarding opportunities which can compete with Jewish living or make it seem irrelevant to their aspirations. They have been well socialized towards the general community, and envision themselves very well fitting into its context as business and professional people and as home- and family-makers. But beyond a minimal Jewish identity to which, indeed, most of them subscribe, they do not envision their Jewishness as an especially active or demanding part of their lives. With the Jewish community weak, it is hard to provide an educational structure for them in which an integration of material, of topics, of time, and so forth, can take strong effect.

If one accepts this hypothesis, how could one act on it within the real constraints of American Jewish life to integrate the contents and enrich the context of Jewish education? The Orthodox community solves this problem automatically, to the extent that it can maintain its children's orthodoxy, by making orthodoxy the contextual framework.

For the rest of the American Jewish community, with its pluralistic themes, I think that a solution in Jewish education might require three revisions of current practice which might both contribute to and result from the paradigm shift suggested above.

One change might be to seek a unifying theme in Jewish education—that is, a theme around which all curricula, all subject matter, and all experiential activity could be designed. The theme might be the continuity of the Jewish people, the privilege of membership, and the responsibilities of a Jewish child for it—now and in the future. Such a theme implies burdens, disciplines, restraints and obligations—but any educational system that promotes community meaningfully must impose serious obligations on its children (and, no less, on their parents).

The second revision, I think, would be to make that theme encompass the whole curriculum—that is, to rationalize everything that is done towards literacy training, text training, Hebrew-language training, customs and ceremonies training, and experiential training in terms of that theme.

And third, it seems to me, it would be well to press the salience of that argument *continuously*—to the child, to the family, and to the community. It is easiest to reiterate to the child because the child is in school; it is harder to convey it to the family because, to do so, the family would have to become an active participant in the life of the school.

Pressing salience to the Jewish community, however, might actually not be as hard. At present, the Jewish community institutionally is quite aware of threats to its strength, if not its actual survival, and might be responsive to efforts by the educational community to involve it directly in trying to create a Jewish community context in which education can work.

Day schools, summer camps, family retreats, and "the Israel experience," in the terms of this essay, are all efforts at *integration* and *contextualization*, that is, at connecting the materials and topics and contents of Jewish thought and experience to one another (integration) and at embedding Jewish living in a broader framework than that of an individual child or, for that matter, of the nuclear family (contextualization).

On the whole, however, these activities have not been connected to each other for the same children or thought through by educators or community leaders as parts of an integral educational process with specific goals, such as increasing the Jewish affiliations of child participants when they leave home and go to college; reducing intermarriage rates or increasing conversion-in rates; increasing synagogue attendance and membership, and so forth.

For most Jews of all Jewish religious denominations, the long term task of Jewish education has abstract religious and spiritual objectives.

But progress towards these goals can only be measured and evaluated in the narrower terms of affiliation and observance. To meet those terms, educators and community leaders need to reconceptualize their task which, I believe, is to integrate and contextualize Jewish education, and to move more systematically towards realizing it.

FROM BENNETT

ON SUCCESS IN HEBREW SCHOOL AND PUBLIC SCHOOL

It would seem that religious education should be concerned fundamentally with the virtuous, moral life of an individual, offering principles of human conduct and interpersonal relationships. But in practice, the Hebrew school avoids any sort of moral education and even reverts to the ways of the secular school system: achievement and grades are accentuated as the motivation for learning.

But a flaw exists: success in the secular system can offer the skills necessary for the acquisition of a job and status within American society which will satisfy utilitarian desires. There is no such motivating force, however, for success within the Hebrew school or the American Jewish community. Beyond the self-satisfaction of competing with classmates, no reward is forthcoming to the successful Hebrew school student.

Reflections II, p. 8–9.

ON GOALS AND OBJECTIVES

It is obvious even to the most disinterested observer, that an educational system based upon and dedicated to teaching beliefs and practices which almost no one accepts, is inevitably doomed to failure.

I insist that elementary Jewish education must be concerned with far more than mere facts and inculcated skills ... Mere accumulation of information pertaining to Judaism without some tangible evidence of their impact upon one's way of life, is not a worthwhile goal of Jewish education. Martin Buber warns, however, that "we who believe that there can be no teaching apart from doing will be destroyed when our doing becomes independent of the teachings!"[1]

Mordecai Kaplan in his presentation of Reconstructionist Judaism as a civilization states that the primary goals for Jewish education must be child-centered and affective:

> ... to cultivate a desire and a capacity for modelling one's life in accordance with Jewish patterns of ethical and religious behavior ...
> to foster in the child a desire and capacity to play an active role in Jewish communal life ...[2]

Reflections I, pp. 4, 9-10.

---

1 Martin Buber, *Israel and the World—Essays in a Time of Crisis* (New York: Schocken Books, 1963) p. 143.
2 Mordecai Kaplan, *Judaism as a Civilization* (New York: Schocken Books, 1967) p. 92.

ON LOYALTY AS OUR GOAL

Successful modern approaches to education insist upon an active, challenging, open, learning environment—one which will emphasize and offer opportunities for both cognitive and moral interaction. But certain choices of means, in the last analysis, also imply choices of ends. The potential growth through new stages of development is considered a crucial aim of such an open system.

In order to apply such progressive techniques to the elementary Hebrew school, therefore, new goals and objectives must be formulated. We must no longer insist upon the ability to pass an objective test, or read and translate modern Hebrew as a requirement for study past the elementary school level. Rather, our goal must be enthusiastic, curious, young people anxious to pursue further study as a means of satiating the desires awakened within them during those first five years. We are concerned with religious education—humanistic, spiritual growth based in Judaic principles. Balancing the emphasis on knowledge (since most of it is forgotten anyway) with increased emphasis on developing more interest, appreciation and loyalty is our goal. Such reconstructed objectives for Jewish education, however, necessitate a concomitant reconstruction of Conservative Judaism in America. We must have the clearness of vision to admit that our present system, which is alienating, must change.

Reflections I, p. 19.

TO BEGIN WITH BELIEF OR CARING?

Louis Newman

I got to know Bennett one summer in the early seventies when he approached me to talk about his interest in doing graduate work in curriculum construction. Over the years we met occasionally and talked shop, especially when we both found ourselves in the greater Boston area. Our last professional conversation was about teaching *tefillah*.

Bennett strengthened my faith in educators. Without exception, every parent and teacher whom I met, who had contact with his school, spoke of the unique positive difference which his leadership contributed to the way his students learned to be Jewish.

What follows is one perspective (adapted from a forthcoming work, "Education for Human Worth"), with its opinions and convictions, limited to a narrow band of the Jewish educational spectrum. I would have tested it out on him.

יהי זכרו ברוך
Yehi Zikhro Barukh

Meaning is Not a Given

This is a plea for non-Orthodox schools that are designed to be fair to the student. It is concerned with the ultimate Jewish educational goal of commitment to human worth, the process of "cloning" by educational institutions, and the need for theological and educational goal clarification so educators may serve more effectively.

The beginning orientation for the non-orthodox Jewish educator must be the awareness that all religious and philosophical positions about cosmic purpose and human worth are subjective choices. They are anchors dropped in a sea, a space where place and boundaries are ultimately indeterminable. There is no one generally accepted way of deriving goals for living from the universe. Because the cosmos is morally incomprehensible, the "good" of the one may be the "evil" of the other. The religious faith of the one may be the "abomination" of the other.

For the religious Jew, evil is what is most difficult to understand; for the investigator of human nature, altruism is most difficult. For the investigator, the human may be no more than a "survival machine" for a long existing gene;[1] for the religious Jew, the human is God's partner in the task of perfecting the world. In this cosmic uncertainty, we Jews cling to our Judaism, or Jewishness, with varying ideational justifications and identities. We hold, however, one faith position, or commitment, in common: a conviction of the inestimable worth of the human being, with its correlate, the imperative to care for others. This position values the person but transcends self-centeredness with a sense of mutual obligation. Powering this ideal are different, idiosyncratically determined, ideological ascriptions of its impelling force. These facts, the indeterminacy of life's meaning with its consequent subjectivity of outlook and simultaneous unyielding devotion to human worth, challenge non-orthodox schools particularly. Basing themselves on the scholarship which seeks to understand the origins, meaning and functions of our received religious texts and practices, different schools' sponsors operate with different ascriptive positions. This is possible because the scholars strive to ascertain history, not theology. Scholarship offers a passageway from which individuals can move onto different theological paths. The various directions to which ideologies advance lead to weighty consequential differences in children's education. With awareness of this variety, the most important ethical question for the educator is whether to replicate her/his perspective onto the learner, or whether to teach the learner how to determine her/his own. This is the issue of this paper.

On the school's level the problem is this: Once it has determined to *respect* the human worth of the student, while it *educates* for human worth in general and *generates* an active concern for peoples' welfare, it requires an educational design which will reconcile itself with the individual. The school wants to transmit its particular ideological motivation but must contend with its recognition of the growing student's right to develop for her/himself a basis for the commitment to human worth.

1 Richard Dawkins, "Selfish Genes and Selfish Memes," in Hofstadter and Dennet, *The Mind's I* (New York: Basic Books, 1981) pp. 124-144.

How are the young to be treated with regard to this issue? In contrast to independent adults who are presumed to be competent and free to choose for themselves among religious and philosophical views, the youngster is neither independent nor competent. Obviously, the student does not have the experiential and intellectual wherewithal to choose among ascriptions. S/he is dependent upon the institutional provision of deliberate education. The educating community, accordingly, must decide whether to offer a program which promotes and inculcates the ideal of human worth while advancing the student's competence to choose, *in time*, from existing justifications of this commitment.

Cloning: Good and Bad

This challenge is not unique. It is one instance of the moral tension that arises when any group which values the integrity of the human being tries to "clone" its ideal image of itself onto its growing children.

How is "cloning" used here? It designates the effort to reproduce in the young a group's axiomatic ideal principles and behaviors, be they helpful or harmful to others. The axioms constitute the essential insurance for the community's continuity. For groups which value decency and compassion, no logical argument, by itself, compels, or is necessarily conducive, to principled behavior. When a group's intent is to achieve, by whatever educative habituation processes are available, specific attitudes and behaviors in the young that will be most resistant to change, the process is here called educational cloning. In deliberate education, it would refer to the part of the normal program which seeks to inculcate the strongest possible predilections for, or aversions to, specific categories of behavior.

In positive form, cloning is recognizable in those spontaneous "do-gooders" who do not offer a philosophical and/or religious compelling reason for their actions. For them, their behavior has become the obvious natural way without doubt or hesitancy. In negative form, it may drive or restrain behavior in a particular situation as it hinders the application of otherwise available, competent intellectual and/or emotional sensitivity. Oft observed instances are the self-elevated "good-citizen" sub-cultures whose ideal cloning incorporates the disvaluing of some outgroup because of ethnic origin, color, religion or economic status.

Clearly a culture cannot avoid a cloning effort. Though ideally, "the individual and society have to be conceived as means and ends to each other,"[2] some thinkers will assert that the individual is intended to serve the group's purpose or destiny. Others will maintain that ultimately the organized community is justifiable only as an instrument for the welfare

2 Mordecai Kaplan, in *Commentary*, Vol 42, No. 2, p. 108.

and dignity of its members. In a forced choice context, where reality cannot be fitted into the ideal, the weight assigned to each position in the design of an ideological and behavioral cloning pattern will depend upon each group's perception of the comprehensiveness and specificity of its empowering or compelling mandate.

When cloning succeeds as part of the socialization process, then, for better or worse, it automatically diminishes the individual's autonomy. It involves some loss of flexibility and freedom. (This decrease has been termed, not pejoratively, an "encumbrance."[3] It may also be termed, more neutrally, "permanent cargo.") The group which wants to guide itself Jewishly is obliged to balance its tendency towards imposition by respecting each individual's worth. Such respect should press it to delimit the cloning of idiosyncratic affirmations to the minimum it deems necessary for its integrity and continuity. In the final analysis, a school must make compatible its version of ascription with its commitment to autonomy and choice.

Cloning for Human Worth: A Framework— Four Tracks in Education

For any community to transmit its reason for the ideal of helping humans while it values the individual being educated, its educational program must contain certain categories of information and experience in a deliberately formed pattern. No matter how little the time available, the school's vision of educating for human worth should be comprehensive. Then, when situationally determined reductions or modifcations must occur, all pertinent factors can be considered.

As it responds to the variables in its immediate context, the adequate school's pattern must operate simultaneously on at least *four interdependent tracks*:

1. Cultivating in students whatever latent general disposition each one has to care for people, i.e., *cloning for caring, compassion and mutual concern*.

2. Habituating an *enduring symbolic-ceremonial maintenance system*, "permanent cargo," that nurtures and sustains the caring disposition. This is the *halakhah* or its modification and/or its replacement.

3. Advancing within the learner the development of the two *natural competencies necessary for responsible independence*:

    a) the *unrestrained use of mind* on the materials to be understood and events experienced, and

---

[3] R. N. Bellah and others, *Habits of the Heart* (Berkeley: U. of California Press, 1985) p. 152.

b) access to *messages of feeling from within oneself*, i.e., emotional health.

4. Transmitting *several categories of knowledge*. Five kinds of knowledge must be delivered at appropriate stages:

   a. The *meaning* and comprehensiveness of the concept, mutual concern.

   b. The *ideational-verbal knowledge about the skills* for implementing this concern: the "how-to" in words.

   c. The enabling *experiential knowledge about the skills* for implementing this concern: the "how-to" in practice.

   d. Knowledge of the school's *goals and strategies*.

   e. Knowledge about *ascriptions*, their bases in texts and/or nature; the motivating, energizing and/or compelling force to which human value is ascribed.

Since the last item, ascription, may allow much or little mental space for individual conviction, it determines much of the content on all tracks which must be consistent with it. (It also determines the guiding principles for the teaching of texts, practices and concepts, e.g., Bible, *halakhah*, prayer, covenant, and reward and punishment. But these are not the focus here.) An immediate result is that the greater the non-forbidden mental space available, the greater the possible modification of, or departure from, traditional *halakhah*.

The relationship of ascription to other educational content is different for each of the three large groups in American Jewish life: the Orthodox, the secular and the non-Orthodox religious. From an Orthodox perspective, the revelational ascription of Torah and Oral Law determines most of the human-worth-program's content. Believed revelation operates as "fact." Individual freedom of thought and behavior is to be found within the boundaries of *halakhah*.

In the secular view, where an ascription does not proclaim the various contents, they must be searched for pragmatically. In between this Orthodox-secular polarity, the religious non-Orthodox theological-philosophical positions need much clarification to be of educational use. New initiatives are needed.

The tension resulting from the conflict within each admittedly idiosyncratic ascription among a multiplicity of ascriptions, together with every non-Orthodox group's valuing of autonomy, ought to evoke from the school educator some general and some very specific questions about the implementation and ancillary goals of a human-worth-program. On the general level, for instance, what is the long-term goal in an optimal program of education, e.g. after a student experiences its ten-year curriculum? Will the school regard itself to be successful only when the student affirms the ascription of the group, or, will the student's deliberate decision either to move into another Jewish group or to withhold an ascription stance also be seen as a sign of the school's sucess?

As stated earlier, there is an even more fundamental question: Is it the school's first goal to be a means toward the individual's competent Jewish ideological independence including his/her ability to make responsible choices, or is it to make the student a means to the perpetuation of its own institutional ideology?

The school, of course, must anticipate the educator's quandary with a decisive conviction on the autonomy-ascription polarity along with the development of an educational process in harmony with its stand.

Subjectivity, Diversity and Opacity

To develop a human worth program for a particular school-community, the non-Orthodox educator must overcome two serious obstacles: the wide range of subjective theological pronouncements and the insufficient clarity of these pronouncements to serve as guidelines for teaching. Arguably, every religious school teacher should be confronted with a minimal introduction to these impediments in order to sense the nature and size of the task.

Towards this end, a sample of the diversity of views and their opacity for educational work follows:

Though all Jewish ideologies are based on ideas from the traditional texts and Jewish history, in some small or large measure every non-Orthodox view is a *negation* of, and a distancing from, the view which is *common* to all versions of Orthodoxy, namely, that both the Torah, as we now have it, *Torah min HaShamayim*, and the Oral Tradition are totally of divine origin.

To the believer, empirical data and reason are not pertinent to the facticity of the Orthodox assertion. As one modern Orthodox scholar put it, *"Torah min haShamayim* ... means that the Pentateuch as we have today is identical with the Torah revealed to Moses at Mount Sinai and that this expression of God's will is authentic, final and eternally binding on the Jewish people."[4]

Another says, "To submit the *mitzvot* to any extraneous test— whether rational or ethical or nationalistic— is to reject the supremacy of God, hence in effect to deny Him as God."[5]

The non-Orthodox groups—religious and secular—take exception to this position. They assert that the Torah we now have is not identical with that revealed to Moses at Mt. Sinai. These views range from the one

---

4 Immanuel Jacobovits, in *Commentary, op. cit.,* p. 105.
5 Norman Lamm, in *Commentary, op. cit.,* p. 110.

which only somewhat lessens the Orthodox view on divine revelation of the Pentateuch and *halakhah*, to those which do not accept any instance of revelation at any time, anywhere. However, all the positions accept the need to inquire into the historical development of the Pentateuch and *halakhah* in order to understand them fully. The result is that with broad-ranging inquiry exploiting all pertinent disciplines, non-Orthodox subjectivity becomes salient and, as stated above, moves adherents along diverse paths of theological understanding and different commitments to *halakhah* and tradition.

Idiosyncratic Diversity: Revelation and The Origin of Halakhah

The many individual ascriptions are bewildering to any serious seeker of a position to identify, and the teacher of the young is no exception. The assertions are made with different mixtures of theological components that are not simple to arrange in an order. The thinkers do not always state precisely their ascriptive views.

As an example, however, with regard to the origin of the commands of the Torah, the possible beliefs can, in fact, be stated simply:

1. All are God's words.

2. Only some of the words are God's.

3. None of the words is God's, but rather all are a human product in reaction to some form of revelation. (One notes that at least three groups in this category claim a substantially different process of revelation and use different terminology: a. "An encounter" with God; b. God's "self-disclosure"; c. God's "inspiration".)

4. None of the words is God's; there is no revelation. It is altogether a human product.

With respect to *halakhah*, one ordering of positions among the non-Orthodox is:

1. a. *halakhah* is from God for eternity, but where "human elements" are identified it may be modified.

   b. *halakhah* is from God for eternity, but to keep Jewish law viable under changed conditions, rabbinic authorities are obliged to modify it.

2. a. The *halakhah* is a totally human enterprise that has value as a guiding tradition, but it can and should be modified by the *community* to render it viable.

   b. The *halakhah* is a totally human enterprise that has value as a guiding tradition and can be selectively modified for personal use by individuals.

For the teacher, the viewpoints of the non-Orthodox groups, from the most traditional to the secularist, can be arranged in different ways, each according to a different component. Two of these will be outlined below. (For the questioning teacher—and others, of course—similar orderings could be made for other religious issues, such as: the functions of prayer, the concepts of covenant and reward and punishment.)

For the present purpose, it will suffice to classify thinkers' views on Judaism and Jewishness around several nodal points: three are religious revelationists, one is religious naturalist-humanist, and one is secular naturalist-humanist.[6] Between these nodes and beyond them at one extreme are many other variant groups and individuals which will *not* be described: the seclusive religious Orthodox, the orthodoxy of the anti-religious, combinations of mysticism and rational empiricism, and yet others. The views, incidentally, which will be introduced, are not necessarily congruent with the ideological boundaries of our organized religious movements, since each is pluralistic and provides for intellectual-emotional-intuitional space for maneuvering within it. Unfortunately, each of the movements still contain large lacunae for the educator working with children.

Essentials for a Human Worth Program in the Extreme Positions

Beginning with the most traditional non-Orthodox position, one finds in the Conservative Movement's pluralistic constellation one conception that diminishes Orthodoxy least and is very much like it, yet is not within it. It maintains that revelation is "the personal encounter between God and human beings ... that God communicated ... in actual words ... [R]evelation's content is immediately normative as defined by rabbinic interpretation. The commandments of the Torah themselves issue directly from God."[7] However, "beliefs about revelation are faith assertions .... [T]hey are outside the purview of empirical evidence ... Even if one accepts the assumptions common to all biblical critics ... one can still view [the biblical text] as a unity because of the way it was accepted in subsequent Jewish history ... One can be a traditionalist without being a fundamentalist."[8]

The diminution from Orthodoxy is in the conviction, based on empirical evidence, that the Torah as we now have it, although revealed,

---

6 I have adapted the categories in Elliot N. Dorff, *Conservative Judaism*, pp. 110-157, for this paper.
7 *Emet Ve-Emunah, Principles of Conservative Judaism* (New York: Jewish Theological Seminary, 1988) p. 20.
8 David Novak, in Dorff, *Conservative Judaism, op. cit.*, pp. 125-6.

shows evidence of composition by different humans and that the contents reflect influences of social processes and religious ideas from neighboring cultures.

One does not know precisely what believers of these statements would do as an educational community. A reasonable speculation is that for this group, as for the Orthodox, the most appropriate action in appreciation of the inherent worth of young people is to inculcate in the student the Jewish ideological essence: belief in God and Torah as revealed at Sinai and obedience to His commands.

This ascription includes total concern for the individual. There is no reason for any ascription-autonomy tension. *Halakhah* is obeyed because it reflects the Jewish community's understanding, through its religious leaders, of God's will. Autonomy is applicable only within the bounds of *halakhah* and whatever freedoms it permits outside of them. Thus, in a school of this ideology, all that *halakhah* requires will be appropriately placed in its human worth program: texts, *halakhah* and generative principles within *halakhah*. Additionally, it may include without limit all secular knowledge and practice that does not violate *halakhah*.

The one "unknown" which might be acknowledged in this position, where unrestrained inquiry with relevant scholarship would be encouraged, is that of the historical development of our religious texts. To understand them most adequately, one needs to know all that one can about the pertinent sociological conditions and intellectual environments within which Torah traditions were transmitted and rabbinic interpretations and decisions emerged.

Two items distinguish this position from the Orthodox: first, the presumed date at which the Torah became the text we now have and, second, the religious body which today is the acceptable determiner of *halakhah*.

Whether practice is consistent with ascription, I do not know. Since this view has a substantial number of adherents, however, their educators ought to have ideological positions available to them on some specific issues. Some of these will be listed after other views have been described.

At the opposite end of theological convictions is that of the Jewish secular humanist-naturalists whose motivational pattern functions without a concept of God. Their ascription is bound to the one empirically observable, deliberate concern for humans: the recurring caring behavior of some people for others. To raw nature, they do not attribute intention. It is judged neither good nor bad—just indifferent. With awareness that there is no compelling reason for compassion, they may attribute their decent behavior to an impelling feeling and/or to the pragmatic view that decency is the most rewarding road towards enlightened self-interest.

The Jewish secularist pattern appears in several guises to convey their ideals: Zionist, Hebraist, Yiddishist or Jewish ethnic. The land of Israel, any of the languages which Jews have used, and cultural forms are valued as carriers of the culture—taken alone or in combination. From the "community memory"[9] all the secular variants retain—in desacralized form—the ancient conviction of human worth and the imperative to help people.

To educate and impassion those who are committed to achieve their aspirations, they extract from classical texts and modern Jewish thought—in widely disparate ways—expressions of human worth and group responsibility. Jewish history yields for them, as it does for all Jews, exemplary individuals and communities which actualized these ideals.

What the many varieties of schools actually do is not readily available in print, nor are the long-term maintenance strategies with which each sub-group looks to the future. But the attachment to a Jewish identity obliges each to teach and preach its own distillation of relevance from the Jewish past. If we envision beyond the cloning process for human worth, one can project different programs which Jewish secular humanists would justify. One such school would be pluralistic, committed to the tradition of *Talmud Torah*. It would offer the full range of Jewish studies in depth and provide opportunities for students, because it respects individual dignity, to observe, examine and participate in prayer and experience other halakhic practices in home and synagogue. It would encourage and enable every student to examine carefully the complete ascriptive spectrum and select a position, or construct her/his own.

The Second Track in the Secular Setting: "Halakhah or its Substitute"

To pursue the human-worth program outlined above, secularists, more than the religious non-Orthodox groups, are deficient in the resources for the second track, the one for "habituating an enduring symbolic-ceremonial maintenance system that nurtures and maintains the caring disposition"—their necessary substitute for *halakhah* and its offshoots. For this task, secularists have not developed a stable pattern.

They need an institutional carrier of their values—a Jewish law for them without theological sanction. They need ceremonial instruments by which the young can appropriate the relevant past, observe and participate with peers *and* adults as the latter express their commitments.

Secularist schools now depend mostly on what they can improvise for each occasion. Thus, regularly, Hanukkah and Passover lend them-

---

9 Bellah, *op. cit.*, p. 153.

selves easily to the freedom theme. Ideally, their schools would have ready for use, in desacralized form if necessary, the humanist and self-discipline components which they have combed out of all traditional thought and practice.

With respect to the rest of the program, what follows can be used by secularists and any Jewish group subject only to the ideological censorship it deems necessary plus its own ascriptive emphasis.

Track Three: Natural Competencies for Responsible Independence

In the third item of the outline, the track for "intellectual competence and emotional health," one would expect to find the special emphases of any serious human-worth program. Here, too, it would diverge from schools with a "fixed" ascription by insuring the presence or absence of certain practices.

Following are some especially relevant items for the training for the unrestrained use of mind in this setting:

1. Avoidance of the ideological cloning process which withholds information that might arouse doubt;

2. Avoidance of cloning internalized intellectual censorship. No intellectual "NO TRESPASSING" signs would be placed in the mind;

3. Analysis of traditional Jewish texts so as to separate the simplest contextual meaning from midrashic interpretations—not using "creative philology" and imaginative additions to reconcile dissonance.

4. Teaching, as soon as students can learn it, the specialized skill of reading for inquiry.

5. Analysis, as soon as students have referents, of the meaning of recurring religious and philosophical terms: e.g., divine revelation, revelation through tradition, immanentism, empiricism, religious truth, *Torah mi-Sinai, Torah mi-Shamayim,* etc.

6. Imparting the skill to discriminate among implications of empirical observations, probability based on incomplete observation, and pure speculation.

With regard to emotional life, in addition to following generally accepted principles and practices, a human-worth school would anticipate the conflicting strains of students' growing in intellectual independence and moral responsibility, simultaneously. These tensions normally emerge from the child's inexperience with autonomy and the uncomfortable pressure of duty.

Illustrative school tasks are:

1. Distinguishing between the purity of concepts and their unavoidable adjustments in daily life situations; Increasing the students' stamina to endure the stress of action decisions in moral dilemma situations, e.g., whom does one help first?
2. Anticipating and ventilating the recurring conflicts and vacillation between self-concern and altruism. Informing students that decency always involves giving to, or serving an other—even in very small measure.
3. Conveying that rewards of decency must be mainly intrinsic. Not every receiver offers thanks.
4. Staying alert to the need for recognition and supportively helping students withstand out-group negative peer pressure.
5. Providing behavioral science information which helps adolescents distinguish between critical and uncritical, i.e., "osmotic" internalization of identities.
6. Indicating the possibility of displaced aggression via critical moralism.
7. Illustrating that striving for meaning is a life-long endeavor. One lives with uncertainty by adopting a "provisional absolute."[10]

The Knowledge Track: Mutual Concern

The first item on the knowledge track, the concept of mutual concern, must be conveyed in its fullness, as must the consequent size of the demand it will make on our individual and communal resources. This includes the historically known, ever present, unsatisfied needs of people's physical and interpersonal security as well as representative social responses and enduring injunctive concepts from different civilizations and cultures.

Jewish historical concerns through people-helping, "social security mitzvot" like the several tithes (*ma'asrot*, מעשרות) and the gleanings, forgotten produce and the corner of the field (*leqet, shikh'ah, pe'ah*; לקט, פאה, שכחה), and all the *mitzvot bain adam la-havero*, must be taught alongside the recent responses of Israeli *kibbutzim* and Jewish community federations all over the world.

This inheritance must be converted to people's situation here and now in the student's life-space: from concern for the one to concern for everyone—from the interpersonal courtesies at any moment to the borders of the "neighborhood" in which one is enjoined to "love thy neighbor."

Generally ignored, but most relevant, are statistics which need to be regularly updated to be a discomfiting sight before the students' eyes. These would include statistics such as:

---

10 Chaim Potok, in *Commentary, op. cit.*, p. 126.

- population in the world without the political forms of democracy.
- population of the world without sufficient daily food.
- levels of infant mortality in different parts of the world.
- annual income categories in the world by percentage of people at different levels.
- the percentile rating, on a world population basis, of the average income of the families whose children attend the school.
- the number of homeless in one's city, state, and country.
- knowledge and observation of the practical aspects of the administration of justice through court visits.

Knowledge of "how-to" implement human-worth activities in words and the planned experiences of the "how-to in practice" to match them are commonplace in the realm of education. A *caveat*: such programs may boomerang when they are perceived by students as childish!

To avoid that reaction, the content should include:
- experience by children in independent planning and execution of helping activities that are recognized by adults as vital and substantial;
- knowledge of how government and private agencies help in cases of special need, e.g. health education, finance, emotional support, etc.

The five "knowledge goals and strategies" (see number 4, a—e, above) which uniquely characterize the program must continually be reiterated to students and parents. New situations arising within the flow of changing circumstances may require unprecedented solutions. The school must seize every opportune occasion to restate why it clones, how it clones, and the reasons for unusual patterning in the human worth curriculum. Moreover, the school will not use any kind of morality rating device such as "mitzvah points."

A counterbalance must be provided for the school's pronouncements. As a synthetic organized personality it must operate with humility. There must be a built-in mechanism for parents and students comfortably to ask questions and criticize.

Finally, with regard to the fifth "knowledge goal", knowledge of ascription in a secularist school cannot be about one fixed ascription, but is rather about the sponsor's considered affirmation of the major Jewish value, that is, helpfully relating to all people. With respect to the student's right to self-determination in the school projected here (and since the affirmation is offered without a logically compelling reason), knowledge about all ascriptions, including the Orthodox, should be provided along with their bases in traditional texts and nature. Simultaneously, facts and questions with which individual ideologies challenge other views should be presented.

Very important, too, is a confrontation with the world. The late Professor Abraham Heschel often said that Jewish schools frequently fail to convey the meaning of Torah because it is a response to questions and issues of which the student is unaware. In the cloning-of-ideological-ascriptions designs which generally prevail, a body of very relevant information is neglected or inadequately presented. It is made up of the stimuli to, and necessary ingredients for, thinking about cosmic organization and purpose.

Examples are:

1. The questions to which neither science nor religion offer an answer.
2. The human potential for beneficence and maleficence.
3. Nature's bounty and beauty.
4. Mutual help and carniverous nature among fauna.
5. Representative samples of the regularities of nature, i.e., the "laws" of science.
6. The unavoidable natural catastrophic cataclysms, e.g., tornadoes, earthquakes, lightning.
7. The known percentage of genetic flaws which limit normal development in humans.
8. The range of individual genetic differences in physique and bodily functions, the several dimensions of mental powers, and the various dimensions of creative potential.
9. The moral incomprehensibility of the universe.

Non-Orthodox Intermediate Positions

A second prominent, revelationist view focuses on divine inspiration. It asserts that the people who wrote the Torah at various times and places "were ... divinely inspired and therefore their words carry the insights and authority of God."[11]

Held with individual differences among its adherents, this position sees the Torah as containing God's communication not in words, not in propositional content, but "verbal formulations by human beings of norms and ideas." The experience of revelation "through an ineffable human encounter with God,"[12] as reported by the human, provides the divine content of Torah. "God inspired human beings with a specific message."[13]

This view is held by segments of the Conservative and Reform communities. For some associated with this view, "[D]ivine inspiration

---

11 Dorff, *Commentary, op. cit.*, p. 126.
12 *Emet Ve-Emunah, op. cit.*, p. 20.
13 Dorff, *op. cit.*, p. 127.

continues on in the form of new interpretation of the Torah in each generation."[14]

Another theological position, influential among Conservative and Reform rabbis, regards revelation, not as divine inspiration, but "as the disclosure of God, Himself. It is not the declaration of specific rules, but rather a meeting between God and man, in which they get to know each other."[15]

One rabbi claims: " The event is self-validating in that its experience is so unique, overwhelming and transforming that the human partner emerges from it reconstituted in his own being and certain of its meaning. It is this meaning, this interpretation of the revelatory event, which the human partner then puts into words."[16]

"The precepts of the Torah are binding ... God did 'command' them, but not by direct communication ... but through the historical experiences of the Jewish people." The Torah was given "not so much *to* Israel as *through* Israel."[17] (Conservative rabbis identifying with this view are loyal to *halakhah* but with individual qualifications.)

Most distant from Orthodoxy among religious views is the naturalist humanist religious position. No revelation is assumed. Shared by most Reconstructionists, some Reform and even some Conservatives committed to a halakhic system, it says that "God inheres within nature and operates through natural law, but is not a discrete supernatural Being."[18] Their religious faith arises from an awareness of the self and of nature and its processes, of human aspirations and of serviceable nature. From anthropocentrism they construct and have faith in a theocentric principle. Some even believe that the capacity and tendency to transcend selfishness through compassion and altruism is a manifestation of divine immanence in people. Stated differently, the faith is that humankind is not doomed to an eternal animal-eat-animal existence.

In his critique of the naturalist religious view, one scholar declares, "No inequity, regardless of its horror, proves that ideals are false or cannot succeed ... Moral activism ... is the fitting response to the problem of evil."[19]

Much like "encounter" believers and very different from the secular naturalists, the religious naturalists have structured approaches to Jewish living through synagogue services and home rituals. Innovating prac-

14 *Ibid.*, p. 126.
15 *Ibid.*, p. 134.
16 Schaalman, in *Commentary, ibid.*, p. 135.
17 Louis Jacobs, in Dorff, *Ibid.*, p. 137.
18 Roland B. Gittelsohn, in *Gates of Mitzvah* (New York: Central Conference of American Rabbis, 1979) p. 108.
19 Eugene B. Borowitz, *Choices in Modern Jewish Thought* (New York: Behrman House) p. 113.

tices in both areas, some, preferring to stay within the halakhic realm, appropriate from tradition via their individual communities and identify themselves as halakhists, while others use the term, tradition, and urge their adherents to choose maximally what appeals to each individual.

The incompleteness of the revelationist conceptions, a fact of enormous consequence in an educational program, has been acknowledged by critics and adherents of non-Orthodox positions. For example: "To hold ... that Torah admits of some human elements and then to offer no way of determining where divine initiative ends and where human interpretation enters, is to avoid the heart of the question. To proclaim that revelation occurs without commitment to follow what revelation demands, or to proclaim the will of God without offering grounds for distinguishing true from false revelation, is to offer a vacuous form—revelation without content or criteria."[20]

And another rabbi concedes:

> We are quite properly asked to explain by what principle one can affirm revelation and yet deny some of the commandments and much of the outlook of the sacred texts in which that revelation is presumed to be recorded.

The plain truth is that there is no clear dogmatic answer ...

> We must say: God exists and He has revealed himself to man through the sacred texts of the Jewish tradition, and yet the individual must be free to make his choices as to what he will affirm as value and what rituals he will obey as representing, for him, authentic commandments.[21]

Educators Need Clarification

Without either the total revelation conviction, on the one hand, and the total non-theological conviction on the other, the educator who must "deliver" the "mixes" of belief and empiricism, without criteria to separate them, needs much specific information about a school's broad vision and guiding principles for curriculum construction.

Orientation for teachers must include, in addition to the questions mentioned above, answers to questions like the following: Does the school aspire to clone its ascription, its theological view? Does the school aspire to clone each student's potential to value humans and train in the competence to do so? Will inquiry into the selected ascription be encouraged? Will there be any censorship, i.e., a limit on the use of mind and emotional sensitivity on any aspect of experience? If the school is in a pluralistic religious movement

---

20 Harold Schulweis, in *Commentary, op. cit.*, p. 140.
21 Arthur Hertzberg, in *Commentary, Ibid.*, p. 100.

(a) will the movement's pluralism be a determining factor in its total curriculum, with all movement views legitimated for adoption?

(b) will non-movement views, including Orthodox and secular, be presented as options?

(c) will the adopter of a non-school view be regarded and treated as a mistaken innocent, a *tinok-she-nishbah*?

Will the school present pertinent behavioral science data on how people develop social allegiances, personal identities, and form enduring faith, belief and behavior?

Will the school maximize a curriculum of existential awareness? i.e., a confrontation with nature, its unknowns, its laws, "wonders," beauty and bounty, as well as its inherent cruelty to humans and animals?

Will the curriculum convey the absence of objective guideposts to meaning in the universe?

Will the school convey the fact of the moral incomprehensibility of the universe?

Will the school convey that all religious-philosophical principles for living are subjective impositions of meaning on the universe?

Will parents be informed diligently of what the school strives to clone?

The answer to such questions should determine within the school's total program, the content of several educational tasks in its human-worth-program. First, in its ascriptive track, the basic theological premises will be clarified. Specified would be what of eternal importance, if anything, is "known," i.e., revealed by God; what God has commanded in general or as specific *halakhot*; what are the conditions under which God has prescribed that any specific *halakhah* may be expanded, modified or nullified; by what criteria one can discriminate what is, and what is not, divine in Tanakh and *halakhah*.

On its clear ascriptive base a school can choose and/or create a methodology in accord with its premises. It can select methods and materials for cultivating a caring disposition. One notes, however, that like the secularists, only much less so, the religious non-Orthodox are also seriously deficient on the track for transmitting a structured maintenance system. This is true not only for the human worth segment, but for the whole framework of Jewish religious identity.

In a successful school, the student knows and feels that he is differentiated out of the nebulous surrounding culture and knows why. S/he subdues any sense of loss with an appreciation of gain.

The "system" obviously consists of certain recurring events and unpremeditated events, from religious ritual celebrations at home and in school to special occasion school assemblies. It succeeds when it infuses the "umbrella" symbol, Jewishness, into the child's consciousness by means of experiences that focus emotion-suffused-attention.

Every school is challenged to make the tradition functional. Religious schools have the resources to choose from, in accord with their views, *halakhah*, "traditional ritual" and/or customs. The secularists and non-halachists are likewise challenged to modify creatively the traditional structure so as to positively condition the symbol, Jewishness, in its many contexts, in order to achieve heightened awareness of what they value.

On the remaining tracks, those for intellectual competence and awareness of emotions, and the five information categories, all that was listed above for a projected secularist school, should be used by every school within its ascriptive limits.

Attempts at Resolution

In part, the dilemma discussed here of non-Orthodox schools can be readily resolved. I know of at least one true *school* of Jewish religion (the emphasis is on school), a sixth to twelfth grade day school. It is a model which can readily be adopted to an autonomy-oriented religious school. With a charter to be an open-ended school, it fosters autonomy. Nothing from either an ideal orthodox curriculum or an ideal Jewish secularist view is, *a priori*, ruled out. What is forbidden is ideological coercion, direct and indirect. The school is not sponsored by any ideological group but by the community at large. Whenever possible it cooperates with the families and synagogues severally by taking into account the different views and practices and offering experiences that are in harmony with their individual ascriptions.

To families which want to clone their particular outlook onto their children, the open-ended ideational atmosphere may induce a feeling of brink-walking. The young may move off their homes' ascriptive foundations. Understandably such parents may decide to avoid the risk.

Such a school, however, is a model for only a partial solution. For better or worse, entering students have already been substantially influenced by a variety of formal and informal experiences. The school's conceptual ideological design and practice are relatively simple. The students have a base in referential knowledge and, though immature, are treated as aspirants for competent responsible autonomy.

With younger students it does not seem possible to devise a practice which removes the autonomy-ascriptive tension in religious schools as they now operate. The really tough decisions for a school intent on minimizing ideological cloning are in kindergarten through grade five. It must choose the appropriate age level and create the setting for introducing the word, God, plus prayers and blessings, while avoiding even indirect adult coercion. Whatever its deliberate program, the school must also be ready with answers for spontaneous theology-related questions which children ask. Regrettably, for this age range, no one has created a comprehensive program which responds to these concerns.

There are at least two options for schools which take the tension issue seriously.

1. Institute a straightforward ideological and human-worth cloning program, religious or secular, in realistic recognition that not all ideal principles can be realized simultaneously. The school judges that it is in the best interests of the individual and community that the young carry its outlook through life as "permanent cargo."

2. A second option for open-ended religionists and secularist is to include an ideological ascription with a built-in "visible escape hatch." The school offers first what every child everywhere should be offered. It tries through information, explanation, inquiry and participatory experiences to arouse and bring to awareness the amalgam of feelings and intellectually active wonder about one's relation to self, to others, to nature close at hand, and to the universe. "God-talk" is deliberately postponed until a planned experiential foundation has been laid. Only then is humankind's quest for ultimate purpose connected for the child to the school's Jewish ascription.

The introduction stresses the unknown, along with the sponsoring institution's religious explanatory "best guess," with a "remainder" still unknown. It assures the children that as they grow they will learn other views and may prefer one of them. They are advised and urged to start their quest for meaning with the "best guess" of their mentors as a "provisional absolute"—in their language—"a good way to live" while they grow and learn. Traditional symbolic rituals are offered to channel expressions of community feeling, gratitude, hope, sorrow and pain.

Viewing Jewishness as the context within which the growing seeking person orients and stabilizes the self—the kind of context which every child everywhere should have—the school pictures itself to the students, and tries to be, a helper in a long-lasting desirable adventure. It avoids the common practice in which assertions are made about God, revelation and Torah that, in later years, have to be "undone" by the school with apologetic recourse to the children's earlier limited capacity for understanding.

Other Issues

Omitted in all that has preceded are the corollaries of different ascriptions in several curricular areas where clearly articulated positions are needed. Within some non-Orthodox positions, the traditional sense of covenant is not consonant with belief, the traditional sense of reward and punishment has lost its base, the traditional sense of prayer is not consonant with belief and "metaphoric prayer" is, for the most part, not understood.

Conclusion

1. Because the meaning of existence is not a given, non-Orthodox Jews freely empower their commitment to human worth with greatly differing idiosyncratic metaphysical and/or philosophical doctrines about God and nature. To transmit this commitment which cannot be compelled by reason, they must—with or without ascriptive components—clone it onto the young. Consequently, any homogeneous ideological community faces a moral dilemma. Is its first educational task to clone for the valued behavior while helping students to become competent choosers among ideological alternative, or is to replicate itself onto the student by cloning both its particular ascription and the valued behavior?

2. For educators, the statements of prominent thinkers are not clear and helpful on essentials needed to resolve the issue. Teachers at a loss among the enormously divergent views on Revelation, Torah and Halakhah need clearly formulated ascriptions and a structured program to guide them in cloning for decent behavior.

3. A school needs to use its ascriptive base on which to create a comprehensive enabling program of information, skills and experiences with which to impel students to internalize a practical human worth disposition.

4. I know of no non-Orthodox religious schools which responds to the issue of individual autonomy versus ideological cloning. At the junior and senior high school level, there is at least one community school which can serve as a model for an autonomy-concerned religious school. At the K-5 level, a curriculum responsive to the issue has yet to be created.

BIBLIOGRAPHY

A substantial variety of positions on theology and practice can be found in the following:

Eugene B. Borowitz, *Choices in Modern Jewish Thought*, (New York: Behrman House, 1983).

_____, *Renewing the Covenant*, (Philadelphia: Jewish Publication Society, 1991).

Elliot N. Dorff, *Conservative Judaism: Our Ancestors to Our Descendants*, (New York: United Synagogue of America, 1977).

Emet Ve-Emunah: Statement of Principles of Conservative Judaism, (New York: Jewish Theological Seminary of America, 1988).

Four essays on "Mitzvah" in *Gates of Mitzvah* (New York: Central Conference of American Rabbis, 1979) pp. 97-115.

Neil Gillman, *Sacred Fragments*, (Philadelphia: Jewish Publication Society, 1990).

"Living with Reform Judaism's Pluralism" in Eugene B. Borowitz, *Reform Judaism Today*, (New York: Behrman House,) pp. 91-139.

"The State of Jewish Belief: A Symposium" in *Commentary* (Vol. 42, No. 2), pp. 73-160.

Theological Foundations of Prayer: A Reform Jewish Perspective, (New York: Union of American Hebrew Congregations, 1967).

WHAT MAKES THE REFORM DAY SCHOOL DISTINCTIVE?

A QUESTION OF PRACTICE AND PURPOSE

Michael Zeldin

Discussion of Reform day schools began in the early 1960s, first as the flight of fancy of one or two, then as a pioneering dream of a few, and finally as a national movement. The first Reform day schools opened their doors in New York City and Miami, Florida in 1970, but it was not until November, 1985, that the concept of full-time Reform Jewish education received the official approval of the Reform movement. Now, a dozen Reform day schools serve more than 4,000 students, and several additional schools are in the planning stages in cities across North America.

Reform day schools face many challenges, but perhaps none more important than identifying the unique characteristics that distinguish them from other day schools. In three decades of debate within the Reform movement over the desirability of Reform day schools, this issue was not settled. But should not Rabbis Alexander Schindler and Jay Kaufman have identified what would make Reform day schools distinctive when they first called for their establishment in 1963? Should not the Central Conference of American Rabbis or the National Federation of Temple Educators have addressed this issue on one of the several occasions when they voiced support for Reform day schools? Should not the task force established by the Union of American Hebrew Congregations in 1983 to prepare a formal position on Reform day schools have clarified the issue?

Perhaps not. As John Dewey suggested, philosophy is at its best when it emerges from life situations rather than from the theoretical speculation of philosophers. Only now that Reform day schools have moved off the drawing boards and into the "real world" can questions of educational philosophy be answered. The distinctiveness of Reform Jewish day schools can be uncovered only by exploring the realities of schools that daily give life to an idea. These schools express the unique character of Reform day schools through philosophy-in-action. However, in light of the historic 1985 resolution sanctioning Reform day schools, there are several reasons why there is an urgent need to articulate what makes Reform day schools Reform.

First, if these schools are to find a place within the Reform movement, they need a clear sense of their identity. Is any school, simply by virtue of its association with a Reform congregation, to be considered a Reform day school? What about a school which is loosely affiliated with several Reform congregations but not part of one? Or a school located in a Reform temple, but which does not concentrate on teaching Jewish tradition? Are all these schools entitled to educational support from the Reform movement?

Second, local community support depends on the Reform day school's ability to justify its existence as a distinctive entity. Reform day schools in some communities must convince funding agencies that they are entitled to subsidies on a par with other day schools. They must assure Federations and Bureaus of Jewish Education, first, that they do not duplicate the efforts of Solomon Schechter or community day schools and, second, that there is a need for, and support of, a Reform day school even in a community that already supports other day schools open to children from Reform families.

While these problems call on the day school to define and justify itself to outside audiences, it may be even more important that the Reform day school be able to articulate its distinctiveness to its own constituency. Policy issues related to religious practice, for example, depend on a school's religious self-perception. What norms and expectations should the school set regarding religious observance? Should the school lunchroom be kosher? Should the school require boys and girls to wear *kippot* while studying Bible or when participating in *tefilah*? Should Rosh Hashanah be celebrated for one day or two? How can the school encourage young children to exercise the "individual autonomy" which is a hallmark of Reform Judaism? To what extent should the school involve these young students in social action projects outside the school?

The need for a clear identity, however, goes beyond issues of religious practice. Educational leaders must be able to articulate the Reform Jewish character of the Reform day school for precisely the same reasons that they articulate other aspects of the school's philosophy: to explain to parents what the school stands for, to communicate to teachers what is expected of them, to make decisions regarding curriculum and materials, to evaluate and assess the school's educational program, to achieve consensus on the goals of the school, and to rally support for the school; in short, to build a coherent school community.

Issues of Practice and Purpose

Several responses to the question, "What makes the Reform day school distinctive?" can be derived from studying educational practice at Reform day schools, and others can come from examining the purposes these schools are designed to address. Issues of religious observance in school, for example, might be addressed by identifying a Reform day school through its affiliation with a Reform synagogue. Religious practice for day school can then mirror the *minhag* of Reform temples. However, customs in Reform synagogues vary. For example, one Reform temple may celebrate one day of *yom tov* while another celebrates two. Day schools affiliated with these temples may observe Jewish holidays quite differently. And many Reform day schools are independent institutions loosely aligned with several local congregations. When these congregations differ in religious practices, the day school faces a serious dilemma of how to design its observances. In addition, few temples have articulated their policies and practices clearly enough to address the unique issues which day schools face, and few have religious policies appropriate to the cognitive, emotional and spiritual level of five- to twelve-year-olds.

One way to discover what is distinctive about Reform day schools is to examine the educational practices shared by the dozen Reform day schools. Unfortunately, the search for curriculum, organizational structures, or pedagogical approaches common to them all would not yield fruitful results. Although the number of Reform Jewish day schools in North America is still small, the diversity among them is astonishing. For example, each school approaches the teaching of Bible differently. Some schools teach *Tanakh* in Hebrew while others teach Bible in English. Some schools use the Biblical text, some teach "Bible stories." Some have a daily Bible class, some integrate Biblical studies into the weekly celebration of Shabbat.

Another example of how educational practices in Reform day schools differ is the way they address the integration of Judaica and general studies. Some schools focus on common themes, some on historical personalities, some on Jewish participation in world or American history, and some on values shared by Jewish and Western culture.

Some schools move students into a special room with a special teacher for Judaic studies, some bring a specialist into the students' regular classroom, and some have a Judaica teacher in the classroom all day alongside the general studies teacher.

No matter what the issue, the search for shared practice as a source of the definition of a Reform day school is likely to be frustrating. However, when the search for distinctiveness is framed by questions of purpose—not practice—a series of commonalities does emerge. Why do Reform day schools exist? What purposes do they serve? What sociological and cultural needs do they address? What religious functions do they perform within the context of Reform Judaism? By examining the historical, philosophical, sociological and religious purposes of Reform Jewish day schools, we can come to a greater understanding of their unique character and distinctive identity.

A Historical Purpose: Transmitting Judaism in a "Holistic" Environment

Judaism originally gave responsibility for transmitting Jewish culture to parents. Concerning the Exodus, the core experience of the Jewish people, parents were instructed, *v'higadta l'vinkha*, "and you shall teach your child." The seder which celebrates this event became the paradigm for the family transmitting the cultural heritage and group identity of the Jewish people across the generations. But in the nineteenth and twentieth centuries, the complexity of modern life led Jews, along with the rest of industrialized society, to delegate responsibility for transmitting culture to schools. While Reform Jews had operated and supported day schools as early as the 1840s, by 1875, they had abandoned day schools. Instead, they sent their children to public schools because these schools had largely succeeded in ridding themselves of the Christian teachings which had earlier dominated their curriculum, because they offered superior educational environments, and because they met the Reform Jews' desire that their children learn about their German cultural heritage. While sending their children to public schools, nineteenth century Reform Jews opened Sunday Schools to teach their offspring about Judaism.

In the twentieth century, unfailing support for public education became a hallmark of Reform Judaism. While Reform congregations often added Hebrew Schools to supplement Sunday Schools, particularly for children approaching Bar or Bat Mitzvah, they resisted any efforts to undermine support for public schools. By the 1960s, though, the faith that Reform Jews placed in supplementary Jewish education began to waver. Many Reform Jews came to realize that a few hours a week of

Jewish schooling were too limited for transmitting a culture that calls for the social, cultural, emotional, and intellectual involvement of the individual.

But the picture of supplementary Reform Jewish education was not entirely bleak. Because of the importance of Confirmation among Reform Jews, Reform religious schools often succeeded in retaining young people in school for more years than their Conservative or Orthodox counterparts. Sustained supplementary Jewish education, especially in conjunction with a strong Jewish environment in the home, played a significant role in transmitting Jewish values and in building strong bonds to Judaism.

But the most significant successes of Reform Jewish education were in educational settings other than the Sunday School or afternoon Hebrew School. Beginning at mid-century, Reform Judaism developed a system of summer camps which have helped tens of thousands of young Reform Jews experience "living Judaism." Following the Six-Day War, Israel trips assumed a significant role in Reform Jewish education, as more and more teenagers spent a summer or semester living and studying in Israel. Recently, Reform temples have built upon earlier experiments in early childhood education and now offer parenting centers for infants, toddlers and their parents, and nursery schools and kindergartens for three- to six-year-olds.

The success of these programs is often attributed to their informal character: they provide "classrooms without walls"; they give children greater freedom of choice; interpersonal relationships are less formally structured. However, these programs share another characteristic crucial to their success: they provide a total, all-encompassing, intensive learning environment. In camps and on trips to Israel, young people live for weeks or months in environments which are infused with Judaism: Hebrew language plays a key role in daily life, Jewish rhythms govern the days, weeks and year, and Jewish sights and sounds are everywhere. Parenting centers help young parents create home environments infused with Jewish values and celebrations for their infants and toddlers. And nursery schools and kindergartens infuse the continual learning that characterizes early childhood with Jewish themes and values. The search for intensive environments for Reform Jewish education over the past 25 years also led to experiments with Hebrew High Schools and six-month post-high school study programs.

Reform day schools, then, are an extension of the decades-old trend within the Reform movement towards creating "holistic" educational environments for transmitting Jewish culture. (They are not, as some have charged, merely a convenient excuse for retreating from the Reform commitment to public education.) Many Reform day schools began as outgrowths of successful temple-sponsored nursery schools. Others were started because congregational or communal leaders sensed that part time supplementary education could not match the achievements of the more intensive day school setting. Day schools offered the opportunity to immerse children in a Jewish environment during the most important hours and days of their young lives. They made it possible for Jewish learning to become an integral part of a child's learning about his or her world. Parental interest in children's education could be harnessed so that the day school could have an impact on the Jewishness of the family environment as well. The day school, then offered Reform Judaism the avenue that it had been searching for to transmit Jewish culture and Jewish values in an all-encompassing environment.

A Philosophical Purpose: Giving Full Expression to Reform Jewish Values

Reform Judaism rests on a complex foundation of values and principles. In supplementary schools, with their limited time and under-trained faculty, it is difficult to translate these values into workable educational programs. In contrast, the intensive environment of the day school offers ample opportunity for teaching the values that are central to Reform Judaism. In the day school, children can study Reform Jewish values and see them modeled daily. Teachers trained in pedagogy and knowledgeable in Judaism can convey Reform Jewish values in a multitude of ways, and the support of the school community can insure that students see these values as central to their lives. First, Reform Judaism rests on the principle that the Jew has a significant role to play in society by working for *Tikkun Olam*, mending the brokenness of the world. For the Jew to play this role in society, he must understand Judaism and the cultural and social milieu of the surrounding society. He must, for example, understand the dynamic interplay between the Jewish community and society, and between the religious values of Judaism and the democratic principles of America. He is then prepared to translate Jewish values into social action.

Second, Reform Judaism suggests that the Jew can work for *Tikkun Olam* only if she survives as a Jew. Jewish learning provides the key to creative Jewish survival, and Jewish survival assures that Jews will remain in the world to work for *Tikkun Olam*. Therefore, she must study Jewish practice, Jewish texts, and Jewish ideas in order to understand her religious and cultural heritage.

Third, Reform Judaism places the individual at the center of its religious world-view. Neither text nor tradition nor external authority can dictate what the Jew is to believe or how he is to act. He may read

Jewish texts, study and participate in Jewish observances, and recognize a transcendent Power in the universe, but ultimately *the individual* must decide how to act, *he* must decide how to interpret a text, and *he* must decide which rituals add richness to the fabric of his life. Deprived of knowledge of the tradition, he cannot make choices that are truly autonomous. But armed with knowledge and the tools of inquiry and autonomy, he is prepared to make meaning of the world and find a sense of purpose.

And, finally, Reform Judaism is based on the idea that individual autonomy has its limits. Unlike secular humanism, which also recognizes the centrality of the individual, Reform Judaism suggests that human beings, and Jews in particular, share in a Covenant with God. The Jew must grapple with that Covenant, try to understand it, and balance its obligations against her own individual autonomy.

In other Reform educational settings, these ideals are acknowledged, but external constraints make them difficult, if not impossible, to teach. The day school is perhaps the only Reform educational setting in North America which makes the full expression of these values possible. The purpose of the Reform day school, then, is to demonstrate that, given adequate time and support, these core values of Reform Judaism can be translated into educational reality.

A Sociological Purpose: Meeting the Demand for Excellence in Education

While historical and philosophical factors called for an intensive environment for transmitting Jewish culture and teaching Reform values, sociological factors have been equally significant in creating the demand for a full-time educational setting within the Reform movement. From its beginnings, Reform Judaism has been committed to adapting Judaism to the social and cultural realities facing the Jewish community. The original reforms introduced in German Jewish congregations were changes in the style of worship designed to make communal prayer compatible with the dignified, cultured settings to which German Jews had become accustomed. In America, Isaac Mayer Wise, American Reform Judaism's founder, fashioned a *Minhag America*, an expression of Judaism suited specifically to American social and cultural mores of the mid-nineteenth century. He developed new synagogue customs, wrote a new prayer book, and experimented with different modes of Jewish education—all in an effort to tailor Judaism to its new American environment. He recognized, however, that in time his innovations, too, might become outmoded, only to be replaced by even newer customs, prayer books, and forms of Jewish education. The Reform movement's continued commitment to the principle of adaptation was reiterated in the title of a UAHC report of the 1960s, "Reform is a Verb."

Two social realities have confronted Reform Judaism over the past two decades: the persistence of ethnic pluralism in America, and the privatization of American education. Ethnicity has always been an undercurrent in American life, but the dominant American ideal of the "melting pot" was that one could be fully American only be dropping vestiges of particularistic culture (except, perhaps, at home). As recently as the 1950s, ethnicity was declared obsolete. But beginning with the Black ethnic movement of the 1960s and the search for "roots" spawned by the television mini-series, public ethnicity has become widely accepted as a legitimate expression of individualism and Americanism. A vibrant awareness of one's ethnic heritage is acknowledged to be a vital element in the personal identity of Americans. One purpose of Reform day schools, then, is to help young Reform Jews adapt to the pluralism of contemporary America by developing strong ethnic identities.

The second social reality confronting contemporary Reform Judaism is the move towards private education. Once limited primarily to Catholics in the Northeastern states, private schools today are more religiously and geographically diverse than ever before in American history. Perhaps the greatest factor contributing to this reality is the perception that the quality of public education has declined. Whether because of integration and busing, or increased violence, or overcrowding, or the intellectual "softening" of America, young parents frequently perceive that their children will not receive a quality education in their neighborhood public school. They therefore "shop the private school market," trying to find a private school that meets their demand for academic excellence in a safe, supportive environment.

In light of these realities, Reform Judaism could either remain steadfast in its opposition to private education for Reform Jewish children, or could adapt to meet the contemporary challenge. It is in keeping with Reform Judaism's commitment to adaptation, that Reform day schools were established in order to meet the new need for quality secular education.

A Religious Purpose: Welcoming Jews into the Jewish Community

One reason that Reform Judaism seeks to adapt to contemporary realities is its desire to involve Jews in Jewish life. Even before Rabbi Alexander Schindler introduced the word "outreach" to the Jewish lexicon, Reform Judaism saw itself as inviting into the Jewish community Jews who might not otherwise be involved. Since the early German attempts to reform the worship service, Reform sought to develop Jewish practices that would feel comfortable to modern Jews with modern sensibilities, thereby attracting them to Jewish life.

One purpose of the Reform day school, then, is to invite a broad spectrum of Jewish families into its orbit. Families already involved in the Jewish community are invited to join in the day school enterprise because of its intensive Jewish education. Others, interested in a quality secular education, are welcome to enroll their children in the Reform day school for its secular program, and may then find themselves involved in its Jewish program as well. Intermarried couples, too, are invited to send their children to the day school, since Reform Judaism recognizes as Jewish the children of one Jewish parent if they are raised and educated as Jews. The Reform day school, as a locus of quality secular and Jewish education in an open and welcoming milieu, can help Reform Judaism fulfill its mandate to be inclusive.

Transforming Purposes into Practice

Reform day schools express their distinctiveness by transforming these historical, philosophical, sociological and religious purposes into educational practice. They provide a holistic environment for transmitting Jewish culture, embody a commitment to the core values of Reform Judaism, meet the demands of today's social realities by providing excellence in secular education with an emphasis on ethnic identity, and concretize the mandate to invite Jews to participate in Jewish life. These concerns guide Reform day schools as they determine their curricula and establish their educational environments. A description of the educational practices of several Reform days schools illustrates how their practices reflect their purposes. (While this portrait reflects elements of practice at several schools, no single school incorporates all these elements.)

Educational policies at a Reform day school, particularly in areas related to admissions, illustrate the school's interest in welcoming Jews and in reflecting Reform Jewish values. The Reform day school makes special efforts to welcome the widest possible spectrum of the Jewish population. No ideological or behavioral tests bar Jews with differing beliefs or modes of practice from attending and feeling comfortable in the school. No test of Jewishness is applied, either: a child need not be born of a mother who was born Jewish or who converted according to *halakhah*. A child with one Jewish parent, mother *or* father, can enroll in a Reform day school.

The question of synagogue membership also reflects the school's welcoming purpose. One Reform day school requires synagogue membership as a co-requisite—but not a prerequisite—for enrolling a child. If a family deciding to enroll its child in the Reform day school is not already a member of a temple, it is required to join a synagogue within a year. If the family chooses to join the synagogue which sponsors the school rather than another local temple, it is encouraged to participate in synagogue life through a variety of programs designed specifically for day school families. One such program teaches them the basics of celebrating the Jewish holidays their children are learning about in school.

Scholarships are the highest funding priority at the Reform day school. To insure that the school does not become an elitist haven, the Reform day school devotes all its fund-raising efforts toward its scholarship fund.

Several Reform day schools also make sure that single-parent families are welcome in the school. They provide them with scholarships and offer early morning and after school care so that they may feel confident that their children are supervised and nurtured throughout the day. They also offer support groups during the school day for children of divorced parents, led by qualified counselors.

Discipline practices provide an opportunity for school policy to reflect Reform Jewish values. One Reform day school commits itself to a discipline policy that provides students with maximum responsibility for their own individual behavior consistent with the group's needs. Teachers do not punish children but make sure that misbehavior is followed by "logical consequences." Teachers encourage but do not praise (since praise has an external source, but encouragement leads a child to develop an autonomous, inner sense of worth).

Curriculum provides the Reform day school with a multitude of opportunities to reflect its purposes. Reform day schools dedicate their energies to developing the finest program of secular studies possible. They realize that being recognized for secular excellence is the key to attracting parents who are part of the mainstream of contemporary society. One school enters its students in national problem-solving competitions—and they win. Another school may pattern its curriculum on the local "country day school," the school recognized as the finest in the area. And it insures that each class is taught by a head teacher and an assistant, both of whom are licensed and credentialed.

Reform day schools also concentrate on integrating curriculum, in which Jewish concerns are infused into social studies, language arts and science whenever possible. The aim is to help students see that their Jewishness can be an integral part of who they are and what they do. Some schools assign a Jewish studies teacher to each classroom all day long so that no opportunity to bring in Jewish themes is missed. The Judaic studies curriculum specialist meets with each teacher at least once a month to plan for integration.

One aspect of making Jewish concerns part of everyday school life is the emphasis the Reform day school places on social action. Each year, one school assigns each class a local community agency to learn about and visit and for which it collects *tsedakah*. Once a year, another school develops a social action theme, such as peace, for the entire school. The aim of these social action projects is to help children see that they can work *as Jews* for the improvement of their community and their world.

The Jewish studies curriculum is a major focus at a Reform day school, where one-third of each school day is devoted to Hebrew and Jewish studies. Some have developed a "spiral" holiday curriculum so that instead of learning the same ideas each year, children at each grade develop a deeper understanding of the holidays. The schools teach Jewish history, values, and post-Biblical texts using the Bible as the point of departure. The aim is to provide a deeper and more thorough grounding in Jewish tradition than is typical of other Reform Jewish educational settings.

Finally, creating an educational environment unique to Reform day schools allows another avenue for transforming purposes into practice. Many Reform day schools meet in synagogues and take full advantage of their religious and cultural environment. Children visit the sanctuary frequently and meet with the rabbi and cantor several times during the year. The school encourages teachers to "take a moment" whenever the opportunity arises to point out positive actions of students in order to label them as "holy." It gives students the opportunity to exercise their autonomy in religious matters, for example, by choosing whether to wear *kippot* for services.

In all these areas—policy, curriculum and environment—Reform day schools link philosophy to action by fashioning educational practices that reflect their purposes. The more successful an individual Reform day school can be in developing policies, curriculum and environments that reflect its *raison d'etre*, the more distinctively Reform it will be. The challenge facing all of the Reform day schools which currently exist and those that will come into being in the years ahead, is to understand their purposes and then to transform those purposes into daily educational practice.

FROM BENNETT

ON AMERICAN AND JEWISH VALUES

Jewish educators have sought to stress [American democratic values as a] unique aspect of American civilization within their schools, connecting it to the basic Jewish religious values of respect for others and freedom for all. Since religious values and American ideals jibe so well, only the so-called rejectionists have found it necessary to isolate their students from American social, cultural and political institutions. In fact, most day school educators have bent over backwards to relate Judaism and Americanism, responding to those critics who viewed day schools as antithetical to the American melting-pot ideal. Therefore, references to the integration of Judaism and Americanism proliferated. It represented an ideal most day schools had to espouse to be worthy of support. It has been variously formulated as:

... a psychologically and intellectually integrated Jewish version of American civilization.[1] (Greenberg)

... harmonious integration of American and Jewish culture not as theory but as a definite pleasant childhood activity.[2] (Dushkin)

The day school is where Judaism and Americanism are fused.[3] (Lookstein)

Critical Review, p. 8-9.

---

1 Simon Greenberg, "The Religious Policy of the Solomon Schechter Day School," *The Synagogue School*, Vol. XXIV:3 (Spring, 1966), p. 8.
2 Alexander Dushkin, "The Educational Significance of Beth Hayeled," *Jewish Education*, Vol. XVI: 2 (January, 1945), p. 22.
3 Joseph H. Lookstein, "The Modern American Yeshiva," *Jewish Education*, Vol. XVI: 3 (May, 1945), pp. 13-14.

UTILIZING RESEARCH IN JEWISH EDUCATIONAL ORGANIZATIONS
BRIDGING A CULTURAL GAP
Susan L. Shevitz

Despite the proliferation of empirical studies—whether demographic, evaluative or survey—intended to inform communal decisions, there is an underlying uneasiness about using this research. Researchers fear the distortion of their findings to suit groups' political and institutional purposes. Decision-makers, on the other hand, expect unequivocal answers to their communities' dilemmas from research which at best suggests directions but cannot prescribe specific action. The tension between research and policy (or put another way, between data and decisions) is basic to the decision-making process.

This article examines aspects of this tension and suggests ways empirical data can be appropriately used in policy decisions related to Jewish education. While the examples derive primarily from the field of education, they are easily applicable to other voluntary, non-profit institutions in the Jewish community.

The Organizational Contexts of Policy-Making

Recent literature about organizations demonstrates how different groups develop cultures which express their implicit and explicit beliefs, limit their views of reality and bind members to the group through the core of shared values, viewpoints and actions.[1] Some of the tension between researchers and policy-makers stems from differences between their professional cultures. In this view culture refers to the:

> level of **basic assumption** and **beliefs** that are shared by members of an organization, that operate unconsciously, and that define in a basic 'taken for granted' fashion an organization's view of itself and its environment. These assumptions are learned responses to a group's problems of survival in its external environment and its problems of internal integration.[2]

These cultural differences are seen at three levels. Most accessible, but not easily understood, are the organization's artifacts and creations (e.g., technology, art, language, etc.). The second level is that of the day-to-day principles guiding people's behavior. The third is the level of basic assumptions and beliefs. These, so basic to the organization that they are taken for granted, are made explicit only with conscious effort.[3] Cultural differences, generally unarticulated, lead to misunderstandings of intention and purpose between research producers and consumers.

The Culture of Research Consumers in the Jewish Community

Consumers of research include both the lay boards and practitioners in the agencies. The boards of individual institutions are legally responsible for the well-being of the institution and thus empowered—or so go conventional descriptions—to set policy which the practitioners are then bound to implement.[4] Both lay and professional leaders are concerned with challenges facing an organization and look for information which will help them understand and deal with their concerns.

The research consumers in the schools and agencies share several characteristics. First are their expectations of research. Research is

---

1 Among others, Allan Kennedy and Terrence Deal, *Corporate Cultures* (Reading, MA: Addison Wesley, 1982); Andrew Pettigrew, "On Studying Organizational Cultures," *Administrative Science Quarterly* 24 (1979); Linda Smircich, "Concepts of Culture and Organizational Analysis," *Administrative Science Quarterly* 38.3 (1983); Vijay Sathe, *Managerial Action and Corporate Culture* (Homewood, IL: Irwin, 1985); Lee Bolman and Terrence Deal, *Modern Approaches to Understanding and Managing Organizations* (San Francisco: Jossey-Bass, 1984), pp.148-189; and especially Edgar Schein, *Organizational Culture and Leadership* (San Francisco: Jossey-Bass, 1985).
2 Schein, *ibid.*, p. 7.
3 Schein, *ibid.*, pp.112-136.
4 This description obscures a more complex reality. As any astute observer of organizational life recognizes, the influence of practitioners on the agency's agenda and leadership is vast. See Michael Cohen and James March, *Leadership and Ambiguity: The American College President* (New York:McGraw-Hill, 1974), pp.206-211.

expected to help raise, analyze and resolve issues. The concerns of lay leaders and practitioners are immediate and framed by action questions: how to respond to a particular reality, shape a community and translate aspirations into viable programs. Research is judged on the basis of its utility: how can it help in these endeavors?

A second characteristic of research consumers is that their concerns relate to a range of institutions in the community even if they are focused on a single agency or school. While individual institutions are autonomous, their policies and programs are frequently interrelated. To use the example of Jewish education: boards of individual and autonomous schools, central agencies, federations and denominational institutions are all involved in policy discussions. While their orientations to the same issue are likely to differ, one institution's decisions affect the others.

Consider the examples of transforming the supplementary school into a center of family education[5] or, more simply, changing a school's schedule. Though these proposed changes appear to affect only the school itself, in fact the concerns, policy options, decisions and programs of a host of other agencies and institutions (including Jewish community centers, after-school programs, denominational offices, training institutions, family and vocational services) would be affected. Similarly, a federation committee's decision to provide supplementary schools with funding for informal education, for example, will affect the synagogue school at least as much as its own school committee's decision to emphasize liturgical rather than conversational Hebrew. Policy decisions affect a wide range of agencies and groups in diverse ways.

A third characteristic of the policy-setting community, especially pertinent to Jewish education, is the historical schism between the communal and denominational spheres of American Jewry, a schism which is today narrowing. The term "organized Jewish community" historically meant the network of non-denominational and secular social, recreational, educational and social welfare agencies; it did not include the synagogue world. This is not merely a semantic convenience but reveals the community's implicit values and beliefs. In this view Jewish communal agencies represent the public, while synagogues represent the private aspects of the community. Communal agencies were assumed to be non-denominational, accountable through independent boards of directors and involving all types of Jews. For decades these were the operative criteria which determined what could—and could not—be funded by a federation.

5 See "Recommendations: Towards Developing a Supplementary Education Action Plan" in Board of Jewish Education, *Jewish Supplementary Schooling in New York: An Educational System in Need of Change* (New York: Board of Jewish Education, 1988) for an example.

Despite the closer links between these two spheres today, each maintains unique characteristics and distinct cultures. While the same research is often relevant to both denominational and communal institutions, each understands and evaluates it through the lens of its own implicit values and beliefs. This is particularly salient when considering the implications of any research.

These three realities are further affected by our limited knowledge of how agency policies are *actually* made and enacted. Conventional notions about policy setting are inadequate.[6] There is no clear line between policy setting (assumed the function of the lay board) and policy implementation (assumed the professionals' domain). Recent research investigating why, facing declining enrollments and escalating costs, some supplementary schools decide to merge with other local schools while other consolidation attempts are aborted,[7] suggests a multi-faceted reality.

Many knowledgeable people assume that, at least in the case of supplementary education, congregational rabbis exert such influence that they are really responsible for the enacted policies. One educator described many cases where it seemed that the position of the involved congregational rabbi determined the official policy and suggested that "when he [the rabbi] needs the school to be his showcase he will block or undermine consolidation efforts."[8] Examination of consolidation attempts in 70 communities, in addition to a detailed case study of consolidation attempts over the last 15 years in one town, suggests a different view. Policy decisions[9] are made by clusters of individuals which vary in the different places. They may include rabbis, principals, school committee members, trustees, valued community leaders or important donors. Since energy and information are scarce commodities in **organized anarchies**,[10] people who are present, persevering and adaptive are the ones who actually define policy, as it is enacted—regardless of official rank and responsibility.

---

6 This is true of the general community, as well, where analysts have called into question views of policy-making which assume a straightforward and linear relationship between decisions and actions, plans and policies. See, in particular, the work of Karl Weick, James March, Chris Argyris, Carol Weiss and others.
7 Susan L. Shevitz, *Supplementary School Consolidation in the Jewish Community: A Symbolic Approach to Communal Decisions*. Unpublished Dissertation, Harvard University, 1987.
8 Interview, 5 May 1986.
9 In this view policy decisions are seen as a series of occurrences and not a single event.
10 This is a category of organizations characterized by three traits: 1) multiple and changing goals, 2) uneven participation and 3) unclear technology. See Cohen and March, *op.cit.*, pp. 206-207.

Policy is then set by changing groups of lay and professional leaders. Many of these people, for good reason, value their own experience over discrete research findings. They remain unaware, unimpressed or unpersuaded by research even when it deals with their specific concerns. In the consolidation case already mentioned, although the schools knew that the local federation had conducted demographic studies, none turned to those data. The town's public school department had also gathered demographic data; the synagogue schools were unaware that this was an available source of information. Indeed, several schools developed elaborate plans to court new members from the nearby neighborhoods; yet there was considerable evidence from the studies that the people they needed to attract (Jewish families with children at or near supplementary school enrollment age) were not living in or moving to the neighborhoods in question. The federation's studies were ignored because some synagogue leaders were suspicious of the federation;[11] the school department's because they viewed the synagogue school in isolation.[12] Individuals firmly believed in their personal explanations for the enrollment decline and its remedies and were not motivated to consider other possible factors.[13]

Using Research in Organizational Decision-Making

Organizational decision-making is often seen as an instrumental activity. Groups analyze issues and information, weigh alternative actions in order to settle on the most beneficial or least harmful policy.[14] A different view of decision-making, however, suggests it is also a ritualized opportunity for group affirmation.[15] As people talk of us and them, ours and others, members are reaffirming the group's values and reasserting its vision. The group's boundaries and its sense of importance are strengthened. Discussions also provide opportunities for participants to reinforce their individual positions: old-timers recall

11 They believed that the federation, through its central agency for Jewish Education, wanted to replace synagogue schools with inter-denominational or communal schools. Shevitz, *ibid.*, pp. 212-217.
12 This tendency to deny or ignore available evidence is not uncommon to groups with a strong viewpoint (consider how the tobacco industry denies evidence, which virtually all scientists agree upon, of the link between smoking and cancer).
13 Explanatory stories included the pressures of single parent families, a hoped for resurgence of tradition, the growth of the Russian emigre community, synagogue politics, etc. See Deborah Stone, *Policy Paradox and Political Reason*. Glenview, IL: Scott Foresman and Co., 1988), chapter 8, "Causes", for a discussion of this phenomenon in American political life.
14 See the literature of policy analysis, for example Edith Stokey and Richard Zeckhauser, *A Primer for Policy Analysis* (New York: Norton, 1978).
15 Bolman and Deal, *op. cit*, pp. 162-163.

mythic events, sages give reasoned advice, jesters defuse tension with humor and tales.

In groups which especially value empirical data, those who conduct and use research will also be valued. As Lindblom and Cohen show in *Usable Knowledge*, however, social science researchers tend to overemphasize the importance of research (what they call "problem solving inquiry" or PSI). They undervalue other sources of knowledge—ordinary social and interactive knowledge—despite clear evidence that PSI is responsible only for a trickle of knowledge. According to Lindblom and Cohen, research can at best reshape "the mountain of ordinary knowledge."[16] Given the important social and affiliative functions of most voluntary groups in the Jewish community, social and interactive knowledge is likely to be more highly valued than research. Research holds a competitive stance with other sources of wisdom; hence its limited role in many policy deliberations.

This suggests a limitation of research which is not often acknowledged by policy-makers seeking "an answer" or researchers describing "the truth." Research findings tend to be fragmentary and incomplete. Taken *en masse*, they are too incoherent to justify a single position. They are often used instead to legitimate particular views or smaller elements of larger doctrines. In a recent contract negotiation involving class size at a day school, for example, teachers and administrators cited the same body of research but selected studies which reinforced their own views. This is not unusual; consider the recent commotion over the US Department of Education's volume, "What Works."[17]

The process of using research to legitimate a position is especially salient when an operational agency commissions research which will influence its program. The experience of the New York Board of Jewish Education's major research about supplementary education demonstrates the inherent tension between the integrity of the research and the action-oriented considerations. The agency's analysis of the data confirmed the direction the agency hoped to take; indeed, the methodology was influenced by the need to invest policy-makers and practitioners in the enterprise to insure that the findings would be accepted by the supplementary school community.[18]

16 Charles Lindblom and David K. Cohen, *Usable Knowledge* (New Haven: Yale University Press, 1979).
17 Gene V. Glass, "'What Works':Politics and Research." *Educational Researcher*, 16.3 (April, 1987) p.9.
18 Sherry Israel, "The New York Board of Jewish Education Study of Supplementary Schools: Reservations and Recommendations," paper delivered at the CJF General Assembly, 18 November, 1987; Alvin Schiff and Barry Holtz, "Symposium on Research and Action," at the Second Annual Conference of the CAJE Research Network, Philadelphia, 6 June, 1988.

Social and educational policies change slowly and in response to diverse forces. Research can only suggest directions and support changes. Consider how mainstreaming became the dominant policy regarding special needs students: social, economic and judicial conditions were largely responsible,[19] despite early negative evaluations; or the continuation of Head Start, in part because pre-school education had become normative in American society.[20]

Similar forces are at work in the Jewish community, despite its absence of legislative authority. Even when research existed, it was hardly the cause for the most significant policy changes in Jewish education over the decades: the gradual development of the five to six hour congregational school, the decline of community school systems, the replacement of spoken by liturgical Hebrew in many Jewish schools, federations' increased support for Jewish education, schools' focus on Jewish identity and the marked growth of day schools. Conditions such as the development of suburbs, establishment of *Medinat Yisrael*, weakened public schools and other forces were among the prime forces contributing to these phenomena. Research, at best, supported or interpreted these changes.

Thus relevant aspects of the culture of policy-setting groups (i.e., research consumers) can be summarized:

1. Policy-making involves varying clusters of practitioners and lay people who necessarily focus on the pragmatic and programmatic implications of data;

2. Autonomous but interrelated groups share the effects of policy shifts;

3. Communal and denominational arms of the Jewish community have distinct values, beliefs and orientations, yet often they are affected by the same policy decisions;

4. Groups' understanding of policy options are limited by their underlying assumptions and perspectives;

5. Policy is set by changing groups of lay and professional leaders who do not necessarily know or value research-based information;

6. Groups engage in decision-making unrelated to the substantive discussion at hand;

7. Groups value diverse sorts of accessible information and wisdom, not only, or even chiefly, research;

---

19 Seymour Sarason and John Doris, "Public Policy and the Handicapped: The Place of Mainstreaming" in *Policy Making in Education* (NSSE Yearbook 81), Ann Lieberman and Milbrey McLauglin, eds. (Chicago: National Society for the Study of Education, 1982), pp. 23–55.

20 Sheldon White and Stephen Buka, "Early Education: Programs, Traditions and Policies" in *Review of Research in Education: 14*, Ernest Z. Rothkopf, ed. (Washington, DC: American Educational Research Association, 1987), pp. 65–79.

8. Policies change slowly, due to a range of economic, social and historical forces; research, if called on at all, frames problems and supports particular positions.

The Culture of the Research Community

A particular set of professional values and practices informs the researcher's work. These include: methodological rigor, the need to be unbiased, the willingness to work in settings isolated from organizations' political agendas, and the desirability of presenting the whole picture especially when it is complex and ambiguous. Each of these leads to dilemmas when research is used in policy debates.

Methodological rigor and technical clarity is often accompanied by professional jargon which distances the non-expert; it keeps the uninitiated at bay. No wonder, then, that practitioners and lay leaders sometimes consider research to be an "ivory tower" or obtuse, while researchers look upon their common language as representing their shared values, reinforcing their sense of group identity and status.

Researchers appropriately evaluate others' work on the basis of a set of technical and methodological standards. Arguments and challenges clarify ideas. Research consumers often lack pertinent criteria for evaluating data and are apt to judge research on the basis of its common sense conclusions, its fit with popular views or its attractive and forceful presentation. Consider the example of how rapidly the notion of the **self-fulfilling prophecy** caught on following the 1968 publication of *Pygmalion in the Classroom*.[21] The concept was quickly used in legal, psychological, educational and sociological deliberations despite evidence of problems with the research and limitations in generalizing from the findings. As documented by Wineburg, the idea, distorted and misused, influenced many desegregation policies. It gained widespread acceptance because it "represented not merely an idea, but an **ethos**, a uniquely American way of looking at ourselves and understanding what we saw."[22] It fit the needs of the era.

Maintaining an unbiased stance, necessary to good research, is at odds with how research is used in policy debates or how it affects practice. Data become a symbol of truth.[23] They are interpreted by advocates of a

---

21 Robert Rosenthal and Lenore Jacobson, *Pygmalion in the Classroom: Teacher Expectation and Pupil Intellectual Development* (New York: Holt, Rinehart & Winston, 1968).
22 Samuel S. Wineburg, "The Self fulfillment of the Self-Fulfilling Prophecy: A Critical Approach," *Educational Research* 16.9 (December, 1987) p.35.
23 Glass, *op.cit.*, p.10.

particular policy to favor that policy. (Hence the situation when partisans of competing policies actually cite the same data to argue their different sides.) The use of research has been likened to the drunk looking for car keys; he searches for evidence wherever the light is brightest![24]

The need to maintain an unbiased stance presents particular difficulties to those who do research while maintaining a keen personal interest in the life of the Jewish community. This is exacerbated by the frequent practice, especially in evaluation research, of expecting the same practitioners who have been instrumental in developing a program to evaluate it. Other research is commissioned and carried out by agencies with a policy agenda and many of the researchers are themselves staff members of these agencies. How can a sufficiently detached stance be maintained? What safeguards should be incorporated into the research process itself to prevent organizational preferences and political realities from contaminating it or presupposing conclusions?

Since this practice is likely to continue, the issues warrant careful attention. Two practices would help to correct the situation. First, descriptions of the conflicts researchers faced, how they were mediated, and other possible interpretations of the data should be included in the research reports. Further, practitioners and researchers who have not been involved in the programs being investigated should collaborate on the studies.

On the latter, when researchers are detached from the pushes and pulls of communal life they have less interest in how the research will be disseminated and used than in the research itself. They may fail to acknowledge that factors which to the researcher seem extraneous—political constraints, groups' attitudes, simultaneously occurring problems, communities' orientations to change—are in fact central to making and implementing policy.[25]

When research is cited in a policy deliberation or used as the basis of a programmatic innovation, it is often simplified. Studies by Coleman and Jencks are examples of this phenomenon.[26] Despite complex data and thorough analysis, findings were often reduced to the inaccurate slogan that "schools don't matter." From this flowed a plethora of reforms which unfairly claimed legitimacy in the research.[27] A similar

24 White and Buka, *op.cit.*, p.69.
25 A fascinating example of this is analyzed in Alan Peshkin, *The Imperfect Union: School Consolidation and Community Conflict* (Chicago: University of Chicago Press, 1982).
26 James Coleman and Associates, "Equality of Educational Opportunity," (Washington, DC: U.S. Government Printing Office, 1966) and Christopher Jencks and Associates, *Inequality* (New York: Basic Books, 1972).
27 Robert Bickel, "Educational Reform and the Equivalence of Schools," *Issues in Education* 4.3 (Winter, 1986).

critique can be applied to the Jewish community's responses to the Bock and Himmelfarb studies[28] about the effectiveness of Jewish schooling. Class size research provides another example. Lay committees and teachers' unions, for example, want to locate research which would resolve the question of maximum class size. The issue, however, is complex and cannot be meaningfully discussed in a particular school without thoughtful reference to the school's situation. Ultimately the value component of the discussion—what kind of school is envisaged? how can it be achieved? what are the trade-offs involved?—is essential to the deliberation. Yet this is not territory in which the researcher can comfortably tread, at least not as an authority.

Finally, the researcher's world values practices and procedures which are seen as rare luxuries to the practitioner: detachment, complexity, careful (read "slow") deliberation, and raising more questions. The practitioner's world values clear and timely presentations, straightforward and unambiguous application of research to a policy question and sensitivity to political and pragmatic ramifications of research—traits which do not necessarily advance one's standing in the research community.

Implications of the Cultural Contexts ... and Some Suggestions

If we consider, then, the different assumptions and values which the research and decision-making groups hold, we might begin to understand the conditions under which research might make more of a difference in Jewish education. Embedded in the description of policy-making suggested in this article are at least four basic tensions between the perspectives of the research and policy-making groups:

1. Complexity versus simplicity

Despite the complexity and subtlety of most research findings, for policy purposes recommendations must be easily encapsulated and simply conveyed. Perhaps this is one reason why the few quantitative studies in Jewish education caught the imagination and remain part of the lexicon of people discussing policy options, especially regarding supplementary education. The decade-old Bock and Himmelfarb qualitative studies (in the 1970's) are examples of this. They have been summarized as concluding that to be effective, Jewish schooling needs a minimum number of hours. It is not as easy to encapsulate an ethnographic account of a Jewish school,

---

28 Geoffrey Bock, "Does Jewish Schooling Matter?" (New York: America Jewish Committee, 1975); Harold Himmelfarb, "Jewish Education for Naught: Educating the Culturally Deprived Jewish Child" (Washington, DC: Synagogue Council of America, 1976).

a philosophical inquiry into the nature of religious education or a model for curriculum and program innovation.[29]

2. Causal versus contextual forces

Those considering policy changes look to research for a direct link between cause and effect. Even in those rare cases when causation (or even high probability) can be asserted, there must be careful attention to the conditions under which the effects will occur.[30] Most studies suggest directions and stimulate meaningful questions. Indeed, that may be research's most potent role.[31]

3. Attention to logical and empirically derived conclusions versus attention to a wide range of political, institutional and social factors

Researchers attend to the logic within and among studies in trying to define and defend their conclusions. Policy-makers, on the other hand, are invariably concerned with a wide range of implicit and explicit factors and consequences. Political, institutional, ideological, social, economic and personal factors have primary roles in their policy debates and decisions. The place of these non-rational forces in a policy deliberation needs to be understood and accommodated.[32]

4. Translation of the research into concrete programs versus the integrity of the ideas

Policy-makers are necessarily concerned with how the ideas which emerge from research can be shaped, molded and sometimes contorted into specific programs while researchers remain concerned about the validity and reliability of the constructs, methods and conclusions.

These tensions suggest a twofold challenge: **more research must be encouraged,** but the **role of research as problem-solver must simultaneously contract**. More support for research, not all of which should be policy-oriented, is critical for several reasons. Deliberations about specific issues would be enhanced and the range of topics about

---

29 See, for example, the doctoral dissertations by Bennett Solomon, David Schoem, Sheldon Dorph and Joseph Lukinsky.

30 See Gene Hall and Susan Loucks, "Policy Research Rooted in Practice," *Policy Making in Education*. Ann Lieberman and Milbrey McLaughlin, eds. NSSE Yearbook, 1982, pp.133-158, for a discussion of contour research. Policy research is transformed when the concerns, perspectives and problems of the practitioners responsible for implementing the solution are incorporated into the research and policy setting scheme.

31 See Glass, op.cit., p. 9, and Donald Schon,"Generative Metaphor: A Perspective on Problem Setting in Social Policy." *Metaphor and Thought*, A. Orthonoy, ed. (Cambridge, England: Cambridge University Press), pp. 254-283.

32 See Jerry Patterson, Stewart Purkey and Jackson Parker, *Productive School Systems for a Nonrational World* (Alexandria, VA: ASCD, 1987), chapters 1-3, for a description of the rational and nonrational approaches. Also see Bolman and Deal, *op.cit.*, chapters 3 and 4; Terrence Deal, "Educational Change: Revival Tent, Tinkertoys, Jungle or Carnival?" *Rethinking School Improvement: Research, Craft and Concept*. Ann Lieberman, ed. (New York: Teachers College Press, 1986).

which data would be available would be expanded. This would reduce the pressure to transform quickly what is learned into a pragmatic policy or program. And, since insight comes in unpredictable ways, it would create a climate which supports creativity and knowledge. Especially useful would be funding to replicate studies so that the knowledge base will grow.[33]

Decision-makers must be conversant with the range, subtleties, protocols and limitations of research while researchers must learn to translate their work into terms which are useful to policy-makers and practitioners. This calls for what might be conceived as a curricular approach: a sequenced, analytical exposure to the relevant ideas with enough time for participants to consider, debate, evaluate and integrate the information. Such a "curriculum" would require the active collaboration of research consumers and producers so that ways can be found to address and expand their different views of what the research entails. Such discussions would be eased by research reports designed specifically to stimulate policy discussions. These should be limited in scope, straightforward and imaginatively produced.[34]

The perspectives of both the denominational and communal spheres must be incorporated in the discussions. On the simplest level this entails developing a set of terms which are used in the same way by both groups. For example, standard categories for different types of schools, sizes and programs need to be adopted. Similarly, the ramifications of any research on each of the two spheres, especially as they relate to implementation, must be systematically considered. There is ample evidence that this does not generally happen.

Given sufficient time and support, a curricular approach might yield more realistic understandings of the limitations and implications of research. The beliefs, assumptions and expectations of each group about the research process would be made explicit, examined and considered. Research consumers would develop a more sophisticated comprehension of the limitations—especially in terms of suggesting professional practice—of research and ways to use findings more selectively. For the researchers the range of non-rational concerns which influences how a

---

33 This has happened with demographic and some other survey research but is needed in other arenas, especially when the concerns suggest more complicated methodologies.

34 Recent experimentation with the "chart essay" is encouraging. This is a restructured form of a methods-oriented report; the main sections are arranged in a series of charts which give detailed yet accessible information and link specific research questions to real policy decisions. By organizing the details, the chart essay tries to avoid the problems which occur when the practical application of research results is far removed from the actual research. See Patricia A. Hanesly, Ann E. Lupowski and James F. McNamara, "The Chart Essay: A Strategy for Communication Research Findings to Policy-Makers and Practitioners." *Educational Evaluation and Policy Analysis*, 9.1 (Spring, 1987).

community understands and uses data might be better appreciated. Researchers might also develop approaches which would help practitioners make better use of the research.

This approach acknowledges the nature of professional practice with its reliance on many sorts of knowledge and wisdom. Ordinary knowledge, reflection on practice, professional insight, interaction and craft—in addition to social science research—offer ways to deal with policy issues. Moving from a technical notion of professionalism in which research findings are expected to dictate practice, Ralph Tyler has recently reminded us that practitioners often find workable solutions to problems through trial and error. As he states, the

> ... professional practice of teaching, as well as that of law, medicine and theology, is largely a product of the experience of practitioners, especially those who are more creative, inventive, and observant than the average.[35]

Schon's work also demonstrates that research-based knowledge is less central to professional practice than making explicit the intuitive way practitioners proceed in the messy world. He argues that individuals and communities need to learn how to reflect on their actions. This "on-the-spot surfacing, criticizing, restructuring and testing of intuitive understandings of phenomena" is what empowers them to remake their world by letting them reformulate the many taken-for-granted assumptions which have structured their work.[36] Empirical data must be carefully used, accompanying other legitimate sources of knowledge.

In many ways Bennett Solomon's approach to teacher training, curriculum development and day school education exemplified the symbiosis of practice and research which is envisaged in this essay. Theoretical questions were starting points but so were the teachers' practical experiences. As a consultant to a curriculum project,[37] for example, he brought the research on moral and adolescent development to deliberations as openly as he brought reports of his observations of teachers using the experimental units. He could sharpen the contributions of each perspective and, through the inquiries he organized, help each enrich the

---

35 Cited in Ralph Hosford, ed., *Using What We Know about Teaching* (Alexandria, VA: Association for Supervision and Curriculum Development, 1984) p. 9. Also see Karl Weick, "Managing Change among Loosely Coupled Elements" in Paul Goodman and Associates, *Change in Organizations* (San Francisco: Josey-Bass, 1984).

36 Donald Schon, "Leadership as Reflection in Action" in Thomas Sergiovanni and John Corbally, eds. *Leadership and Organizational Culture: New Perspectives on Administrative Theory and Practice* (Urbana: University of Illinois Press, 1984), p. 42. Also see Donald Schon, *The Reflective Practitioner: How Professionals Think in Action* (New York: Basic Books, 1983).

37 Susan L. Shevitz, *Why Be Good? Sensitivities and Ethics in Rabbinic Literature*, First Edition (Boston: Bureau of Jewish Education, 1977). Second revised edition, by Kaye, Rabinowitch, and Towvim, 1984.

curriculum. He fought attempts to oversimplify research on moral development as zealously as he guarded against dismissing teachers' experiences because they represented challenges to the ideas of the curriculum developers. Both perspectives informed his work and enriched the units and related teacher training sessions.

Solomon's work on curriculum integration for the day school is an even clearer example of this. While it is based in research on curriculum and learning, it emerged from his own teaching and the inquiry—or in Schon's term, reflection-on-practice—which he conducted on his own work. Teaching enriched the concepts; concepts enriched the teaching. Neither was simplified for the comfort of the other. Even when the work developed so that other educators were using his ideas, he insisted on both the integrity of the research and the wisdom of practical experience. Time to collaborate, discuss, debate, experiment, reflect, plan, proceed and evaluate were maintained so that his ideas were not simplified in educators' rush to try a new approach in the classroom. Solomon could succeed at this because he understood and respected the cultures of both the research producers and the consumers. What he did as an individual is a model for how the community needs to move if it is to learn to use research more beneficially in its policy discussions.

Solomon, of course, fastidiously built a school and a faculty committed to this kind of inquiry and procedure. Communities and institutions within these communities face the challenge of using research responsibly in a research-poor environment. This analysis suggests that the actual process of how the Jewish community uses information becomes a legitimate subject for study. How is information used? What experimentation ensues? How do researchers and decision-makers learn to bridge implicit cultural gaps and help each other define, understand and shape reality? With the Jewish community facing unprecedented challenges and opportunities, diverse sources of knowledge and reason need to bear on particular issues. Making the contributions of the research community more useful while broadening the research consumers' understanding of research are compatible and timely goals.

This article is based on an invited paper presented at the First Annual Conference of the Research in Jewish Education Network, June, 1987. I appreciate the comments of Professor Bernard Reisman in reviewing an earlier version of the essay, and my discussions with Professor Isa Aron on this subject.

II. CURRICULUM

FROM BENNETT

ON CURRICULUM

THE SACRED/SECULAR DILEMMA

... One's philosophy of education will be directly influenced by one's philosophical view toward the sacred/secular dilemma ... it must be emphasized that no single curricular plan will satisfy these varying attitudes toward the question of integrating the sacred and the secular. The challenge confronting day school educators is the elucidation of a consistent policy on this fundamental issue which will then serve as the basis of the philosophy of education from which the curriculum will flow.

It is almost universally accepted among contemporary philosophers of education that knowledge does not exist as one single unity, but rather consists of distinguishable patterns or structures which are ordered in precise ways ...

The epistemological positions of these thinkers suggest that efforts toward integrating religious knowledge with other forms of knowledge are not as simple as merely juxtaposing similar content. More importantly, according to Hirst, Phenix and Schwab,[1] the fundamental means of establishing the truth of assertions is what actually separates each discipline one from another. Merging content without regard to these truth criteria and means of verification would represent a very superficial and sloppily constructed integration.

Following this line of thought, it is crucial to distinguish "religious knowledge" from "knowledge about religion." William James[2] distin-

---

1 Paul Hirst, "Liberal Education and the Nature of Knowledge," *Knowledge and the Curriculum* (London: Routledge and Kegan Paul, 1974); Philip Phenix, "The Architectonics of Knowledge," in Stanley Elam, ed., *Education and the Structure of Knowledge* (Chicago: Rand McNally and Co., 1964); Joseph Schwab, "Problems, Topics and Issues," in *Education and the Structure of Knowledge*.
2 William James, *The Varieties of Religious Experience* (NY: Modern Library—Random House, 1902/1929).

guishes the immediate, personal, intense religious experiences of man from the second order "science of religion" which attempts to generalize and systematize these experiences for classification and comparison. Knowledge about religion can be logical and/or empirical, as it deals with the psychology of religion as well as with the sociology, history and philosophy of religion. Its truth criteria are open to the public and verification is possible through rational discourse and investigation. But actual religious knowledge is limited to the inner personal experience of the individual. Its proof is not empirical, but rather deeply embedded within the believer.

The unique substantive and syntactic structures of religious experience have been the topic of contemporary theologians, both Christian and Jewish. Rudolf Otto characterizes the holy [as] indefinable—inexpressible ... The appreciation for the holy, the religious, is *sui generis*, irreducible to any other form—it is linked neither to the moral nor rational spheres. It cannot be taught, it can only be evoked, awakened in the mind ...

Abraham Joshua Heschel calls this inexpressible awareness of the divine the "sense of the ineffable"—a realm which lies "within our reach but beyond our grasp."

For Otto and Heschel the essence of the religious can only be expressed through analogy. Religious language is symbolic, for it deals with a realm far and beyond the ken of ordinary language and perception. Therefore, both the substantive and the syntactic structures of the religious realm are special and unique.

This short sketch of the issues separating religious knowledge from other forms of knowledge suggests that notions of curricular integration are far more complicated than implied by the simplistic references found throughout the literature on the Jewish day school. We have noted that the "science of religion"—study about religion—can be undertaken from the perspective of the social sciences, literature, philosophy and history. Therefore, such study about religion might be easily "integrated" or taught alongside of, or as part of, general courses. But the sphere of the religious must not be mistakenly equated with this cognitive, empirical study of religion. Jane Martin reminds us that "we must distinguish between understanding a form of knowledge and understanding something by means of, or in that form of knowledge; for example, understanding the discipline of science as opposed to scientifically understanding some phenomenon."[3] The goal of integration must not overwhelm the distinctions which do exist and which must be retained for the various forms of knowledge to remain authentic.

Critical Review, pp. 13-15.

3 Jane R. Martin, *Readings in the Philosophy of Education: A Study of Curriculum* (Boston: Allyn and Bacon, Inc., 1970), p. 155.

RELIGIOUS SYMBOLISM IN THE CURRICULUM

The day school, by focusing on the variety of symbols and their significance for man, can help forge unity out of diversity. It can also help develop the specific skills needed for appreciation of symbols in their respective domains.

> The principle of symbolism, with its universality, validity, and general applicability, is the magic word, the Open Sesame! giving access to the specifically human world, to the world of human culture. Once man is in possession of this magic key further progress is assured.[1]

Although symbols do exist throughout every realm of knowledge and they all serve to explain the universe, there are differences in the way they function.

Religious symbols differ in purpose and essence from scientific and artistic symbols. They combine aspects of each, however, as they transmit their message.

> The meaning or value of any given (religious) symbol is not a denotative, precise meaning, but a connotative one—a meaning in a language designed to speak to the mind, but having more immediate relation to the emotions than to verbal thinking. Beyond simply arousing emotions, however, these symbols carry potent ideas ...[2]

In other words, the religious symbol connotes a specific phenomenon (like the scientific symbol) and also evinces an emotional response (like the artistic symbol). The specific phenomenon which religious symbols connote is the ultimate reality symbolized by God.

Only one symbol in Judaism relates directly to God, that being the four lettered Tetragrammaton which relates God's essence. All other symbols relate to God indirectly, for they refer to commandments, rituals or observances within which God's presence is revealed. Greenberg explains this unique aspect of religious symbols:

> The Sabbath symbolizes first a created universe and only secondarily Him who created it. The fringes directly symbolize the commandments that are to be remembered and only secondarily Him who is the author of the commandments. Circumcision symbolizes directly the covenant between God and Abraham and only indirectly the God with whom the covenant is thus renewed in every generation.[3]

---

1 Ernst Cassirer, *An Essay on Man* (New Haven: Yale University Press, 1944), p. 35.
2 Erwin R. Goodenough, *Symbols in the Greco-Roman Period*, Vol. IV (New York: Pantheon Books, Inc. 1954), p. 37.
3 Simon Greenberg, *Foundations of a Faith* (New York: Burning Bush Press, 1967), p. 185.

The significance of these symbols can be transmitted to the young, with their similarities to and differences from other symbols stressed not in a detached, cognitive fashion but rather through participation within and among these Jewish symbols and ideas. The fact that they are shared by the community of Jews around the world and throughout history will give these symbols even greater cogency. At the same time it will be vitally important to point out to the students that symbols—all symbols—create certain barriers in addition to the bridges which they construct ...

A conscious pursuit of the role of symbols throughout the entire day school curriculum will be yet another integrating thread, one which will help forge unity of purpose while building important skills into the foundation of the children's education.

Dissertation, pp. 94-98.

CURRICULUM INNOVATION

As the principal of a community sponsored K-9 Jewish day school, I have worked with our faculty to create integrative experiences within our entire school setting and to create a curriculum which will foster the development of integrative individuals.

...

During the last 10 years numerous researchers have studied the effects of curriculum reform efforts in America. Millions of dollars have been spent on the development of new material and yet, as Ann Lieberman of Teacher's College states, "relatively few new ideas can make it behind the classroom door."[1]

> **Editors' Note:** Bennett proceeds to review the literature on this topic, citing, *inter alia*, Goodlad; Tyack, Kirst, and Hansot; Berman and McLaughlin; Sarason; Lortie; Apple; Eisner; and Huebner.

Lieberman and Loucks have identified three major concepts which characterize successful implementation efforts: Developmentalism, Participation, and Support.[2]

...

1. *Developmentalism* recognizes that teachers and school staff who are involved in curriculum implementation develop personally and professionally as they deal with new ideas. First they orient and prepare themselves while responding mechanically. Later, as the curriculum becomes routine, a few changes are made. Finally the curriculum is refined and/or adjusted to better meet the needs of the students and the teachers. Understanding the various developmental aspects of change can help educators design an implementation process which anticipates teachers' questions and needs throughout the process. This can occur only in an open and trusting environment.

2. *Participation*: Research indicates that when teachers participate in decisions made prior to and during the process of implementation the likelihood of successful implementation is increased. The significance of teacher participation in school improvement has more to do with how the activities are handled than with the content itself. Sensitivity to who the faculty are; their past experience with improvement activities; and assessment of what the social context of the school is and an understanding of the interpersonal relationships among the staff will help determine how one organizes an innovation project. Participation by

---

1 Susan Loucks and Ann Lieberman, "Curriculum Implementation" *Fundamental Curricular Decisions*, ASCD, 1983, p. 125.
2 Loucks and Lieberman, *Ibid.*, pp. 129-133.

the teachers will result in their investment in the project and thus enlist their support toward a successful conclusion.

3. *Support*: Material support is usually given prime importance, with human support too often overlooked. Both research and common knowledge indicate that the principal functions as a key element in the successful change effort. The principal must consistently remind the staff that the new curriculum is a *high* priority of the school. Both formal and informal encouragement must continually be given by the principal. Awareness of the developmental nature of change will help principals be more realistic in their expectations, especially in the first year. It will also help them to be more understanding of the personal issues involved in making changes in the classroom. The principal must delay the introduction of additional curricular programs until the original innovation is firmly in place, usually within three years. The all too common routine of overloading teachers with innovations has led to many failures. One must also recognize that trying to create new materials or methods at the end of a school day is inefficient. Released time, or special curriculum workshop time, is a more productive way to use teachers' time and expertise.

Peer support also helps facilitate the process of change. While teaching can often be a lonely activity, particularly in self-contained classrooms, sharing ideas, solving problems and crating new materials can be invigorating and positive. Curriculum personnel who work with teachers as resources and facilitators also help sustain the project.

In addition to these recommendations, the Crandall study lists three additional factors which contribute to the successful institutionalization of new practices in schools: Creating line items on budgets to guarantee money for the project; orienting new personnel to the project; and writing the new programs into existing curriculum guidelines, scopes and sequences.[3]

The results of these findings have also led to a new emphasis within discussions of staff development. Rather than focus upon the individual teacher and in-service courses for teacher training, the emphasis is now focused upon staff/organization development.

...

Teacher development is seen, therefore, within the context of the social political and educational environment of the entire school. All personnel must be involved in the change process within that dynamic environment. This is a crucial lesson learned from research which must be applied to curriculum reform efforts in Jewish schools.

Curriculum Innovation, pp. 1-9.

---

[3] David P. Crandall et al., *People, Policies and Practices: Examining the Chain of School Improvement* (Andover, Mass: The Network, Inc., 1982).

TEACHING OF RABBINICS IN THE DAY SCHOOL

Mark Smiley

This paper reviews aspects of the teaching of Rabbinics in the Conservative Day School.[1] The founding vision for the teaching of Jewish tradition in the Solomon Schechter Day School aspired to an intensive communication of Judaic knowledge and an emotional commitment to Judaism. The growth of the Schechter network has been accompanied by numerous experiments in translating the aspirations of the founding thinkers into programs, staff development and curriculum.[2] Indeed, the founders of the schools dreamed that the schools would become sanctified arenas for the teaching of Jewish tradition and responsibility.

The Solomon Schechter Day School Manual describes one avenue for translating the vision into an educational program whereby these schools would:

> provide a natural setting where many of the mitzvot can be lived rather than simply discussed. Opportunities for the realization of the interpersonal mitzvot of fair play, sympathy, concern, help for one another, avoidance of entrapment, and the like, as well as the opportunity for daily *tefillah*, observance of *kashrut*, hospitality to visitors, respect for elders and for property of others, must be fully exploited.[3]

---

[1] Robert Gordis, "The Philosophy of the Conservative Day School," *Understanding Conservative Judaism*, ed. Max Gelb (New York: Rabbinical Assembly, 1978), p. 162.

[2] Bennett Solomon's writings serve as the clearest evidence of this claim. Indeed his writings, his practical models and our personal contact were important factors that influenced many of my professional aims.

[3] Pesach Schindler, *Solomon Schechter Day School Manual* (New York: United Synagogue Commission on Jewish Education, 1970), quoted from 2nd edition, 1983, renamed, *Manual for Organizing and Administering the Solomon Schechter Day School*, chapter IX, p. 64.

These goals coupled with a desire for integrating Jewish and American experience formed part of the educational rationale for the new day school movement.[4]

Early Curricular Visions

While encouraging a well-rounded curriculum, the early visionaries believed that Rabbinics instruction should not be the primary source for the development of cognitive skills and emotional dispositions. In differentiating the new day school from the Yeshivah, Bokser challenged the centrality of Talmudic study as a major focus of Conservative Day School education and suggested that a number of subject areas be given more or less equal emphasis.

> A Solomon Schechter School will surely understand the crucial role of rabbinic literature in the unfolding of Judaism. But it will include as elements of basic emphasis other branches of Jewish literature: the Bible, the Hebrew language and literature: including the modern creations emanating from Israel; the moralistic and philosophic literature; poetry and the arts; historical studies which embrace the total sweep of Jewish history with attention to the modern epoch and the rebirth of a free Israel.[5]

Siegel suggested that the Bible might serve as a better means for the "appreciation of (Judaism's) moral message." Yet, he emphasized the need for mastery of cognitive skills in the Rabbinics subject area.

> The student of the day school should have the ability to read the Talmud, certainly the Mishnah and to understand the categories and the methodologies of the text, albeit in a simple but nevertheless comprehensive fashion. Furthermore, Rabbinics education should provide the child with the ability to identify basic Mitzvot.[6]

Bokser, among others, also saw a need to suggest a "Conservative Day School" approach to text study that would be in accordance with the ideology of the movement and the positive historical methodology taught at the Jewish Theological Seminary. "Our movement long described itself as historical Judaism which focuses on historical factors in the development of tradition." Bokser saw the need to emphasize the role of

---

4   For a discussion of the goals of the Solomon Schechter School see Morton Siegel, "What Kind of a Child Do We Want To Produce in the Solomon Schechter School?" *The Synagogue School*, Vol. 25.3, 1967, pp. 6-7. See also Bennett Ira Solomon, "Curricular Integration in the Jewish All-Day School In the United States," (unpublished doctoral dissertation, Harvard University, 1979), Chapter Two.

5   Ben Zion Bokser, "The Solomon Schechter Day School and the Conservative Movement," *The Pedagogic Reporter*, Vol. 19(4), 1968, p. 24.

6   Siegel, "What Kind of a Child Do We Want To Produce in the Solomon Schechter School?" p. 7.

the human *and* the Divine in the evolution of Jewish tradition. "Historical Judaism ... does not negate a Divine initiative in the precipitation of the visions in which Jewish beliefs arose. But it acknowledges a 'creative human' dimension working in symbiosis with the Divine."

This delineation of Conservative ideology led to the assertion that the student should gain:

> a) the recognition of historic development in the genesis of tradition, corresponding to the human factor which is always finite and transient and
>
> b) the recognition of the compatibility of change with loyalty to tradition, which is grasped as a fluid and unfinished system, which is continually remolded to reflect new religious experience.[7]

Bokser's statement suggests the importance of appreciating the text as the embodiment of various responses to important religious questions. The task of the educator is to uncover the questions of faith that the classic Jewish texts have preserved.

Siegel also suggested some educational principles for Conservative day school instruction. First of all, inquiry should underly all instruction. Moreover, inquiry should be accompanied by "freedom," that is, the ability to make choices within the Conservative ideological framework. A doctrine of permanent revelation should allow the educator to present Judaism "as an evolving faith and not a closed system." Text instruction should inform the student that "Judaism has standards, approaches, and mandates" that must be considered. Furthermore, Siegel saw the possibility of the student using the text as a "matrix from which he can draw forth solutions to moral problems which present themselves in his (one's) daily life."[8]

Greenberg encouraged the view that the school should also be developing the spirituality of the student. He proposed a learning environment that would be informed with a sense of wonder and awe.[9] Greenberg's writings on Bible instruction influenced a curricular movement that believed that the curriculum could be arranged to deal with Judaism's "main patterns of thought and life" and to promote an understanding of:

- one's attitude to God and to the world He created;
- one's relationship to the family as a child, sibling or future parent;
- one's relationship to his fellow man and his people;
- one's relationship to basic human needs such as food and shelter and
- one's relationship to time.[10]

---

7   Bokser, *op. cit.*, p. 24.
8   Siegel, *op. cit*, pp. 4-8.
9   Simon Greenberg, "The Religious Policy of the Solomon Schechter Day School," originally published in *The Synagogue School*, Vol. 25.3, 1966, pp. 14-16.
10 Simon Greenberg, "Bible Study and the Conservative School," in Walter Ackerman and Norman Schanin, eds., *New Insights into Curriculum*

Greenberg would achieve such an understanding of man's relationship to his world not by philosophical proofs but by a study of Jewish tradition.[11] Toward this end, he proposed that the curriculum be structured around the following themes:

1. The Moral and Ethical Laws
2. The Sabbath and Festivals
3. The Dietary Laws and
4. The Laws Affecting the Structure of the Jewish Family.[12]

Thus, it was proposed that the Conservative day school would teach Judaica in a new way—different from the pure academic approaches in the universities and seminaries, and different from the humanistic approach of the Israeli public schools. The Conservative day school, it was proposed in theory and in practice, would be different from Yeshivot, the Orthodox day schools, and the state religious school system in Israel, distinguished by its historical approach to the tradition.

Early Implementation

The aspirations of the founders of the Conservative day school movement has proved to be difficult to implement fully in the school. The resources needed to translate modern approaches to Judaism within a theoretically sound educational framework have presented an enormous challenge. The lay and professional leaders of the Schechter movement have found that there is a need to educate a generation of teachers and administrators who, by reflecting the philosophies of the founders, would be able to create appropriate Judaic studies curricula.

Solomon notes that the early curricular innovations "merely mirrored existing curricular models, i.e., the structure and content of the congregational school and the Orthodox day school."[13] While the founding thinkers cautioned against a Talmud centered curriculum, Abramson observed: "Our day schools tend to be Hebrew and Bible oriented ... This is so even though the Conservative movement has considered the rabbinic period and its literature normative."[14]

Development, 1964 Year Book, Part One, (New York: Jewish Educators Assembly of the United Synagogue of America, 1964), p. 11.
11 Citing Kadushin, he maintained that a philosophical approach would be "absolutely foreign" to Rabbinic thought. He wrote "there is no need for philosophical appreciation of the relationship between God and man, or to an understanding of the nature of God, of His existence and of His involvement in the affairs of man." See Greenberg, "The Religious Policy," *op.cit.* p. 9.
12 *Ibid.,* p. 13.
13 Bennett Ira Solomon, Dissertation, *op. cit.* p. 40.
14 Robert Abramson, "An Educational Rationale for a Rabbinic Value Concepts Curriculum Grades 3-4," unpublished paper, p. 1.

Though there have been a number of pioneering efforts, very limited work has been done in curriculum development in the formal Judaic studies program. Adar suggests that the disappointing level of curricular work in the Conservative day school stems from the fact that the schools "have not developed an educational conception of Jewish culture."[15]

He comments:
> Mishnah and Gemara were not introduced into the curriculum on the basis of serious educational considerations, but rather because of the simplistic belief that adding the study of Mishnah and Gemara means that one is presenting a better Jewish education.[16]

In spite of these observations, seminal curricular experimentation began to take place in isolated Schechter schools. Indeed, Frost's curricular thinking exemplifies the unique type of deliberations that were taking place in the early years of the Schechter movement.

In a statement of goals and objectives for the Solomon Schechter Day School, Frost suggests a direction for a Rabbinics curriculum. For the teachers, his goals included demonstrating "various strata of the Oral Law ... exposing our students to an appreciation of Talmudic reasoning, the development of halacha and its impact on the growth of Rabbinic Judaism."[17] Frost shifts the previous goals of religious and moral education, as articulated by Siegel and Bokser, to more of a "structure of the disciplines"-based instruction. Though this approach stresses the cognitive aspects of subject matter, it remains closely related to the ideology of the Conservative movement. Frost's suggestions view text study as a means to teach the "positive historical"[18] nature of Jewish tradition. As such, this approach would add the means of historical analysis to the list of ends of Rabbinics education.

Reflecting on practice, Frost asserts that the positive historical focus is the best direction in creating "proud authentic Jews, who are ethnically and religiously non-apologetic yet citizens of the Western world participating in its intellectual life." The Schechter school "should be characterized by an interpretation of Judaism, its religious and cultural legacy, that is broad, nondoctrinaire, open and nonparochial." Therefore, Frost

---

15 Zvi Adar, *Jewish Education in Israel and in the United States* (Jerusalem: Magnes Press, 1977), p. 202.
16 *Ibid.*
17 Shimon Frost, "Goals and Objectives for the Solomon Schechter Day Schools," in A. Gittelson, ed., *Jewish Education in the 70's: Challenge and Promise, 1970 Yearbook* (New York: Jewish Educators Assembly of the United Synagogue of America, 1970), p. 50.
18 Gordis defines the term "positive historical" for the purposes of the day school in the following way: Judaism has a history, it is a historical religion, the product of growth and development, and we must take a positive, affirmative attitude toward this problem. See Gordis, *Understanding Conservative Judaism, op.cit.* pp. 162-165.

defines education in a Schechter school as "nonfixed ... an evolving task ... a process ... which parallels the evolving nature of the tradition."[19]

For Frost, "our schools are not neutral as far as Judaism is concerned." Judaism should be made challenging in the area of *emunot ve-de'ot* (Jewish philosophy) and meaningful in the area of *mitzvot*. The Jewish day school cannot only reflect the needs of the society at large but must "move Jewish society out of its present reality and not perpetuate a reality we consider Jewishly inadequate."[20]

Frost's views are reflected in *The Curriculum Compendium*.[21] It illustrates some of the varying attempts at introducing the study of Rabbinic literature in the Solomon Schechter Day School curriculum. A review of a number of curriculum outlines contained therein supports Solomon's assertion that schools utilized materials found in the Orthodox day school and in the supplementary school. However, even in the *Compendium*, one sees a movement to a "historical" approach in the goal statements included in the subject area of Rabbinics-Mishnah. One school's stated aims include:

a. To enable the student to understand and appreciate the developmental aspect of Jewish religious law based upon the "Basic Law" as suggested in the Torah.

b. To enable the pupil to understand the systematic and organizational creativity that went into the development of this system of "Torah She-b'al Peh."

c. To enable the pupil to understand that the "Halacha" is a disciplined "road" upon which to travel; a disciplined lifestyle to adopt and live with.

d. To enable the pupil to understand that Mishnaic law was for the purpose of meeting the needs of the people in the days of the Tanaitic period in our history. It is important to know the depths to which the Tanaim went to evolve a religious law suitable and appropriate for their time.

e. To provide the student the insight into the corporate products ... and an appreciation of its spiritual inspiration and ethical teaching and guidelines to human relations and their relevancy to the student's own life.

f. To help the pupil understand the Mishnaic structure; "argumentation, query" is the method of determining the law.

g. To help the pupil follow the development in the interpretation of the Torah Law into the Mishnaic Law.

19 Shimon Frost, "The Needs of the Solomon Schechter Day Schools: A Practitioner's View," *Conservative Judaism*, Vol.33.3, 1980, pp. 74-75.
20 *Ibid.* p. 75.
21 Chanoch Shudofsky, ed., *Curriculum Compendium for Solomon Schechter Day School K-8* (New York: Solomon Schechter Day School Association, United Synagogue Commission on Jewish Education, 1978).

h. To guide the pupil into an understanding and appreciation of the historic period in which the Mishnah was written.
i. To become familiar with Mishnaic personalities and schools of learning during the Mishnah period.[22]

These aims stress the developmental aspect of Jewish law and the skills to understand this historical process. This list may, however, only illustrate the ease of translating certain discipline skills into behavioral objectives and not the ultimate intentions of the curriculum developer. The moral or spiritual education of the student seems to have given way to the aims and content of "university-type" courses.

The translation of the positive-historical approach into methodologies for the purpose of teaching classical texts in the Schechter day school thus appears to lack the dimension of spirituality and search described by both Greenberg and Bokser. While text skills were emphasized by the founding thinkers, their acquisition seemed to be secondary to the creation of a caring, committed individual. The process of translating the "structure of the discipline" of Rabbinics study into day school curricula appears to meet some of the original aspirations of the Schechter founders, but still requires additional levels of deliberation on the ultimate ends and goals of instruction.

In addition to Frost's contributions other efforts emphasize the structural-cognitive approach: many local schools have invested in the development of independent curricular outlines and units;[23] a number of research directions have been developed in the area of Rabbinics in cooperation with the Department of Education of the Jewish Theological Seminary;[24] and the forthcoming Solomon Schechter Day School Curriculum[25] will be continuing a subject-centered approach to curricular development in the area of Rabbinics. These developments appear to reinforce a structure of the disciplines conception of Jewish learning in the Schechter movement.

---

22 *Ibid.*, pp. 110–111.
23 A number of curriculum outlines are recorded in the *Compendium*. A recent collection of curriculum outlines was presented at the 1988 Solomon Schechter Principals' Conference. See "A Curricular Unit on Rabbinics for the Haggadah", one of three unpublished papers on Teaching the Haggadah, Jewish Theolgical Seminary, 1981.
24 See for example, David Kraemer, "Critical Aids to the Study of Talmud," *Jewish Education*, Vol. 49.1; Joseph Lukinsky, "Integrating Within Jewish Studies," *Jewish Education*, Vol. 46.4; David Resnick, "Jewish Law in the Conservative Schools," *Conservative Judaism*, Vol.34.1; and C. Alexander, "Halakhah and Aggadah in Conservative Curricula: A Response to David Resnick," *Conservative Judaism*, Vol.34.6.
25 See *Compendium, op. cit.* See also *Catalogue of Publications* (New York: United Synagogue Book Service, undated), p. 11, for a description of forthcoming curricula.

Some Recent Developments

In a recent survey of Solomon Schechter schools, it was found that many within the Schechter movement are adapting materials created by the Jewish Values Project of the Hebrew University's Melton Centre for Jewish Education in the Diaspora. Indeed, Hillel Day School of Metropolitan Detroit, a Solomon Schechter school, co-sponsored with the Melton Centre a conference on the teaching of Jewish Sources according to the Jewish Values Approach. This curricular direction appears to have refocused Rabbinics instruction from the imparting of technique and information to an inquiry into the value implications of our textual tradition, the curricular direction advocated by the founding thinkers of the Schechter movements. Indeed, this curricular direction can be found in other materials within the Conservative Jewish educational community.[26]

Much of the research energy devoted to the improvement of the Solomon Schechter Day School has been aimed at forging a relationship between education and Judaism. This seminal work was needed to provide the school movement with some philosophical basis in its curricular planning.

Both Solomon and Abramson have suggested new curricular directions which enrich educational theory and practice. Aware of the subject-centered nature of the day school, they suggest alternative directions for utilizing the wisdom of the disciplines.

For his part, Solomon traces the bifurcated nature of the school experience and the role of the "structure of the disciplines" in the Solomon Schechter Day School.[27] He suggests moving towards integrative experiences based "on the commonality which exists within knowledge—both general and religious." For him, some of the skills and dispositions which foster a unified perspective include rationality and objectivity, emotional commitment, rational thought, creative imagination, joy, surprise and awe.[28]

Abramson believes that the present regularities of the Schechter Day School call for the adoption of "generative foci, the articulations of purpose around which the school can focus its educational energy. Generative foci would be values or concepts that ... would capture a faculty's imagination and engage their energies in dialogue about the meaning of the school ... teaching ... the subject matter ... and educa-

---

26 See, for example, Chaim Potok, *Ethical Living for a Modern World: Jewish Insights* (New York : Jewish Theological Seminary, undated), a republication of earlier Leadership Training Fellowship materials.
27 Solomon, Dissertation, *op. cit.* Chapter Two.
28 Bennett I. Solomon, "Curricular Integration in the Jewish All-Day School in the United States," in Michael Rosenak, ed., *Studies in Jewish Education*, Vol. 2 (Jerusalem: Magnes Press, 1984), pp. 150-174.

tional formats."[29] Abramson chooses as an appropriate generative focus of the day school the development of the "the capacity to sense and live with holiness, '*Kedushah*', and obligation, '*hovah*'."[30]

Solomon and Abramson try to forge the integration between education and Judaism in order to provide the practitioner with some philosophical direction for curricular planning. However, even adoption of both of these approaches to curricular thinking for the Conservative school would not dismantle the current subject centered structure but would rather inject it with purpose, ultimate aims and ideals.[31] In this context, the Rabbinics curriculum still remains an important curricular area open for new investigation. Slowly, it seems, the Schechter school network is working its way through curricular deliberation and experimentation—closer to the ideals of its founding vision.

29 Robert Abramson, "Generative Foci—A Way of Thinking About the Day School," unpublished paper presented at the Second Annual Colloquium of the Jerusalem Fellows. May 20-22, 1986, pp. 2-3. See his follow up article, below.
30 *Ibid.*, p. 5.
31 See, for example, Bennett I. Solomon, "Curricular Integration." See also Bennett I. Solomon, "A Critical Review of the Term 'Integration' in the Literature on the Jewish Day School in America," *Jewish Education*, Vol.46.4; Joseph Lukinsky, "The Jewish Day School Confronts Modernity," *Jewish Education*, Vol.51.2, pp. 23-24, 26; *idem*, "Integrating Jewish and General Studies in the Day School: Philosophy and Scope," in Max Nadel ed., *Integrative Learning: The Search for Unity in Jewish Day School Programs, Proceedings of an Invitational Working Conference, May 15-17, 1978* (New York: American Association for Jewish Education), pp. 1-34.

TEACHING MIDRASH IN THE DAY SCHOOL

Alvan H. Kaunfer

Midrash is an essential process and product of the Jewish tradition, yet its study has been neglected in the elementary non-orthodox Jewish day school. It is an irony of modern day school education that, although Judaism is essentially a rabbinic religion, rabbinic literature tends to be ignored in the lower grades. We will explore a rationale for teaching midrash, as well as suggest some methods for its teaching.[1] Our contention is that midrash ought to be taught, that its style and mode speak to the thinking of young minds, and that its methods suggest teaching strategies appropriate to the material.

Why Midrash?

Midrash is central to Judaism in many respects. First, midrashic literature embodies ideas basic to Judaism. One must turn to midrashic compendia for examples of what the rabbis of ancient Judaism thought about such key ideas in Judaism and God, Torah, and the Jewish People.[2] In a period when abstract philosophy was not yet the mode of transmission of significant ideas, ideas were expressed in the form of story, parable, interpretation, myth and homily.[3] Midrash, then, became the dominant mode of expression of ideas in the Judaic world, and the essential genre for the formulation of Jewish thought

---

1 Although our focus will be the day school setting, a number of the discussions and conclusions are applicable to the supplementary Jewish school.
2 For examples of the use of midrash in a presentation of Jewish philosophical concepts, see Ephraim Urbach, *The Sages: Their Concepts and Beliefs* (Jerusalem: Magnes Press, 1975); Solomon Schechter, *Aspects of Rabbinic Theology* (New York: Schocken Books, 1909), and George Foote Moore, *Judaism in the First Centuries of the Christian Era* (New York: Schocken Books, 1927, 1958).
3 See Henri Frankfort, et al., *Before Philosophy* (Baltimore: Penguin Books, 1949), and Isaac Heinemann, *Darkhei Ha-Aggadah*, (Jerusalem: Masadah, 1970).

throughout history, even after Judaism had embraced the world of abstract thinking. Similarly, values basic to Judaism cannot be studied or taught without citing midrashic literature. Justice and mercy, tzedakah, mitzvah, and study, are all values which are embodied in midrashic homily.[4]

Midrash is fundamental to Judaism not only because it contains its central ideas and values, but because it speaks to the heart and soul of the Jew. Where Jewish law provided structure, midrash aggadah[5] provided an outlet for emotion, creativity, and imaginative thought. Whereas halakhah was written in dialectic and apodictic prose, the aggadah was written in the imaginative language of metaphor and story. The halakhah challenges the mind; the aggadah speaks to the heart. As Abraham Joshua Heschel describes:

> Halakhah is the rationalization and schematization of living .... Aggadah deals with man's ineffable relations to God, to other men and to the world. Halakhah deals with details ....aggadah with the whole of life, with the totality of religious life.[6]

Finally, and most significantly, midrash represents the response of Judaism to a changing world. The Bible has been the central sacred text of Jews throughout the ages. New understandings of the Bible and reinterpretations of its laws and stories were based on the belief that the Bible is an eternal book with eternally valid divine messages. *The reinterpretation of Scripture from age to age, in light of the new circumstances, new culture and societal realities, and new understandings of Judaism is the process as well as the product we call midrash. Midrash is the enterprise of making the Bible relevant to each new generation.*[7]

In the age of classical rabbinic Judaism (first to sixth centuries) these interpretations were recorded, first orally, then in writing, in compilations of midrash. Midrash is thus both a literature and an interpretive mode. It represents the flexibility of a tradition confronting change. Midrash addresses eternal questions and timeless issues of Judaism and of life.[8] That process of reinterpretation of Scripture may be seen as a

---

4 See the works of Max Kadushin.
5 **Aggadah** is used here to refer to the narrative and non-legal forms of midrash. **Midrash**, as will be defined later, is a broader term encompassing the entire interpretive literature.
6 Abraham Joshua Heschel, *God in Search of Man* (New York: Harper and Row, 1955), pp.335-337. See also his introductory chapters to *Torah Min Hashamayim* and Bialik's "Halakhah and Aggadah."
7 For definitions of Midrash which emphasize this point, see Joseph Heinemann, "The Nature of the Aggadah," in G. Hartman and S. Budick, eds., *Midrash and Literature* (New Haven: Yale University Press, 1986); Renee Bloch, "Midrash," in William S. Green, ed., *Approaches to Ancient Judaism* (Missoula: Scholars Press, 1978); and Addison Wright, *The Literary Genre Midrash* (Staten Island: Alba House, 1967).

wider interpretation of Judaism itself.[9] Midrash both contains the concrete record of Judaism's response to a changing world over the ages, and provides a model and method for continuing that response.

Midrash in the Curriculum

If midrash is such a significant part of Judaism, it should be a prime topic for study in the Jewish school. If we want our children to begin to understand the ideas and values basic to Judaism, they should study midrash as the source of those ideas and values. If the task of education is to prepare youth for the challenges of a changing world, then the topic of midrash would seem necessary for that task. If we are to initiate the young not only into the skills and facts of Jewish tradition but also into its dynamism, interpretative tradition, and evolving nature, then an understanding of and participation in the process of midrash would be a necessity.[10]

Although the day school curriculum devotes significant time to the study of Jewish sources, midrash and aggadah, if taught at all, have been peripheral to other subjects.[11] Stories about the sages, legends, and fables are sometimes included in collections of Hebrew stories. When midrashic interpretation is presented in connection with the Biblical narrative, it is sometimes presented in a manner which blurs the line between Biblical text and legend. Midrashim contained in the commentary of Rashi are often taught without distinction between what "Rashi says" and the midrashic sources upon which he draws.[12] Students in the non-Orthodox day school, despite the emphasis on critical analysis of text, are rarely if ever taught to distinguish midrash from biblical text, or Rashi's use of midrash from Rashi's own interpretation.

In short, the day school curriculum lacks a well-defined program in the important area of midrash.

8   See I. Heinemann, *Darkhei Ha-Aggadah* where he discusses the idea of "trans-historical truth" (*emet al-historit*).
9   See Gerson Cohen, "The Shattered Tablets," *Moment*, Vol.10:9 (October, 1985), pp.17-21; and Neil Gillman, "Toward a Theology for Conservative Judaism," *Conservative Judaism*, Vol.37:1 (Fall, 1983), pp.4-22.
10 For the idea of education as initiation, see R. S. Peters, "Education as Initiation," in Donald Vanderberg, ed., *Theory of Knowledge and Problems of Education* (Urbana: University of Illinois, 1969) pp.60-65.
11 The neglect and even denigration of midrash can be partially traced to the prejudices of haskalah writers. One interesting example of such a tendency is Elijah Morpurgo's strong discouragement of including aggadah in the school curriculum, quoted in Asaf, *Mekorot Letoldot Hainuch Be-Yisrael*, Volume 2, p. 231. This attitude has unfortunately influenced the traditional day school curriculum.
12 See, for example, Rashi on Genesis 6:9, "in his generation," and on Genesis 22:2, "your son, your only one," which both quote midrashic sources but are usually taught as "Rashi." We would suggest that the study of midrashim in their original sources would lead to a better understanding of Rashi's commentary.

Midrash and Children's Thinking

Isaac Heinemann has described the essential characteristic of midrashic thinking as "organic thinking."[13] Organic thinking expresses the abstract in the concrete garb of story, parable, metaphor, drama, dialogue. It makes extensive use of word play, and the telescoping of time and place. These modes of thought would seem to parallel the thought patterns of young minds. The young child thinks concretely, freely, employs creative imagination, metaphors, stories, parables, drama and word play.

As Glenna Davis Sloan suggests in *The Child as Critic*:

> We are constantly told that if we expect instruction to be successful, we must begin where the child is. *Imaginative literature is exactly where he is*. Not only are his interests and emotions aroused by it, but it is also closer to his natural mode of expression ... The imaginative writer, particularly the poet, instantly makes use of the analogy and identity, simile and metaphor. So does the child. Children, if they are freed to do so, recapitulate the experience of primitive literature ... The child grasps analogies that more experienced and practical minds reject as absurd ... They are themselves poets and storytellers.[14]

Midrashic literature in its mode and technique seems parallel to the natural poetic and imaginative thought of the child.

Teaching Strategies Appropriate to Midrash and its Methods: Creating Midrash and Analyzing Midrash

How can students begin both to experience the process of midrash and to appreciate the literature of midrash? We suggest that the teaching of midrash should have a dual focus: creating midrash and analyzing midrash. By creating their own midrashim, children are able to get "inside" the myths and metaphors of midrash, and thus become initiated into the midrashic mode of thought.[15] The analysis of traditional midrashim will introduce the child to the themes and interpretations of the rabbis. The methods of midrash can serve as a basis for classroom

---

13 See I. Heinemann, *Darkhei Ha-aggadah*, who uses the term to mean a non-analytical type of thinking characteristic of midrash. Max Kadushin uses the same term in a different sense.
14 Glenna Davis Sloan, *The Child as Critic* (New York: Teachers College Press, 1984) pp.2-4,8.
15 For the notion of participation in the Biblical story and Jewish myth, see Joseph Lukinsky, "Fairy Tales, Myths, and Jewish Education," *The Melton Journal*, No.13 (1982), p.9.

strategies which will stimulate midrashic creation in children, while the techniques of inquiry and discussion will provide the child with an entry into midrashic literature.

Creating Midrash: Creative Writing— Filling in the Gaps in the Biblical Story

Erich Auerbach in comparing the style of Biblical narrative with Homer's literary style,[16] illustrates how the biblical narrative, in its attempt to be dramatic in style, avoids details, descriptions, character motivations and feelings. This laconic narrative style leaves much to the imagination, much to be read "between the lines." This biblical style provided the opportunity for the midrashic homilist to expand and elaborate on the Biblical narrative. As Joseph Heinemann comments, "Biblical aggadah does not deal exclusively with exegesis, it also expands and elaborates the Biblical narrative ... In fact there is almost no Biblical story that did not undergo aggadic amplification and no Biblical figure whose character is not portrayed more fully in the aggadah."[17] Thus, the famous midrash of Abraham and the idols fills in the "missing part" of Abraham's early life not included in the Biblical narrative, just as the midrash on Moses reaching for the coals rather than Pharaoh's crown provides the reader with details of Moses' childhood in Pharaoh's court.

If midrash is often a response to gaps in the Biblical narrative, then it would seem appropriate to allow students to respond to the textual stimulus created by those "missing" details in the narrative. Students can be asked to compose midrashim to fill in parts of the Biblical story by answering such questions as:

- What do you think Abraham was like as a young boy?
- How do you think he might have discovered God?
- What do you think Abraham and Isaac discussed on the way to Mt. Moriah? Write your own dialogue.
- Moses spent so many years in Pharaoh's court that we hear nothing about, invent one episode that you think might have happened during that time.[18]

This writing process should be followed by a study of traditional midrashim which respond to the same textual question or gap in the narrative. Students might better respond to traditional midrashim after suggesting their own interpretive midrashic story.

16 Erich Auerbach, "Odeseus' Scar" in *Mimesis* (Princeton: Princeton University Press, 1971), pp.3-24.
17 J. Heinemann in Hartman and Budick, *op.cit.*, p.45.
18 For further examples of midrashic writing exercises, see Howard Schwartz's "Write Your Own Midrash" sections in Lillian Freehof, *Biblical Legends: An Introduction to Midrash* (New York: UAHC, 1988).

Synectics—Mashal, Metaphor and Imagery

Nearly every chapter of midrash contains the refrain *mashal limah hadavar domeh* (to what this might be compared). However, *mashal* in its more general sense as parable, allegory and metaphor represents a basic methodology of midrash.[19] Poetic imagery and imaginative comparisons as well as parables and allegories fill midrashic literature. Maimonides refers to midrashic literature as being essentially "poetic metaphor."[20]

William J. J. Gordon[21] has developed synectics (a Greek word meaning metaphor) as a technique for enhancing creative thinking. This process of synectics and making strange comparisons would seem appropriate in helping the student create midrashim. As in synectics, the use of metaphor in midrash is part of the creative process of exegesis. Midrashic *mashal* often employs "strange" analogies in developing creative exegesis:

> What did Abraham resemble? A bottle of perfume closed with a tight fitting lid and lying in a corner so that its fragrant smell was not spread. When it was moved, however, its fragrance was spread. Similarly, God said to Abraham: "Travel from place to place and you have well become great in the world."[22]

An adaptation of the synectics model could be useful in helping students to generate midrashim. One of the advantages of the synectics model is that it involves students in a group process of midrash creation. The sharing of ideas and metaphors among students is a particularly attractive aspect of this strategy.

Role-Playing and Dramatic Strategies—Midrashic Drama

One of the techniques of midrash is the use of drama and dialogue. Such dramatic situations as the *Akedah*, which is elaborated in the midrash with dialogues between Abraham, Isaac, God and Satan, suggest the use of dramatic and role-playing strategies in the teaching of midrash.

---

19 See J. Neusner, *The Enchantments of Judaism* (New York: Basic Books, 1987) p. 127; and *What is Midrash?* (Philadelphia: Fortress Press, 1987) pp. 102-105.
20 Maimonides, *Guide for the Perplexed*, Part III, Chapter 43.
21 See William J. J. Gordon, *Synectics* (New York: Harper and Row, 1961) and *The Metaphorical Way of Learning and Knowing* (Cambridge, MA: Synectics Education Press, 1970). For classroom use, see the student workbooks, *Making it Strange*, and *Strange and Familiar*, (Cambridge, MA: SES Associates). For further examples of the use of synectics in teaching midrash, see my "Synectics: An Approach to Teaching Midrash," *Melton Newsletter* 11 (Fall, 1980): pp. 2-3. For other applications of the synectics technique to Jewish education, see Esther Netter in *The Melton Journal* 14 (Spring, 1982): p. 26, and her masters essay, Jewish Theological Seminary, 1982.
22 *Genesis Rabbah* 39, 2.

Simkha Weintraub suggests using dramatic and role-playing techniques "to involve the kids directly in biblical text, with the understanding that the way to get the core experience of the text, in its *p'shat* power, it to explore its endless midrashic potentialities."[23]

Seymour Epstein in "Midrashic Drama: Experiencing the emotional content of biblical Narrative,"[24] suggests a similar model which he terms "Midrashic Drama." Epstein, however, suggests the more extensive use of improvisational theatre techniques, especially as warm-up to the midrashic drama session.

The use of role-playing and dramatic techniques to enhance participation in a story has been developed by Samuel Laeuchli.[25] Laeuchli adds a significant aspect to the dramatization of the story. After participants act out a dramatic turning point in the story, Laeuchli invites his audience/class to participate in the dramatic reenactment of the *Akedah*, audience participants might ask Isaac how he felt when he went with his father, or Abraham why he did not challenge God. This technique can be adapted successfully for use in the classroom using other dramatic Biblical stories such as the story of Moses and Aaron's confrontation with Pharaoh.

The Arts—Creative Expression

The ability to make free associations, and connections, to imagine images, to create stories and interpretations, is basic to midrashic method. The freedom of thought operative in aggadic creation is emphasized by Judah Goldin:

> In haggadah, one is at liberty to draw cheerfully on his own intellect or imagination ... on anything congenial to his own spirit to interpret a Biblical verse or create a homily ... The key word here is *free*, be it explanation or musing.[26]

In general, the rabbis saw infinite creative interpretive possibilities in each and every verse and word in the Torah. Even their expression of this interpretive idea itself was imaginative and figurative:

> Just as a hammer smashes a rock into many pieces so too one verse may yield many meanings.[27]

23 Simkha Weintraub, "Ah-Kay-Dah: A Midrash-Making Experience," *The Melton Journal* 13 (Winter 1982).
24 Seymour Epstein, "Midrashic Drama: Experiencing Emotional Content of Biblical Narrative," in Models of Jewish Learning, (unpublished doctoral dissertation) Toronto, Ontario Institute for Studies in Education, 1976.
25 Although Laeuchli has not published his technique, his workshops exemplify the method described here. I am indebted to Joseph Lukinsky for bringing Laeuchli's work to my attention.
26 Judah Goldin, "Freedom and Restraint of Haggadah" in Hartman and Budick, *op. cit.*, p. 63.
27 *Sanhedrin* 34a.

The uses of the arts would seem appropriate to experiencing the creativity of midrashic process. One such technique has been suggested by Jo Milgrom.[28]

Milgrom asks participants to imagine a Biblical scene, then she has them recreate a portion of that scene using only torn paper. The group then shares explanations of their art. Milgrom claims that this technique relates the Biblical text to very personal experiences, which to Milgrom is the essence of the midrashic process.

We have presented here brief descriptions of a number of classroom strategies which both parallel midrashic method and present opportunities for students to create their own midrashim and help them relate to the text personally.[29] If midrash is essentially the process of making the Biblical text relevant to the lives of each generation, then these midrash-creating strategies would be helpful in involving the student in that midrashic process.

The Validity of Children's Midrash

If children are asked to offer their own free and creative interpretations, what range of children's midrashim should be considered valid and acceptable? For instance, if students are asked to write about what they think Abraham was like as a young boy, as an introduction to teaching the traditional midrashim on Abraham, would any answer be acceptable? In our experience with this assignment, we have found that children often relate familiar settings such as stories about Abraham going to school or tending to a pet animal. Once the door is opened to children's interpretations, some bounds must be set by the teacher.

First, we would suggest the questions which teachers ask have some specific direction, while leaving room for the child's imagination. The question about Abraham's childhood might have been better phrased, "How do you think Abraham might have discovered God as a young boy? What incident might have happened to him that would make him believe there was one God?" Such a question might exclude far fetched stories, while leaving room for the child's creative imagination. Synectics, role-playing, or art techniques can be directed towards specific textual issues, and, thereby, they may elicit creative yet appropriately valid

---

28 Jo Milgrom, "Hand-Made Midrash," *The Melton Journal* 17 (1984): pp. 16-18.
29 For a general approach to personalizing midrash, see Arthur Waskow, "How to Teach the Making of Midrash," *New Traditions* 3 (Summer, 1986): pp. 61-69. We feel that this approach is too general and is to distinct from the text. Sherry Werb has suggested similar approaches to personalizing Biblical narratives based on the "mythic" thought of the Bible: "Toward an Approach to Bible Teaching in the Afternoon Elementary Hebrew School," unpublished masters thesis, Brandeis University, 1970.

midrashim. In older grades, students may even be asked to create a midrash using a specific midrashic style, such as a play on words or a *mashal limah hadavar domeh* (parable) format. In the final analysis, the issue of validity is a subjective category, and there will always be a tension between free creativity and directed textual interpretation. The basic criterion must be that a student midrash must relate to the text being interpreted. It cannot be exclusively an expression of the child's own personal experience.

Analyzing Midrash: Inquiry and Discussion

In addition to creating midrashim, students must also have the opportunity to analyze traditional midrashim through discussion and inquiry. Numerous models of inquiry exist.[30] Although many of those models relate to science and social studies rather than to literature, literary analysis models of inquiry may be applied to the study of midrash. Harold Herber[31] has suggested that the analysis of a text be based on three levels of inquiry: (1) Literal comprehension, (2) Interpretive comprehension, (3) Applied comprehension. Similarly, Ruth Zielenziger in her *Genesis Teacher's Guide*[32] suggests that Biblical inquiry focus on three questions: What does the text say; What does the text mean; and What do these ideas mean to me?

Some example questions in midrash on three levels of inquiry might be:

Literal Comprehension
- What details does the midrash add to the Biblical text?

Interpretive Comprehension
- How does the midrash we read answer the question/problem in the Biblical text?

Application and Personalization
- How is the midrash you read different from the one you created? Which do you like better? Why?

Questions developed for class inquiry should be specific to the particular midrash being studied rather than formulaic for all midrashim. The questions should be based on a careful literary analysis of the midrash. Finally, the class inquiry should involve the student in the emotive and participatory nature of the process of enquiry. Joseph Schwab[33] has offered insight into the significance of student involve-

---

30 For a definition of the term "inquiry" and an overview and analysis of several inquiry models, see D. C. Orlich, et al., *Teaching Strategies*, Chapter 8.
31 Harold L. Herber, *Teaching Reading in the Content Areas* (Englewood: Prentice Hall, 1978).
32 Ruth Zielenziger, *Genesis: A New Teachers Guide* (New York: Melton, 1979).
33 Joseph Schwab, "Enquiry and the Reading Process," in *Science, Curriculum, and Liberal Education: Selected Essays* (Chicago: University of Chicago, 1978), pp. 149-163; and "Eros and Education," *Journal of General Education* (October, 1954).

ment in the discussion and enquiry process. His suggestions must be considered in the development of classroom discussion.

A Sample Lesson : Creating Midrash— A Synectics Exercise

The following sample lesson will illustrate some of the suggestions presented regarding the creation of midrash and the analysis of midrash. It is based on the *s'neh* burning bush episode (Exodus 3:1-7).

The teacher should begin this session with some synectics warm-ups. Then introduce the following exercise, holding a thorn or a picture of a thornbush:

- I want you to imagine you are a thornbush with sharp, prickly barbs. Be the thorn. How do you feel?
- A person comes and tries to reach for something inside of the thornbush, what happens? How does he feel?
- Now think about the situation of the Israelites in Egypt. How was Egypt like a thornbush?

An alternative midrash-creating exercise might be a torn-art project on the burning bush based on Milgrom's method, using torn paper to illustrate the burning bush scene followed by a sharing discussion.

The teacher may then continue by discussing the following midrash from *Exodus Rabbah* 2, 5:

(Simplified student text:)

מדוע דבר ה' אל משה מתוך הסנה?
רבי יוסי אומר: סנה קשה מכל עץ, ואין צפור נכנסת
ויוצאת בשלום. כך שעבוד מצרים קשה לפני הקב"ה
מכל שעבודים שבעולם.

(Full text:)

ר' יוסי אומר: כשם שהסנה קשה מכל אילנות וכל
עוף שנכנס לתוך הסנה אינו יוצא בשלום, כך היה
שעבוד מצרים קשה לפני הקב"ה מכל שעבודים
שבעולם.

Just as the thorn bush is the sharpest of all trees, and any bird that enters the thorn bush does not come out unscathed (in peace), so too the slavery of Egypt was sharper and more difficult before the Holy One, than any other slavery.

[*A note on Hebrew:* In a day school, discussions should take place in English, though texts should be in Hebrew. The simplified student text here attempts to retain the flavor, style and language of the original, while using a vocabulary familiar to the American day school student. A full Hebrew text of the original source should be provided to the teacher.]

Read the text first, then begin with the general question:
- What does the *s'neh* symbolize? Students may answer "slavery," but they may also say "Egypt" or "Pharaoh." Any of these may be possibilities. Elicit from students why they think the *s'neh* symbolizes what they have suggested.

The second key question should be:
- What does the bird symbolize? Students will most likely suggest "Israel." Then ask:
- What do you think happens to the bird that comes out of the thorn bush?
- What do you think the midrash means (is referring to) when it says—"it does not come out in peace"—אינו יוצא בשלום?
- Did the Israelites "not come out in peace"—how so?

Students may raise a number of possibilities of how the slavery in Egypt affected the Israelites (their families were destroyed, people died and were hurt, their morale was broken, etc.).

The final question might focus on how this midrash might be talking not only about the condition of the Israelites in Egypt, but of Jews throughout history in exile and under foreign domination and persecution. The teacher can introduce this transition in this way:
- The person writing this midrash might be trying to tell us something not only about the Israelites in Egypt but about Jews who are "enslaved" in some way in his time—and in our own time. What might this midrash be saying in general about the Jewish people?
- How might the thorn bush represent Jews enslaved today?
- Can you think of any Jews caught in a "thorn bush"?

This may lead to a discussion of contemporary issues (such as Soviet Jewry or Ethiopian Jewry or assimilation in America).

Conclusion

This sample lesson illustrates a number of guidelines we feel are crucial to the creation of a midrash program for day schools:

1. Since midrash has always been a way of making the Bible relevant to each new age of readers, midrash should not be taught in isolation, but in connection with Biblical studies. However, a distinction between *p'shat* (literal meaning) and *derash* (interpretive meaning) should be maintained.

2. Students should be given the opportunity to create their own midrashim both as part of participating in the midrashic process and as an introduction to the study of classical midrashim. Students should also discuss and analyze traditional midrashim and compare them to their own creations.

3. Inquiries of midrashim should include both a literary analysis of the text and discussions of wider eternal questions which the midrash addresses (such as the question of slavery and freedom in the sample lesson).

We feel that the approach outlined here is the first step in the creation of a midrash curriculum for day schools.[34] Introducing our students to midrash and initiating them into participating in the midrashic process is crucial to their understanding and appreciating the most dynamic and central aspect of Judaism in both ancient and modern times.

---

34 The next steps in creating a midrash curriculum would be the development of in-service programs for teachers both in the techniques suggested here and in the study of midrashic literature. In addition, appropriate student and teacher materials would have to be written.

FOOTSTEPS ON THE CEILING AND IDOLS ON THE FLOOR

INTEGRATED STUDY OF HISTORY AND STORY IN THE CONSERVATIVE JEWISH DAY SCHOOL

Benjamin Edidin Scolnic

Introduction

In both his theoretical and practical work, Bennett Solomon was vitally interested in the concept of integration in Day School education. He understood that education in a Conservative Jewish Day School is not only an opportunity to absorb the best of two worlds, the secular and the religious, but also to integrate those two worlds into a system of thinking and living.

In his doctoral thesis, Curricular Integration in the Jewish All-Day School in the United States,[1] Bennett suggested several ways in which a Day School curriculum could be integrated. He did not stop, however, at the obvious level of integration, say, that of comparing Sukkot and Thanksgiving. Bennett pursued a more difficult goal, the integration of educational approaches.

It is my purpose here to present some thoughts towards a model for the integration of Jewish and secular education in the Conservative day school. I shall explore the distinction between, and the relationship of, history and story, in Conservative Jewish study of the Torah. Modern

---

1 Bennett's thesis was in Philosophy of Education at Harvard University, Graduate School of Education. It was submitted on May 17, 1979. Also see his "A Critical Review of the Term 'Integration' in the Literature of the Jewish Day School in America" which was the lead article in an issue of *Jewish Education* devoted to Integration in Day Schools (Vol. 46, 4, Winter, 1978).

critical scholarship has known, for a very long time now, how to adapt the tools of the study of secular history to the study of the Bible. It is time, I will suggest, for the study of secular history to learn from the study of the Torah. I am not referring to a topic such as "Abraham Lincoln and the Jews." Rather, I shall propose how the study of Abraham Lincoln can benefit from a use of Jewish categories of exegesis and thought, and how critical Torah study can benefit from the examination of parallels in the American past, understood from a perspective of history as story.

In other words, what can the study of secular history derive from the study of the sacred Torah text? There are levels of history: there is *what happened* and, then, there are the *stories about what happened*. We must learn to distinguish between the two levels. Clearly, we must "know" the "facts," but we must recognize that the story level has its own important purpose—to interpret and give meaning to the history. The stories are told not to provide more information but to reveal greater levels of understanding.

The Idol-Maker's Son

On my daughter's bookshelf, standing side-by-side, are *A Child's Introduction to Torah*[2] and *Abraham Lincoln*.[3] This juxtaposition prompted the thoughts which follow.

A Child's Introduction to Torah, a product of the Melton Research Center, presents a great deal of material which is not found in the Torah. The student learns stories which Moses and even the Biblical editors would probably not recognize. Midrashim about young Abraham take up twenty-four pages of the book, more pages than are devoted to the last four books of the Torah.

What is the main purpose of the midrashim that are selected? To explain how Abraham made the leap from his father's polytheism to his own, new religion. Abraham, as the first monotheist, would not have suddenly stumbled upon his faith as an old man. He must have discovered, or been led to discover, his belief in the one God through a long process of thought and inquiry.

The young Abraham, struggling with his questions about the heavens and his society on earth, became a prototype for the Jewish child of the twentieth century, who also struggles with questions about heaven and earth. From his struggle, Abraham emerges as a believer; he is a model for his descendants.

2 This textbook was written by Shirley Newman and edited by Louis Newman, with Joseph J. Schwab as Consultant. It was published for the Melton Research Center of the Jewish Theological Seminary of America by Behrman House (N.Y.: 1972)
3 Anne Colver, *Abraham Lincoln: For the People*, Discovery Series of Scholastic Book Services (Champaign, Ill.: Garrard, 1960).

Abraham, son of an idol-maker, persecuted by a pagan king, has endured terrible trials before he can be free to worship his God as he sees fit. Most famous of the stories about his childhood is that in which he is left in charge of the family idol shop by his father Terah. Abraham destroys the idols and later gives his father a lesson about the meaninglessness of fetishism.

To her credit, the author, Shirley Newman, explains the "history-legends" of Abraham, simply and lucidly. Newman writes:

> We can read all that the Torah tells about Abraham and his family ....Then we can try to imagine some other things that might have happened in Abraham's life. Then we can make up a story. We call such a story a "history-legend." It's a legend because it is a story that has been made up. It is history because it is about real people or real things ... Americans have history-legends about George Washington, Abraham Lincoln, and heroes of the Wild West.[4]

The term "Torah," as used in the title, *A Child's Introduction to the Torah*, encompasses more than the Torah, the first five books of the Tanakh/Bible. In this definition, Torah is at least partly story, as opposed to history. Part of the Torah is no more historical, no more a reflection of events which actually happened then, say, stories in the Midrash.

This is a valid approach. It reflects good Conservative Jewish teaching. Conservative Judaism has, as its intellectual foundation, the idea that Judaism has evolved. Evolution in this case means that our understanding of personalities and events in the Torah has developed over time.

This is a sophisticated approach to the distinction between history and story. As such, it should be applied equally to the study of secular history. What follows is an example of the application of the tools of exegesis of Jewish texts to an event in secular history—a second set of traditions, if you will—commonly included in the elementary school curriculum.

Young Honest Abe: The Funeral of Nancy Hanks and "Footsteps on the Ceiling"

If we have been raised in the United States we know the stories of Young Abe Lincoln. We heard them as children, and now, as parents, we share them with our own children. We talk about Young Abe walking twenty miles to borrow a book (when we can't get our kids away from the VCR) or of Abe's struggling to read by firelight.

In every book I have read about Lincoln, whether for children or adults, there is at least a passage about the death of Nancy Hanks Lincoln, Abe's mother, when he was only nine years old. There was no funeral as

---

[4] Newman, p. 23.

such when they buried her. According to these books, Abe was extremely upset that proper honor was not done to his mother. Some writers maintain that he wrote to a preacher to request a more dignified ceremony at a later date.

The fact is that Lincoln never wrote to a preacher, as "history-legend" has it. Young Abe couldn't have done so; he did not know how to write (he would not learn until five years later). What we know about the culture of his time and place indicates that Lincoln probably wasn't even familiar with the concept of a funeral as we think of it. If he was concerned about such things, he had a strange way of showing it; there would be no monument or marker of any kind over his mother's grave during his lifetime.[5]

This is what history does to meaning. It levels it, often destroys it. There is no history about Nancy Hanks Lincoln's death except that she died. And since that is a terrible fact, it cries out to be cried over, it demands interpretation and analysis. How did young Abe feel? How did he cope? Did he cry? Did this death affect him in lasting ways?

So story fills in the gaps, somewhat like *derash* fills in the *p'shat*. The modern writers superimpose their own feelings about what a funeral should be like and assume that Lincoln must have been terribly disappointed that a proper service was not conducted.

Less than a year after his mother's death, Abe's father left his sister and him totally alone. They were living in an unfinished cabin, without a real ceiling or floor. His father returned with their new stepmother, who immediately insisted that the cabin should be finished. She was especially happy with her new, whitewashed ceiling. Young Abe decided to have a good time. He got his older cousin to lift him upside down so that Abe could make footprints across the clean white ceiling. How would his new stepmother respond? She looked at the footprints and laughed. "Nobody but Abe Lincoln would ever have thought up such a thing," she said. They cleaned up the ceiling together.

What does the story tell us? The new stepmother appreciates Abe. Footprints on the ceiling test her, and a family is created.

The story of the footprints on the ceiling is a cute story, but no cuter than any that most of us have in our own family memory-book. It is only in the context of Abraham Lincoln's life that the story attains historical importance. The roof of the Lincoln cabin was finished because of Abe's

---

[5] For the lack of a stone marking on Lincoln's mother's grave, see Albert J. Beveridge, *Abraham Lincoln: 1809-1858*, Vol. I (Boston: Houghton Mifflin, 1928), p. 49. On the customs of the Kentucky Baptists, see William E. Barton, *The Life of Abraham Lincoln*, Vol. I (Brooklyn: Bobbs-Merrill, 1925), p. 116; Stephen B. Oates, *Abraham Lincoln: The Man Behind the Myths* (N.Y.: Harper and Row, 1984), p. 36; Richard R. Current, *The Lincoln Nobody Knows* (N.Y.: McGraw Hill, 1958) p.30.

stepmother, it was unfinished before she came. She made them turn a hut into a house. Footprints on the ceiling mocked her efforts.

It is not important whether this story is historically true or not. As a written record, it carries the truth of literature or text. It is not a superimposition of meaning which runs counter to the custom of Abe's environment. This cute story becomes important because it represents the new stage of Abe's emotional life with a new mother.

History tells us that Abe never read by firelight. History tells us that Abe Lincoln only went to school for a short while, so he did not walk six miles back and forth for years, as the legends tell it.[6]

But history is not just what happened. History is also what we say happened. History has selected and developed certain stories about Abraham Lincoln's life. That selection process tells us more about American dreams and myths, about the values we want our children to have, than it does about Abraham Lincoln's actual experiences.

The same holds true for young Abram in the Torah. It no longer matters what young Abram's spiritual experiences actually were. Tradition fills in a gap in a meaningful and provocative way. There is no young Abram. There is only young Abraham.

We are the stories that we tell about ourselves. Do we really think that the patient on the psychoanalyst's couch is accurately reporting exactly what happened to him? Memory is much more complex than that. In many ways, the patient "creates" his history by interpreting his memory and experiences. The analyst interprets his patient's case-history as story. Even a case-history, then, becomes a literary form.[7]

Each historical figure is a separate case, but the literary traditions about the Biblical Abraham and Abraham Lincoln are fairly typical in the way they develop answers to questions which may never have been asked when the Torah was written or Abraham Lincoln was living.

Conservative Jewish Approaches

The *p'shat*, the "literal" interpretation of the verse or passage, is the first level of the story. The *derash*, either the acontextual interpretation or a derived/attached teaching, is a second level of the story, building from the foundation of the *p'shat*.

What actually happened, the historical event, is also a first level, something to be interpreted and explained by levels which build from it. The student in the Conservative Day School, in both his/her religious

---

[6] Counting every day Lincoln had of school in his sporadic education, we get a total of about a year of formal training of any kind. See Oates, *ibid.*, p. 37 and Beveridge, *ibid.*, p. 63. Cf. Oates for why Lincoln could not have read by the fireplace.

[7] James Hillman, *Healing Fiction* (Berrytown, N.Y.: Station Hill, 1983), pp. 3-49.

and secular training, can be brought to the understanding of how history and tradition work. He/she will not be limited by the question, "Yes, but did it really happen?" There are different planes on which history happens, and only one of them is the scene of actual events.

Let us suggest two approaches to the study of both religious and secular history.

1. History is an accurate retelling of real-life events. Since history is often amplified by story, history must clearly be separated from what people say about it.

2. History is more story than we think. Finding meaning in history, for example, the religious-theological plot line in Jewish history, is making a story out of history. Otherwise, all we have is a meaningless series of unconnected events.

Which is the Conservative Jewish approach? One would have to say that the first approach has been the primary one, that it is good Conservative Jewish educational practice to separate midrashim about Abraham from the narratives in Genesis. But it is important to go further. Our Day School students should be brought into the text so far that they can understand where midrash comes from. The impetus for midrash is not just a question which arises in later generations. The impetus for midrash is the text itself, which demands interpretation.

And yet, once we have brought the students back to the point at which meaning was created, once we have been true to the flow of history, the second approach takes over, and history and story are categories which begin to overlap and even merge to a certain extent.

Religious Difficulty with Integration

There is the potential for some religious discomfort in all of this. A nagging concern in the drive for integration is the tendency towards levelling, wherein all subject matter to be integrated is treated as being of equal value. The Torah, however, is a Sacred Text. I am troubled religiously when the Torah is equated with "just stories" or taught as history-legends. It's *not* all just legends; it is God's truth.

My daughter's teacher, in referring to a sacred event in Jewish history, said: "Maybe it happened, maybe it didn't." For all of my scholarly training, the parent in me got nervous.

The difficulty of integration is that we are working with two very different content areas, with two completely different structures. One is history, which, without detracting from its significance and integrity, can separate from legend. The other is traditional Judaism, which, as it adds level upon level of interpretation, sees each level as an integral part of the process of God's original revelations of His Will to Israel.

What we have to do, while *integrating* the two worlds, is to learn how to *separate p'shat* and *derash*—history and story, if you will—without requiring the debunking of religiously important material. Distinguishing between critical and literary approaches to texts (or events) should not result in any text or approach being devalued.

The recognition of levels of the text or of history will provide the student with a grid for understanding the nature of truth. If *derash* can interpret *p'shat*, if story can build on historical event, then the student can feel encouraged to bring him/herself to the search for knowledge.

Fantasies of Rebellion

We cannot be content with these thoughts about history and story at this stage, because we have not yet sufficiently emphasized the psychological impact of the text under discussion.

Bruno Bettelheim's *The Uses of Enchantment*[8] is a fascinating study of how and why children respond to fairy tales. He explores the nuances and symbolism employed by the makers of fairy tales, and investigates how these stories may be interpreted by a child.

Bettelheim distinguishes between the heroes of fairy tales, myths, and history. A fairy tale hero does not have a real name, because he represents the child. A mythical hero has superhuman dimensions, so the child knows that he cannot parallel the hero's deeds; he is not pressured by the demands of the story. Bettelheim states that "the real heroes of history, however, having been people like the rest of us, impress the child with his own insignificance when compared with them."[9]

A story such as "Footsteps on the Ceiling" shows, in a most reassuring way, how human Abraham Lincoln was. The story helps the child to counter the feelings of inferiority. The impact of the story may be that "Abe Lincoln was just a prankster and look how he turned out."

How do the stories of the "two Abrahams" we referred to resonate within the child's imagination?

Think about Abraham smashing his father's idols. Bettelheim reminds us that "the child's mind is filled not only by deep love, but also by strong hatred of his parents."

Stories such as those about the two Abrahams allow children to act out fantasies of rebellion. And they're safe, because the heroes are great men—the founder of a religion, the Great Emancipator. It becomes acceptable for today's children to rebel when child rebels of the past turned out so well.

---

8   Bruno Bettelheim, *The Uses of Enchantment: The Meaning and Importance of Fairy Tales* (N.Y.: Knopf, 1977), p. 41.
9   *Ibid.*, p. 123.

Conservative Judaism and the Fantasy of Rebellion

There is another level, especially of the story of Abraham and his father's idols, which we should consider. The story says, "Children, your truth may not be that of your parents. You may smash your parents' idols in constructing your own life. And that's fine with us, because Judaism began with the little idol-smasher himself."

The Conservative movement, in all of its educational endeavors, has as its basic obstacle the gap between its emphasis on Halakhah and the failure of most Conservative Jews to follow Halakhah. Every Conservative Jewish school, afternoon or all-day, every camp, every youth group, is faced with the reality of this gap. The school can only do so much to bridge the gap between the movement's ideals and the parent's practice. But it can struggle mightily to win the child's heart over to its side of the great divide.

So what have the day schools done? I would submit, as a Conservative rabbi who does the same thing, that we do not approach the problem of the great divide frontally. We can't say: "Your parents are not doing the right thing." Instead, in ways that we might not even suspect, we send subtle messages, often through stories, to the students. If this is true, we should be aware of what we're doing. And if we are not doing so, why not? Have we simply given up?

Let there be a discussion about smashing one's parents' idols. The discussion is not just a negative one. The religious tension between parents and children often yields important results. Many of our greatest figures, Rosenzweig, Scholem, Buber, and Kafka, have created their own paths because they found their fathers' lives so lacking in religious meaning.[10]

I do not ask for teachers of history to be psychologists. But teachers must attain a greater awareness of the complexity of the stories which tradition and history demand that we transmit. These stories have become a vital part of the culture because of their enduring complexity, their perpetual human appeal to every generation. If history is partly that which we have chosen to remember about the past, our memory includes many stories which never actually happened. We may carefully separate midrash from the Torah, legend from objective historical reporting, but we must also understand the power of that which we might be tempted to call "untrue" or "made-up."

---

10 Michael D. Oppenheim, "Sons Against Their Fathers," *Judaism*, Vol. 29, 3, Summer 1980, pp. 340-352.

Educational Model

An outline of the educational model I am proposing would begin with Abraham in the Bible, where we receive no information at all about his childhood. The next steps would be to examine the important midrashim about young Abraham, then to turn to a contemporary children's textbook, such as the one by Newman, to see what stories it tells about young Abraham. The student would see for herself how traditions develop, how certain stories are emphasized and others neglected. She would ask questions about the purpose and meaning of the stories.

The class would turn to a rigidly objective biography of Lincoln which, to use our examples, would tell the stark facts of Lincoln's early life, without Lincoln reading by firelight or writing letters to a minister. When the student would then be presented with a book such as that by Colver, he/she would see how stories are superimposed on history. "Why," the student might ask, "has history been changed? Why is a story such as 'Footprints on the Ceiling' so heavily emphasized? Why have generations of writers and students responded to it and transmitted it with such great care and affection?"

In the separation of levels of meaning, all meanings become clearer. After all is said and done, we are trying to create American Jews who can integrate their religious beliefs with their understanding of the modern world, who are not left with inner dichotomies. In bringing children back to the point where meaning is created, by following the same methodology whether the subject is religious or secular, we will enable the students to achieve their own versions of integration. We are trying to create human beings who understand the implications of history and of classic texts for their own lives. Each child, in his imagination, will achieve his own synthesis of the stories he is told.

Conclusions

"Education," Joseph Lukinsky has written, "should give us generic memories of the human race that supplement, enrich, and, most of all, inform those which belong to each of us alone. To do this it needs to recreate those crucial moments at which we stand on the verge of the creation of meaning."[11] This important principle must be part of the process of integrating secular and Jewish studies.

We stand on the verge of the creation of meaning every time we separate *derash* from *p'shat*, legend from accurate reporting. Why was the midrash created? Of all the midrashim on a particular passage, why

11 Joseph Lukinsky, "Law in Education: A Reminiscence with Some Footnotes to Robert Cover's 'Nomos and Narrative'," *The Yale Law Journal*, Vol. 96, 8, July 1987, p. 1858.

was this one transmitted by tradition? What does it tell us about the *p'shat*? What does it tell us about Judaism? What do we learn about the process we call Torah? Stating that a midrash is a midrash does not make it "just a midrash." The student can learn how meaning in Judaism is created and developed.

The same idea holds true for the study of secular history. What can we learn about America from the tales it tells about its heroes? Study of Abraham Lincoln would take us back, as William Safire's brilliant novel *Freedom* does, to the real-life Lincoln, with all of the controversy and turbulence associated with his leadership. But what objective history has to say about Lincoln is only part of what America remembers about him. We can learn a great deal about the values of our country by examining the process through which the Lincoln legends were developed. Standing on the verge of the creation of meaning, from the perspective of Lincoln's own time, we can understand not only how but why those legends sprang into existence. The American dream will attain a new and different level of meaning and, thus, a new and different reality.

Thus we must consider carefully what stories we tell, because the student's mind is constantly reaching for personal integration, growth, and expression. While his eyes are on the teacher, his imagination is making footprints on the ceiling and smashing idols to the floor. We cannot dictate what the imagination does. But we can realize how important it is.

What the school can do is provide a model of integration. It is to Bennett Solomon's lasting credit that he emphasized the concept of integration in his tragically brief career. It is up to those of us who care about the future of Judaism to go on from there.

I wish to express my thanks to my daughter, Rachel Yaffa Scolnic, for her encouragement and kibbitzing during the writing of this paper.

FROM BENNETT

ON INTEGRATION

We have pointed to the numerous references to integration throughout the literature on the Conservative day school. But what does the term actually mean?
... It is impossible to pinpoint one descriptive or pragmatic definition of integration for no standard interpretation exists within the literature. Jewish educators have neither set forth a specific connotation, acknowledged one generally accepted theme, nor recognized an accepted practical methodology for the implementation of the idea. We must ... view its usage as an educational slogan.[1] Throughout the literature, almost every statement regarding the purpose of the day school stresses this concept.
... It is not clear what educators envision as an integrated or unitary curricular experience. Do they see forging a totally new entity out of the separate elements of the curriculum, or are they rather merely advocating a close coordination among the subjects of instruction?
In a cable, various strands are brought together and intertwined. Each element contributes to the whole by becoming part of that whole. Each strand remains intact, standing in relation to its fellow strands. This image of a substance, each of whose consitutent parts retain its unique characteristics, is not equivalent to the image of chemical elements vanishing as a new "synthetic" compound is formed.
... We shall suggest, however, that in practice, the Schechter Schools maintained a picture of knowledge similar to that of the congregational schools. The Judaic curriculum was totally separate from the general studies, and was perceived, in fact, as an addendum to the overall education of the children. In fact, there has been very little integration within the day schools.

Dissertation, pp. 49-59.

1 Israel Scheffler, "Educational Slogans," in *The Language of Education* (Springfield: Charles Thomas, 1966), pp. 36-47; Paul Komisar and James E. McClellan, "The Logic of Slogans," in B. O. Smith and Robert H. Ennis, eds., *Language and Concepts in Education* (Chicago: Rand McNally, 1961), pp. 198-214.

... The child's day is bifurcated into "Jewish" and "English" or "American" times. Students often generalize from this that all experiences outside of school must also be so dichotomized.

But the day schools affiliated with the Conservative movement of Judaism need not maintain such a schizophrenic school program ... This perspective emphasizes the similarities among the various forms of knowledge and the skills and dispositions which can help the student unify his educational experience. The concepts, skills and dispositions described and analyzed include rationality and objectivity, reason and emotion, creative imagination, symbolism, *verstehen* or empathetic understanding, communication among a community of investigators and the so-called "cognitive emotions" of Scheffler, the "rational passions" of Peters and the "intellectual passions" and "personal knowledge" of Polanyi. These concepts, competencies and affective inclinations are crucial not only to the general studies but also to an authentic understanding of (Conservative) Judaism. All of them must, therefore, be introduced and reinforced throughout the entire day school curriculum, so the student will be able to fully participate in and contribute to a vibrant Jewish American civilization.

Dissertation, pp. viii-ix.

... the educational objectives of the Solomon Schechter Day Schools under examination include an integration by the student of his general and Judaic educations. We have noted, however, that the goal has not been the organizing principle which has actually directed the construction of the educational program. But if the aim of the school is the full development of rational autonomous individuals, knowledgeable of and inclined toward an integrated American Jewish life experience, then the school must plan its programs accordingly. To base the program on some other principle, or worse, to develop a program without a guiding aim or purpose, is to plan ineffectively. As integration is the unique aspect which the Conservative school wishes to foster, its curricular structure and content must reflect this commitment.

Dissertation, pp. 58-59.

Integration can only occur within individuals. Therefore, the specifics of each school program must depend upon the particular talents of the teachers, the concerns of the community and the needs and abilities of the individual students.

Dissertation, p. ix.

For some [Jewish educators, the term integration] was a response to a basic theological view which saw the unity of God in a unified world. For some, it emanated from a desire for enculturation into American society. Still others saw it as a response to John Dewey's well-known call for unity of theory and practice, mind and body, community and school. Others employed the term in response to the revolution in curriculum theory which stressed unifying structures of knowledge and spiral curriculum.[2]

From these numerous perspectives Jewish educators continually found integration to be a well respected and desired goal of the Jewish community. The obscurity of terminology enabled individuals to interpret the idea according to their personal points of view. So long as these views remained popularly accepted, the inclusion of this goal in Jewish day school literature rallied support and helped fill classroom desks. As Shimon Frost noted, "the term 'integrated' or 'integration' is ... charged with the magnetic power of an affirmation or manifesto."[3] But it was as if the educators were selling tickets to the ballpark without publicizing what type of game would be played on the field.

... the student needs opportunities to forge his own integrations. These will develop the skills to recognize the need for unity in real life situations and the propensity and ability to respond accordingly.

Therefore, a wide ranging and in-depth knowledge of Jewish sources, practices and beliefs is a necessary requirement for integration to occur. The result of each individual's integrative effort will be unique, for each will bring to bear his/her own insights and experiences, but all will revolve around the basic commitments of Judaism if they are well known.

Dissertation, p. 103.

Lipman[4] lists similar conditions which must exist in the classroom for the philosophical thinking inherent to integrative thinking to occur. These conditions include:

---

2   Jewish education has consistently borrowed methodologies and approaches from general education. For a critical review of such applications see Daniel J. Margolis, "Covenant—A Religious Entry into Curriculum Design for Jewish Education in America" (unpublished doctoral thesis, Teachers College, 1976).
3   Shimon Frost, "Integrating the Judaic and General Studies Curriculum," *The Synagogue School*, Vol. XXIV:3 (Spring, 1966), p.29.
4   Matthew Lipman, A. M. Sharp, F. Oscanyan, *Philosophy in the Classroom* (West Caldwell, N.J.: Institute for the Advancement of Philosophy for Children, 1977), p.61.

> commitment to philosophical inquiry;
> avoidance of indoctrination;
> respect for children's opinions; and
> evocation of children's trust.

If these conditions do not exist—if the milieu is not conducive to and encouraging of open thought—no educational experience will be an integrating experience. No matter how the content, schedule or role models are integrated, the child will not be initiated into the process unless the criteria outlined by Scheffler and Lipman are produced.

This is the most crucial pedagogic recommendation that can be made! It is the basis of the rationality which is the integrating force or dimension within the child's life in school and outside of school

> The ideal of rationality is capable of providing a unifying and liberal focus for education.[5]

But it can be fostered only under optimal conditions!

Dissertation, p. 107.

The importance for us, therefore, is the difference between teaching Judaism, versus teaching *about* Judaism. The school which teaches Judaism involves the child in actual practices and particular worship services. Beliefs are acted upon through the performance of ritual and through the study of Hebrew, identification with Jewish communities around the world and the collection of funds for their support. The unique close relationship with the land and the people of Israel is actualized through the same Hebrew language, holiday celebration and special prayers. Studying Judaism *involves* the child in the Jewish heritage whereas teaching about Judaism merely would elucidate its concepts and practices. Teaching religion, on the other hand, *advocates* participation within it.

Dissertation, p. 108.

---

5 Israel Scheffler, *Reason and Teaching* (Indianapolis: Bobbs-Merrill, 1973), p.63.

ON HONESTY IN TEACHING

Today, children listening to the teacher's half-hearted avowals of belief and ambiguous explanations, are not influenced to practice Judaism. They either intuitively realize that the teacher does not actually believe what he is saying, or inwardly revolt at the demands upon their credulity.

No differentiation is made among Jewish religion, Jewish religious folk-tales, and Jewish history ... Instead of pointing out and discussing the substantial conflicts between positions of tradition and reason, teachers allow most children to remain engaged with Judaism at only a superficial level as a result of the confusion created in their minds between fact and fiction, outlived and permanent values. Today the average child (and adult) assumes he has repudiated Judaism if he rejects the historicity of the Bible. We must, however, accustom the child to identify religion as not only certain traditions about God, but also as a particular type of personal reaction to life. Such an approach would serve the cause of Judaism far better, for the present policy of evasion only alienates the child from Jewish life and thought and defeats the very ends of Jewish life ... To the present student of the Conservative school, Judaism is, unfortunately, something that many Jews used to live, and that few Jews, including their parents, now study or take seriously, and they themselves will soon outgrow. Such conclusions negate the possibility of children becoming practicing Jews.

Reflections I, pp. 12–13.

STARTING WITH YOURSELF

A MODEL FOR UNDERSTANDING THE JEWISH HOLIDAYS AND TEACHING THEM

Joseph Lukinsky
Lifsa Schachter

> *It is important that students cooperate and become conscious of their cooperation. They also have to realize what they are doing in the class and in their research. They have to realize that it is not so much the method that is important, but learning how to use themselves as instruments and how to think things through ... The teacher has to get it across that the students are their own instruments and that they have to be sensitive to their own interactions and to what they are doing methodologically.*
>
> — Anselm Strauss[1]

Introduction

We have sought a practical, "heuristic" way of thinking about the Jewish holidays, a model that could function as a speculative and integrative tool. In this model, the holiday material itself would become, along with feedback of others committed to the approach, the criterion of authenticity.

Such a model would be a resource for generating new educational applications, an instrument in the hands of an educator for interpreting and "creating" tradition.

The model would be empowering rather than exhaustive, enabling Jewish educators to construct the meaning of a holiday through explora-

---

[1] "Teaching Qualitative Research Methods Courses: A Conversation with Anselm Strauss," *International Journal of Qualitative Studies in Education*, 1:1, January-March 1988, p. 96.

tions of symbols, personal experience, and texts without being or needing experts. They would reach an independent level of inquiry before turning, as needed, to the latter. Scholarly works of interpretation would be activated in the context of the students' and teachers' independent judgment, as a more pertinent response to their concerns.

We believe that we have conceived, through explorations in courses and workshops that we have conducted over the past several years, such a paradigm-model for our students and for teachers who create curriculum for the holidays.

Our Plan: A Workbook

Each holiday has its laws, customs, concepts, stories, histories, and folk experiences. There may be a primal story, "myth," or historical event such as the Exodus from Egypt or the salvation of the Jews of *Purim* or *Hanukkah*. Understanding the array of elements for even one holiday may be formidable and bewildering.

Let us look at one "bewildering array" associated with a Jewish holiday unfamiliar to most readers. We will first present, randomly and without interpretation, a description of the *Maimuna* festival of Moroccan Jewry. Then, since we want to demonstrate how *initial* access to a holiday's meaning can be gained with reduced dependence upon books, we will describe how we developed our model for doing so prior to using the approach on the *Maimuna* material. To illustrate the process of creating the model we will show how we generated substantive paradigms that interpret the material of *Purim*. This exemplification of process will also have broader pedagogical implications for dealing with the raw materials of the other holidays.

In the following section, we will discuss the model and the process in a more formal way, stressing structural concepts, "meta-themes," which we first elicited from our *Purim* research. Our claim is that these meta-themes are a relevant starting point for the examination of any or all of the holidays.

At the end, we will come back to the example we started with, the *Maimuna* festival, using it as a test-case for the aptness of the model.

The article should be viewed as a work-book through which the reader experiences a process for probing the data for meaning, creating new educational practices, and developing criteria for judging their authenticity. The method avoids the limitations of approaches that start with interpretations derived from scholarly research which may be intimidating to both teachers and students.[2]

---

2 We need to stress that this article is *not* anti-scholarship. To the contrary, it aims to create a receptivity to scholarship, enabling it to play a more effective role in the curriculum process.

Some Raw Data for a Test-case: *Maimuna*

The brief description of the *Maimuna* holiday which follows is based upon accessible popular sources and personal experiences in Israel; it is random material to which the paradigmatic *schema* we create will be applied. We will make that application at the end of the article. We chose the *Maimuna* festival of Moroccan Jewry because the reader is less likely to have prejudged its meaning on the basis of previously gained knowledge.

Moroccan Jews, in Morocco and in Israel, celebrate the day after *Pesah* as a special festival called *Maimuna*. Scholars have tried to explain the festival in different ways. In Israel explanations of *Maimuna* generally take the "quaint custom" route which seems condescending to groups comprising the *edot hamizrah* (Jews from Asian and African countries). Popular speculative treatments are unsatisfactory in that they describe the practices without a modality of access to a deep level of the holiday.[3]

Beyond the obvious relationship between the *Maimuna* and *Pesah*, everything else is open for exploration. Starting with this assumption, consider the following selected characteristic elements:

The source of the name, *Maimuna*, needs further research. Some try to relate it to Maimonides, but other interpretations are equally unconvincing. There is a generational conflict among the *edot hamizrah* today, with many of the younger generation not wanting to bother with the observance. In Israel it has an aura of being just revelry, a "good time," somewhat vulgar, losing qualities of the native Moroccan version. For practical purposes, in our description of the *Maimuna*, we have collapsed elements which may be more characteristic of either Morocco or Israel. The differences now, we feel, are essentially a matter of emphasis. We do not mean to imply that Moroccan Jews in either place would agree with our interpretation.

Moroccans finish *Pesah* quickly as the last day of *yom-tov* ends in order to get ready for *Maimuna*. Some eat lunch on the last day of *Pesah* early to get on with the work and the preparations, a violation of the spirit of the *halakhah* but a choice among priorities. Women do most of the preparation, which perhaps rationalizes aspects of the violation in people's minds. (*Mutav she-yihyu sho-ga-gin*, "Better that a violation be done mistakenly than intentionally.")

Arab neighbors (in Morocco) bring the *hametz* (leavening and leavened food, forbidden on *Pesah*) which is to be used for the *Maimuna* refreshments. Sometimes they bring it to the back porch a bit before the end of *Pesah*. Husbands overlook this; they know that if they are too strict and foolishly raise

---

[3] "Maimuna", in *Encyclopedia Judaica* (Jerusalem: Keter Publishing House, Ltd., 1971), p. 781. The *Jerusalem Post* and other journals annually describe the festival, missing the point in our opinion.

the issue, there won't be a *Maimuna*. After sundown when *Pesah* is over, there is "open-house," and sweet cakes (*mufletas*) and other sweet foods (made from the *hametz*) are served.

Other *Maimuna* Customs

There are special *Maimuna* dishes, such as lettuce leaves in honey; vases are filled with flowers and coins (the coins may be used in various games of chance); glass dishes are filled with yeast (leavening, *hametz!*); there is a festive meal; special clothes are worn; guests arrive; musicians go from house to house. There is a distinctive synagogue service for men before the feast. Besides bringing the *hametz* for cooking the *Maimuna* foods, Arabs, especially in Morocco, are involved as visitors to the open house and at the picnic the next day.

During the day after *Pesah*, the festivities continue. In Israel (especially in Jerusalem) there is a large communal public celebration which includes belly-dancing, gambling, and barbecue. Other national groups besides the Moroccans have come to participate in the merry-making over the years, which is a "must" for politicians of all parties.

We will return to the *Maimuna* festival after we present our model for the study of the holidays. We shall then apply that model to the *Maimuna*.

The First Level of the Model: The Substantive Paradigms of Purim

The model has its origins in our graduate curriculum course at the Jewish Theological Seminary where we examined the practices and texts of one holiday, *Purim*.[4]

There were two steps in the process which we will present in the next two sections. We started by looking for substantive issues and concepts in *Purim* (paradigms) and then, based upon them, hypothesized general "meta-themes" that could apply to all the holidays.

In our exploration of *Purim* with our first class at JTS and in succeeding workshop settings we found that starting with the experienced *observances* and practices of Purim draws upon something people know. While the students may not have the trained insight to see underlying structural commonalities, these experiences are an accessible starting point, at least at first.

---

4   The first time we conducted the workshop, in a Spring semester in the mid-seventies, the next holiday on the calendar was going to be *Purim*, and much of what we developed later originated in that experience. We struggled with *Purim* in our own planning and with our students. Later, we decided, on principle, whether in graduate courses, in-service workshops, or in parent and adult education, following the calendar, always to work on the next holiday, whatever it was.

Taanit Esther, the *Megillah* reading, *Seudat Purim*, *Mishloah Manot*, and *Matanot La-evyonim* are the "official" core practices of *Purim*. Associated with these are various customs that have evolved. The latter (even the former!) are often presented as quaint, expressions of joy or other feelings, independent of one another, supposedly aroused by the holiday's message. They are seen as broadly *related* to the meaning of the holiday. They *celebrate* this meaning and may be given esoteric interpretations, which, in general, are external to the student and sometimes even to the holiday itself. The practices and the interpretations are presented as givens, assumed rather than grounded in some kind of principle.

Typically, we do not legitimate our subjective experience of the holiday as a resource for understanding it. To do this would be too contingent and personal to have much value. We are embarrassed sometimes with negative feelings. At the very least, "no one else would be interested" in such material. This point is especially relevant to day schools, where, paradoxically perhaps, the more we rely upon knowledge authoritatively conveyed "by tradition" the less likely is personal experience to be considered as a valid resource for finding meaning.

To the contrary, we have found that one's personal experience of the holiday is a most meaningful starting place, a concrete and felt clue to interpretations that ring true. An examination of personal responses to the experiential dimensions of Purim is likely to arouse considerations such as the following collective summary of material, drawn from group discussion in various trial inquiries past. (Some of it relates to specific practices such as the reading of the *Megillah* in the synagogue; some applies to *Purim* generally.)

Drinking

Drinking to the point of drunkenness has not been characteristically Jewish. Yet, on Purim it is the fulfillment of the mitzvah of "*Adloyada*," (to drink until "one does not know the difference between 'Cursed be Haman' and 'Blessed be Mordecai.'" B.*Talmud Megillah* 7b). Why is the blurring of this distinction normative, a *mitzvah*? Is it just some kind of arbitrary bursting forth of feeling because of the joy we feel at the Jews' salvation, or is something more involved? Normally, we maintain a clear distinction between good and evil; *Purim* itself is, at its most obvious level, about this very distinction. So why blur it here?

Most students at the college level are aware of the drinking associated with *Purim*, and perhaps with some interpretations associated with it. No one is likely to be a *tabula rasa*. With respect to this and other practices they are likely to have a hodge-podge of facts, experiences and interpretations with a minimum of connections. (In the unlikely event that students know nothing about or have not experienced a holiday in *any* way, some basic reading would obviously be in order.)

Noise in the Synagogue

There may be noise during the synagogue service even when it is not *Purim*, but it is usually unwelcome. Here we are talking about noise that is encouraged. Though rabbis try to control it so that every word of the *Megillah* may be heard, they overlook noise that would not be tolerated at other times. The *grogger*-noise at the mention of Haman's name is *supposed* to be deafening, a literal and symbolic blotting out the name of *Haman*, descendant of *Amalek* whose name we are commanded "to eradicate"(Dt. 25:19). But the *noise* goes beyond this explanation and the mere mention of Haman's name, jarring our expectations for synagogue decorum. Behavior is tolerated that otherwise would not be.

Costumes

Masquerade has become part of the experience of Purim for young and old, but we can ask questions about the generic phenomenon; *Purim* is analogous to other "Mardi Gras" style celebrations and a prior question needs to be asked: why do *these* include masquerade? What is the purpose of being "in costume" at these celebrations and on *Purim*? Is a kind of hiding involved here? When you "let go" and behave other than normally, is there a wish to conceal one's identity? Gilbert and Sullivan say: "things are never what they seem; skim-milk masquerades as cream." In costume, masked, a person is "another"; the outside is not the same as the inside.

Seudah

The *Purim seudah* (celebratory meal) seems connected to the *seudot* that Esther gave for King Ahasuerus and for Haman. (Est. 5:8) But why? She, indeed, conceals her purpose, but this does not fully account for characteristics of the *Purim seudah* that have evolved over the centuries: It comes at the end of the holiday rather than the beginning! It includes satire (*Purim kiddush*, *Purim* Torah, mimicry of *Shabbat* and other holidays).

There is, however, another aspect to the satire embedded in the *Purim seudah*, one which connects *Purim* itself to the *next* holiday in the calendar—*Pesah*. Which other holiday has a special formatted meal, in which there is a "program" of sorts? The *Pesah seder*. On Purim the Jewish people were saved as they were on *Pesah*. Also, on Purim, *Pesah* is on people's minds; it is only one month away. Jews start preparing for *Pesah* right after Purim.

There are other connections to Passover. Ahasuerus recalls Pharaoh. Esther goes before the King to save her people, as Moses goes before

Pharaoh. There seem to be various conscious and unconscious connections between the two holidays and their meals. The *Purim seudah* seems in some respects to be a parody of the *Pesah* seder.

Satire, Ridicule of the Sacred

This has different forms such as *Purim Torah* (satiric religious instruction) at the *seudah*, parodies of the *nushaot* (melodic modes) of the *tefilot* (prayers) and of the *tefilot* themselves such as the *Purim kiddush* (satirical version of the Sabbath prayer accompanying the drinking of wine); rabbis and teachers are parodied (Cf. the incident of the *N'tsiv*, headmaster of the famous Yeshiva at *Volozhin*, halting the *Purim Torah* because it was getting out of hand). There is a letting off of steam, the freedom to do what is not normally permitted. Negative feelings, otherwise not openly expressed, may be always present, resentment, anger, cynicism, disillusionment of various kinds. The tradition seems to have used *Purim* as a safety valve.

But, it may be asked, why *Purim*? There is something about Purim that lends itself to this possibility, that goes beyond the mere *carnival* (carni-vale: hail the body, the physical!) aspect of the holiday. The sought-after cleverness of the *Purim Torah* goes beyond the mere idea of permitting license as a safety valve. *Purim Torah* becomes a kind of Torah or "anti-Torah" in itself.

A great deal of material of this sort is accumulated through explorative discussion. We look for some commonalities. All of this derives both from the formal knowledge of the participants in the inquiry and from their own personal experiences and perceptions. As the leaders of the inquiry we have, of course, our own thoughts and experiences which we contribute sparingly, but we are prepared for alternate directions the discussion might take. It has not always turned out the same.

There are potentially many ways of working with this material. What then, would be an example of a common feature in what has been presented above? From the varied possibilities, there is one that often strikes participants when they see what has accumulated before them. The overwhelming impression is that the observance of *Purim* is a reenactment of the theme that *things are the opposite of what they seem to be or what usually is the case*. We view this as a "substantive paradigm."

This leads us to the text of the book of Esther and we ask whether anything similar can be found there. We go to the text and *find* the idea there, crystallized in *Esther* 9:1 as *vi-nahafokh hu*, "The opposite occurred," generalized as "The world is upside-down."

We therefore arrived at what we call the *nahafokh hu*, or *olam hafukh* (or "upside-down world") paradigm. *Vi-nahafokh hu* is the term that best represents the construct we are dealing with, that characterizes and sums up at least one dimension of the practices and the texts we have examined so far.[5]

We are not saying that this is all there is to *Purim*. The ideas presented in scholarly and interpretive books can provide leads here in the spirit of Dewey's concept that "the subject matter is for the teacher."[6] But it is one possible way of starting to think about a holiday. People have worked through the development of an idea that "fits" the material and is generative and relevant. We shall develop this claim in the next section.

Meta-themes

Out of the paradigm-ideas constructed from the *Purim* research we extrapolated "meta-themes" (general themes or "codes") which we then tested on other holidays. The early versions of these "meta-themes" and the crystallizing *Purim* paradigm-concepts from which they were derived

---

5 Cf. Golinkin, N.A. in *Hadoar* (March 17, 1989) P.18–20. Golinkin finds many examples in the text of *Esther* but does not apply *vi-nahafokh hu* to the *practices* of *Purim*.

   Examples of *vi-nahafokh hu* in *Megillat Esther*. This is our list. Golinkin has additional examples.
   a. Esther is chosen to be an obedient queen, not like Vashti, who didn't come when the king called her. Later, Esther comes when he doesn't call her (1:20,22; 4:11ff.; 5:2; 8:4).
   b. Esther doesn't tell she's Jewish (2:10,20). But Mordecai tells her to do so (4:13,14 and see 7:3).
   c. Mordecai saves the king's life, but he endangers the life of a whole people by not bowing to Haman.
   d. The *Purim*, the Casting of the Lots to determine a propitious, "*mazeldike*" day for killing the Jews, turns out indeed to *be* propitious, but *for* the Jews (3:7; 9:26).
   e. Jews are to be destroyed by their enemies, and they destroy *their* enemies. (3:13)
   f. Mordecai mourns, Esther fasts, (*Avel Gadol La-Yehudim*) (4:1ff.; 4:3; 4:15). But then, Mordecai becomes prime minister (8:2).
   g. God not present explicitly, but is implicit in 4:14, 16.
   h. Haman thinks he's going to be honored by king, but Mordecai gets honored instead (6:1; 8,10).
   i. Haman thinks he's being honored by being invited to the party (5:5,9). But it is the beginning of his downfall.
   j. Haman builds gallows to hang Mordecai (5:14), and he is hanged there instead (7:9,10).
   k. Haman's wife predicts his downfall (6:13).
   l. Jews defend themselves on day they are supposed to be wiped out (Chapters 8,9).
   m. *Vi-nahafokh hu* (9:1).
   n. Anti-semitism seems rampant, but many people convert to Judaism (8:17).
   o. *Mishloah Manot* and *Matanot La-evyonim* (9:22.16).
   p. Jews promise to observe *Purim*, but then Esther has to "sell" it again (9:29).
   q. Mordecai saved the day, yet was only *Ratsui li-rov ehav* (admired by "most of" his brethren) (10:3).
6 J. Dewey, *The Child and the Curriculum/The School and Society* (Chicago: University of Chicago Press, 1902, 1956).

were clarified reciprocally. *Olam Hafukh*, "an upside-down world," described in the previous section, is an example a substantive *Purim* paradigm. *Kol Yisrael arevim zeh ba-zeh* (Tal. B. *Shavuot*, 39a), "all Jews are responsible for one another," was derived similarly, centered on the experience of *Shalah Manot*, the "sending of portions" (Esther 9:22). The formulation of the meta-themes, yielding an instrument of greater breadth and applicability, began at our first *Purim* curriculum workshop. We refined the meta-themes and the process gradually, as we used them in workshops and courses, sharpening both the emerging meta-themes and the diverse holiday concepts in these early interactions.

Our method was similar to Glaser and Strauss' "Grounded Theory,"[7] but we didn't know it then. It would be ingenuous to claim that our backgrounds and training as workshop leaders were not a factor in the derivation of both the substantive (*Purim*) and the formal (meta-theme) paradigms. Notwithstanding, because we start with the participants' personal connections to the raw material of tradition, they are more engaged in the construction of the argument, which they are less likely to perceive as "sprung" upon them from an external source. We feel that the process can be internalized; moreover, people may contribute ideas for new substantive paradigms even from the beginning.

A Summary of the Process

First, there is a construct (paradigm) suggested by the primary materials, which, refracted through personal experience, reveals connections in them. The first try at application refines the construct which then "loops" back onto the material, and so on, in a shuttle effect. We accept that there is a subjective element, that there *could* have been other constructs that would have elicited different circuits.

At stake here is the control for authenticity. Since there are many possible constructions, are the paradigms and meta-themes authentic? There is a long-range balancing principle operating: does the paradigm work, does the meta-theme illuminate, do they take us someplace we haven't been? There is a continuous reworking of the primary materials, the substantive paradigms, and the meta-themes. An inauthentic construct would break down, from thin support and the weight of counterexamples. Conversely, the more it works, the more trusted and suggestive it becomes.

---

7   B. Glaser and A. Strauss, *The Discovery of Grounded Theory* (Chicago: Aldine, 1967). See also "Teaching Qualitative Research Methods Courses: A Conversation with Anselm Strauss," *International Journal of Qualitative Studies in Education*, 1:1, January–March, 1988, p. 96.

Extrapolation of the Meta-themes

Earlier, we demonstrated the derivation of a *Purim* paradigm of "an upside-down world" (*olam hafukh*), a "substantive" paradigm connecting directly to *Purim* content. It derived from study and from the experience of the members of our curriculum workshop. At first the *meta-themes* which came to constitute our theoretical "model" emerged from these *Purim* paradigms as hypotheses. These were refined in their referral to other holidays.[8] The first versions of the meta-themes were tentative and experimental; they came together in their present form (as follows) when we became confident of their overall usefulness.

The Meta-themes[9]

The Medium is the Message. The mode of celebration and observance exemplifies, is, the meaning. Methodologically speaking, this is the key meta-theme, deriving from the self-referential examination of personal experience described in detail earlier. We assume that the observance, *halakhah*, or custom as we have it, is an embodiment of a paradigm-concept or a reenactment of an "historical" experience; the ritual *manifests, is* the meaning, and is not merely a celebration *of* or a response *to* that meaning. The personal experience of the holiday has been affected and energized, according to our hypothesis, by the intuitive folk-wisdom embodied in the substantive paradigm, even prior to the explicit articulation of it. The implicit paradigm has sparked the media of observance which become, in turn, the experiential ground from which the paradigm itself may be *learned*. The early explorations leading to the "upside-down world" paradigm, at the heart of this paper, derived from this *assumption*. Since this meta-theme and its derivation have been exemplified already we will say no more about it here.

Meaning is historical and developmental, manifested in history, literature, law, custom, and philosophy. This meta-theme avoids the genetic fallacy. We realized in our preliminary exploration of *Purim* that our understanding of the holiday doesn't evolve only from Biblical and rabbinic sources. *Purim* has to be grasped in terms of its actual observance in different historical periods and places, especially in the *Galut* (the Diaspora communities in which Jews have lived in different periods of Jewish history).[10]

8   Clearly, the meta-themes were not available to us for our first *Purim* explorations. They did not *precede* the exploration of the specific materials; we render them here, necessarily in this linear presentation, at a later stage than when they were first proposed.
9   The expanded model we use in courses and workshops has five overlapping meta-themes. In this paper we stress three of them here, subsuming the other two.
10 Purim itself is a *Galut* holiday in a *Galut* setting. It is modelled in part upon the Joseph Story. Some examples of parallels to the Joseph story:

Staying with the "upside-down world" paradigm for now, the phenomenon of "special Purims" is an instructive source for illustrating and comprehending its significance. When Jews, individuals, families, or communities, were saved from danger during *Galut* Jewish history, they declared a "*Purim*."[11] Instead of creating a new holiday, they assimilated the new "miracle" to the old paradigm.

Why did *Purim* become the archetypical paradigm of choice? Jews probably "lost" in crises many more times than they "won;" yet, *Purim* exemplified hope in the face of despair. Jews knew that miracles *could* happen, because of *Purim*, even though they hardly ever did, and this kept hope alive. Observing Purim became a testimony to the faith that their vision of the world as it *ought* to be was right, even as it contradicted the evidence of their own senses. Indeed, the world as they experienced it fell short of the ideal; it was "upside down."

This is one example of how the meaning of *Purim* reflects the way the Jewish people grasped that meaning through the centuries. Historically, Jews found meaning consciously or intuitively in deep-seated paradigms and adapted them to generate practices that spoke to their current circumstances.[12] Historical *remembrance* enables *us* to participate in that intuitive historical process which nurtured a web of Jewish meaning for all time; doing this is richer than merely understanding a "concept" or "idea."[13] In fact, it is the necessary grounding for any critical understanding.

Concepts are not just historical remembrances but paradigms for the construction and understanding of today's reality, a challenge for all times. The meaning commits us to do, think, reflect, and feel, to some form of action response *now*, at the very least a refinement of perspective or

Takes place in *Galut*;
Esther and Mordecai are parallel to Joseph;
Jews rise to power in *Galut*, have shaky status, easily overturned;
Appointment of Joseph is like appointment of Haman and later Mordecai;
They bow to Joseph as he rides through street, like Mordecai;
Jacob says "If I'll be bereaved, I'll be bereaved;" Esther says, "*Im Avaditi*," etc., "If I'm lost, I'm lost;"
Esther doesn't reveal her Jewishness; Joseph suppresses his.

What's the point of these and the many other parallels? They associate the Book of Esther with the Joseph story as a paradigm of the Jew's life in *Galut*, always at risk, always in danger, never secure; yet, God is there in the *Galut*, too, and ultimately looks after them.

11 See "Purim," in *Encyclopedia Judaica, op.cit.*, for long list of "special Purims," pp. 1397-1400.
12 See David Roskies, *Against the Apocalypse: Responses to Catastrophe in Modern Jewish Culture* (Cambridge, Mass.: Harvard University Press, 1984).
13 Cf. J. Lukinsky, "Jewish Education and Jewish Scholarship: Maybe the Lies We Tell are Really True?" in N. Cardin and D. Silverman, eds., *The Seminary at 100: Reflections on the Jewish Theological Seminary and the Conservative Movement*, (New York: Rabbinical Assembly and Jewish Theological Seminary, 1987), p.205.

sharpening of capacity. Even rejection or modification of a paradigm idea is a legitimate response after confronting it on its own terms.[14]

Historical remembrance, as suggested, is a good in its own right. This is not disputed; our first task is to understand the historical paradigm in its own terms (that is, as it functioned in its historical context), without imposing our own perspective upon it. However, the paradigm is not only of historical or sentimental interest. We also assume that the paradigm must speak to our present situation, or it will not last.

As described earlier, we looked at the concept of the *olam hafukh*, the upside-down world, and asked what meaning it may have had in Jewish history. "*Nahafokh hu*—the opposite occurred" (Esther 9:1) or "*Olam Hafukh*—the world is upside down." Things are not what they seem. It seems as if the Jews are always on the bottom, but that is not the "real" world. The real world is the opposite; we will triumph over our enemies and be on top. Even if we don't triumph materially, our victory is spiritual. *Purim*, then, throughout its history and with all the variety of its observances, preserved the sense of the world as upside-down.

What might this paradigm of the "upside-down world" mean to us today, especially to Jews who live in Western democracies and identify with Western values and a majority culture? We are, of course, still challenged to identify with Jews of the past and with those who are oppressed today. The tension between the world as it is and our vision of what it ought to be confronts us with this challenge. It is a clue to the famous *midrash* (*Mishlei Rabbah* 9) that only *Purim*, of all the *moadim* (festivals), will be observed in the days of the Messiah. It is then that the true order, now embodied in the deep structure of *Purim*, will come to light.

But there is more. That our view of the world is the correct one—that we are not "losers" as other people may think but ultimately the winners; that if we hold to our covenant with justice, peace, and truth, we will be vindicated—remains provocative. *We* may be seduced more by the attractions of material culture, narcissism, the "new" morality, and the like, away from our ideals, than by the pressures of persecution. This expands and opens up the paradigm, but it maintains its core of authenticity. We are challenged by *Purim* to do everything we can to promote the Jewish world-view in the face of competing values, as well as in the face of persecution.[15]

General extrapolations like these came up while working with *Purim*, and we hypothesized that we could apply them as "meta-themes"

14 But cf. J. Goldstein, "Even the Righteous Can Perish by His Faith," *Conservative Judaism*, XLI:3, Spring, 1989.
15 This was one part of the educational and life credo of our colleague and friend, Bennett Solomon z"l, to whose memory we dedicate this article. *Yehi Zikhro Barukh*.

to the other holidays, even if not all of them. This was the beginning of an emerging process of comparative analysis. The paradigms tried out "worked" as we used them to interpret the raw data; moreover, trying them out, tentatively assuming that they *did* work, led to understandings that might not have arisen from the sources alone. We attempted, in other words, to formulate the substantive meanings, derived first from *Purim*, as constructs of a general sort, i.e. as "meta-themes" that go beyond time-bound contextual factors.[16]

Where do the *meta-themes* come from? They are constructions just like the substantive paradigms. Admittedly, it is possible that the average student or layman might not have arrived at *these* meta-themes. *We* created them as a heuristic device. The creation of additional paradigms and meta-themes is not ruled out. Anecdotal feedback from students leads us to believe that the method can be learned.

Back to the *Maimuna*

Let us return to the *Maimuna* festival with which we started and apply the model to it. The reader may judge whether the model indeed "works."

The Medium is the Message: (meta-theme #1)

What do we find when we look at the experience of observing the *Maimuna*? The holiday involves eating *hametz* again, the return to eating it after being prohibited from doing so on *Pesah*, and the resumption of relationships with Jewish and non-Jewish neighbors. During *Pesah*, the quintessential holiday of "separation," some Jews who are very strict with *Kashrut*, and the additional stringencies of *Pesah*, separate themselves even from their Jewish friends, let alone non-Jews! The experience of *Maimuna* is about the tensions among the different levels of community of which the Jew is a part. It is about the reconstitution of the broader community and the affirmation of the Jew's and Jewish community's place in it. This is manifested in the eating of *hametz* in a celebration with Jewish and non-Jewish friends. The varied observances cited earlier celebrate this phenomenon of communal solidarity. There is more to *Maimuna*, but this is a start, educed from the application of our first meta-theme.

---

16 We have indeed applied these meta-themes to the other holidays, but will not present the results here. We hope to do this in a future article. Our purpose here is to explain the *process*. Our application of it to the *Maimuna* is illustrative for present purposes.

The Holiday must be Understood Historically: (meta-theme #2)

Maimuna originates in *galut*. Jews were concerned for the Jewish role and presence among the nations. There were considerations of *Darkhei Shalom* (peaceful relationships with neighbors). (Further exploration of the history of Moroccan Jewry would be enlightening here.) *Pesah*'s observance has a strong particularistic dimension. There is a great deal of curiosity about it on the part of outsiders; it has rituals that seem strange and secretive to them. Gentiles, for the most part, have not participated in it. Jews, even when it was not *Pesah*, could not eat much in the homes of Gentile neighbors. The limitation has been even more rigorous on *Pesah*. *Pesah* has been central to Jewish consciousness and, in its intensity, has functioned to separate Jews from their neighbors. In tense historical settings, and even in friendly ones, there must have been a felt need to overcome feelings of alienation.

The Concepts are Paradigms for Today: (meta-theme #3)

What are some paradigmatic concepts that flow from the other two applications of the meta-themes? What can all of this mean to us? What can we learn about the folk observance of the *Maimuna*, and which general learnings can we extrapolate for ourselves? Looking at the material with the assumption that it has imperatives built into it, leads to some suggestive hypotheses.

We must dedicate ourselves both to the particularistic and the universalistic aspects of Jewish life. We are entitled, indeed obligated, to separate ourselves for purposes of intensive Jewish life and education as we do on *Pesah*. That is what makes us Jews and enables *Pesah* to have, ultimately, its compelling *universal* significance. But we also are part of the wider community. That status should be celebrated. It is not only necessary; it is *desirable*. Such celebration would be a way of nurturing the commitment to the universal which may sometimes be in danger.

Thus the return to normal life from the special life of *Pesah* should be celebrated. *Havdalah* after *Shabbat* or holidays is a weekly expression of this idea, but *Shabbat*, also a kind of separation from the wider community, is familiar and taken for granted; it is also *brief*. *Pesah* is more exclusivist and mysterious in its separating. The return from sacred to the profane is thus not only a "downer." It should be marked in a positive manner which restores the Jew to a role among friends, Jewish and non-Jewish, in community. *Maimuna*, then, is a contrast to *Pesah* which is a special realm just for Jews; but, after the unforgettable Exodus, the move from "slavery to freedom" that *Pesah* celebrates, the return to everyday life is commemorated too.

The analogy to *Sukkot* is relevant here, for *Sukkot* represents the return to normal life after the spiritual peaks of *Rosh Hashanah* and *Yom Kippur*. But *Sukkot* also celebrates the wandering in the desert and the harvest. The difference inheres in the identification of *Sukkot* with a special meaning of its own. It is the remembrance of *that* forty years of wandering in the desert which goes beyond the "celebration of normality" of the *Maimuna*. *Sukkot* enables us to identify with and enact our people's preparation in the desert for becoming a nation in Land of Israel.

Thus, we have applied our meta-theme structures to *Maimuna* and found an interpretation that rings true: *Maimuna* is a celebration of the return to everyday life after the separation from it that characterizes *Pesah*. *Alice in Wonderland* has a character that celebrates his "un-birthday" because there are so many more of them. *Maimuna* partakes of this frame-of-mind, the return from the intensive and celebratory restrictions of *Pesah* to the ordinariness of everyday life. American Jews would probably not want to make another holiday immediately after *Pesah*, the most difficult holiday, especially for women, that we have. Understanding the different kind of mind-set, represented by the *Maimuna*, gives us an insight into the way the different ethnic groups in Israel think. This understanding enables us to go beyond the "quaintness" which characterizes prevalent approaches to observances such as *Maimuna*. Whether a holiday like *Maimuna* should be developed by other Jews is a moot question, but its *function* needs fulfilling; it is a challenge to us.

We are not claiming that this preliminary exploration has exhausted the meaning of *Maimuna*. The study of *Maimuna* from this perspective, however, raises issues about the nature of the celebratory experience that are often avoided and opens up possibilities for creative extension to our own situation.

Conclusions: The Model

Our paradigm-model derives from the experience of creating curriculum with students and teachers, a focus which led us to view the holidays from an educational perspective. We started our research with one holiday, *Purim*, and, as we derived paradigmatic substantive commonalities, we extrapolated trial "meta-themes" that we tested on other holidays, modifying and sharpening the particular holiday materials concurrently with the formal instrument as we went along. As we have described, we started with the familiar and accessible practices of *Purim* as a methodological strategy. We then combined and generalized until we had a functional, though not finished, instrument (the meta-theme model).

We assume that additional meta-themes could be added to the model, and indeed hope that others will use it, expand it and keep us informed. We have found that these meta-themes work for us and for the students and teachers who have participated in our courses and workshops. We feel that it is a generative and initiating framework for thinking about any of the holidays and/or all of them. With material that has seemed difficult to understand, where the standard understandings and interpretations have seemed forced, we have found that using the meta-themes has produced results that otherwise might not have emerged. Increasing applicability of the tentative model gave us enough confidence in it to trust the process. We are convinced that it can help others make sense of what often seems a hodgepodge of detail. Though we have used it extensively with the other holidays, we have exemplified our claim here, in addition to showing its derivation from our *Purim* research, by extending the model to the *Maimuna*.

The model creates opportunities for connections and integrations that might be missed by starting from a prior understanding of the basic "ideas" of a given holiday.

The model, moreover, has the potential for generating *new* substantive ideas from the deeply-felt connections that emerge from the participants' own experience that have the ring of authenticity about them. By looking at the Jewish people's intuitive applications of the underlying holiday paradigms in history, and by presupposing that these paradigms always make normative claims upon the present, we generate interpretations, as in the discussion of *Maimuna*, that would probably not have arisen.

INTEGRATION

DOING IT

Lifsa Schachter

As Bennett Solomon has amply demonstrated, the term integration means different things to different people.[1] It is a term with strong appeal. From its Latin root we get the idea to make whole, to renew. It is related to the word integrity, implying the virtues of soundness and moral principle. By itself the term implies desirability and has become a positive slogan in the day school world. But, because of its ambiguity, when school people get together to discuss the merits of integration or whether to increase the amount of integration within a school, they rarely have a useful definition.

This was amply demonstrated when I was asked to consult with members of a day school education committee. Preliminary conversations with the committee and with the school principal found all participants using the concept of integration in sharply different ways. Consequently, they differed in their evaluations of the school's existing practice with regard to integration. They also had different ideas about the direction the school should take. I came to realize that if I was to succeed in facilitating a productive discussion with the entire committee my first task had to be bringing the committee to a shared working definition of the concept of integration. At the same time, I had to avoid sacrificing the complexity of the term in the process of seeking clarity and consensus.

I found a method for achieving this goal through the development of a matrix that laid out the components of the concept of integration. The matrix served to structure and focus our discussion. It enabled the committee to analyze the components of schooling relevant to integration, to locate its presence within the school, to raise the crucial issues related to the various positions one might take regarding it, and to generate further study and planning. In this article I will elaborate on

---

1 Bennett Solomon, "A Critical Review of the Term 'Integration' in the Literature on the Jewish Day School in America." *Jewish Education* 46:4, Winter, 1978.

the matrix in order to raise issues regarding integration and to demonstrate a process that can be useful with other groups.

A Matrix for Understanding Possibilities for Integration in the Context of the Jewish Day School

Most often when integration is discussed, it is in relation to the curriculum of the school.[2] As Robert Dreeben states, what is learned in school derives from many more dimensions of schooling than curriculum alone.[3] Learning also derives from the way time is structured, relationships among staff, types and distribution of teaching strategies, methods of inquiry used in the various courses of study, the quality and distribution of resources and materials, arrangements of the physical environment, parent involvement and informal activities. A consideration of the possibilities for integration within a school must relate to all of these dimensions of schooling.

My plan for working with the education committee had as its starting point the identification of all these dimensions of schooling. Together we generated a list that included the following terms; time, staff, teaching strategies, subjects, resources, physical environment, climate, informal activities, world view and parents. I then explained the value of a matrix as a tool for studying the various components of the problem and we placed these terms along one side of a matrix.

In order to form the second side of the matrix, we then identified the attitudes towards integration which are held by different members of day school communities. These attitudes covered a wide range. At one extreme we placed the total separation of Judaic and general studies, virtually dismissing general studies. This position acknowledges that general studies are useful only to the extent that they prepare the student for the world of work and are included only to comply with the requirements of the state. It sees Judaic studies as the source of the real values of the school and of the community.

A second position compartmentalizes the Judaic and the general. It sets up two totally separate, but equal realms with no interaction between them. Each is seen as possessing independent value. A third position

---

2 See for example Fradle Freidenreich and Abraham J. Gittleson, *Interdisciplinary Integration in the Jewish School: The Process of a Pilot Project*. AAJE and CAJE, 1979; and Bennett Solomon, "Curricular Integration in the Jewish All-Day School in the United States." in M. Rosenak, ed., *Studies of Jewish Education*, Vol. 2 (Jerusalem: The Magnes Press, 1984).

3 Robert Dreeben, *On What is Learned in School* (Reading, MA: Addison-Wesley, 1968).

values *both* the Judaic and the general, seeing each as possessing value and positing some interaction between them. Examples of this kind of interaction include having a general studies teacher lead the class in writing stories about Jewish holidays as part of an English language program, or having the science and Judaic studies teachers jointly plan an ecology trip to coincide with and relate to Tu B'shvat. Finally, we identified the position of total integration, a position which professes one world view incorporating both the general and the Judaic as two fully valued sources of knowledge and approaches to the world.[4]

We completed our diagram by arranging the attitudes towards integration along the second side of the matrix. We followed a sequence of attitudes ranging from that which expressed the least amount of integration to that which expressed the most complete integration. This led to the creation of a figure with 40 cells (Fig. 1). Every one of these cells represented a possible application of the idea of integration within a school. Exploring the implications created by each of the cells helped us see integration as a highly differentiated concept. It gave us a picture of integration that was multi-dimensional and more susceptible to meaningful examination.

THE MATRIX

	Rejection	Compart-mentalization	Interaction	Integration
Time				
Staff				
Strategies				
Subjects				
Resources				
Physical Environment				
Climate				
Informal Activities				
World View				
Parents				

Figure 1

---

[4] For a similar typology see Joseph Lukinsky, "Integrating Jewish and General Studies in the Day School: Philosophy and Scope" in Max Nadel, ed., *Integrative Learning: The Search for Unity in Jewish Day School Programs* (American Association for Jewish Education. 1978).

The matrix helped us see that, rather than having one undifferentiated attitude, any given school might hold a range of attitudes toward integration, with different positions for the various dimensions of schooling. Some specific examples will clarify this point.

A school might have a fully computerized Talmud program with students utilizing the latest innovations in technology at the same time that it conveys an attitude of rejection towards the non-Jewish world. On the matrix, in the area of resources and use of technology this school might be described as totally *integrated*, while in terms of world view it might be placed on the *rejectionist* end of the matrix.

We saw a similar complexity when we looked at the dimension labeled school climate. Starting from the *integration* end of the matrix, we recognized schools which have one approach to classroom management in the entire school, where there is one set of expectations applied equally in the general and Judaic studies classes as well as in all of the public spaces within a school. For example, in this school type, there is no difference in the quality of respect given general and Judaic studies teachers, and methods of reward and punishment are consistent across departments, at least according to school policy.

As we moved across the matrix to the *interactive* model, we recognized schools which lack a unified approach to school climate, but where one can find general and Judaic studies teachers working together on issues of classroom management.

It was more difficult to label the following dimension clearly, however we were able to identify two forms of *compartmentalization*. In one, the school is sharply divided along Judaic and general lines. This school type functions as two independent institutions under one roof. In some instances there is a climate of respect and control within the Judaic studies but not in the general; in others the situation is reversed.

A second form of *compartmentalization* in school climate is found in schools where every class is virtually a self-contained unit. Every teacher decides independently how children should behave and what behaviors should be rewarded or punished. Children go from class to class without knowing how good behavior is defined, what is expected in the classroom, what is the cause for or the nature of reward or punishment. In schools such as these one may find a cooperative learning environment where children seem relaxed and where one rarely hears raised voices side by side with classrooms run like military academies.

Finally, we identified schools which fit the *rejectionist* model, where respect and status are extended only to the teachers of one department or the other. The children learn early on that either Judaic or general studies is the valued area in this hierarchy and act accordingly.

In a similar way we identified the range of attitudes expressed by arrangements of the physical environment of schools. When the use of space within a school is fully *integrated* the needs of the general and Judaic studies are equally honored and the physical environment displays both departments in a seamless interrelated way. Where there is *interaction*, the two realms are separated but there will be some sharing, for example, of bulletin board displays and other such artifacts. A school that *compartmentalizes* divides the use of space between both realms while in a *rejectionist* situation physical allocations and visual displays favor one realm over the other.

A good test of integration of space can be conducted by taking a walk through a school building with questions such as these in mind: Which flags are in view? Whose portraits adorn the hallways? What kind of student work in displayed in hallways and classrooms? If the classroom is shared, how much of the bulletin board goes to the Judaic studies teacher and how much goes to the general studies teacher? How are materials arranged in the classroom? Who has primary use of the teacher's desk? Thinking of the schools with which we are familiar from the prospective of their allocation of space, we saw once again the complexity and differentiated nature of the concept of integration. In some cases it is the school that most prides itself on integration which allocates space in ways that do disservice to one portion of the school's agenda.

Using the Matrix

After constructing the matrix with the participation of the education committee and examining the situation indicated by each of the cells in a general way, we began the deliberative process designed to help the school confront its own current reality and plan for the future. Members of the committee identified the school's current staff patterns as compartmentalized. They agreed that the school's general studies and Judaic studies faculties are characterized by minimal interaction. During the early stages of the discussion, members of the committee indicated a preference for a totally integrated faculty. They described the most integrated staff that they could envision as one in which the same person teaches both the general and the Judaic studies. But when they examined the feasibility of such a staffing pattern in their own school they realized how unlikely it was that they would find people with expertise in both general and Judaic studies.

They then began to examine the option of increasing the interaction between the general and Judaic staff. They explored what would be involved in increasing staff interaction and faced issues like the need for more staff meetings than they currently have. They saw that this, in turn, would create the need for different scheduling patterns from those that currently obtain and an increased financial commitment in the form of staff salaries. The committee concluded that they wanted to examine the impact of the need for additional faculty hours and the resulting increase in faculty salaries on other aspects of the school program before making a commitment to the new pattern. Some members expressed the sentiment that a well-run compartmentalized staffing design might be preferable to an interactive design which was not supported by financial resources for additional staff time.

The matrix helped the committee examine the ways increased interaction among staff would affect other aspects of schooling. They reflected on the effect increased interaction among staff would have on parent contacts and relationships, on school climate, on the use of space within the school.

With regard to subject matter, the group concluded that integration was not always desirable. Some people talked about the specific modes of inquiry appropriate to different disciplines. Others asserted that they did not want their children to study Humash in the same way that they studied history, placing an emotional weight on the study of Bible that they did not put on other subjects. At the same time, the committee as a whole expressed the desirability of children being able to integrate the skills acquired while studying one subject with the study of other subjects. In the past, discussions of this sort caused deep controversy within the education committee. The matrix gave legitimacy to a wide range of viewpoints and made possible a non-confrontational dialogue, and created a framework for further productive discussion.

Extending the Use of the Matrix

A school wishing to use the matrix would need to modify the matrix to reflect the local situation. The matrix would then be used to structure the ensuing deliberation. Based on the experience described in this paper, structure of such a discussion can be outlined in the following way:

1. Place the school's current position with regard to a given dimension of schooling in one of the cells.
2. Mark the school's desired position for that dimension on the matrix.
3. Describe the qualities of that desired position, what the school would like if it reflected the realities of that position
4. Identify what it would take to move the school to the desired position with regard to cost, feasibility, availability of material and personnel resources.
5. Estimate the length of time needed to make this change.

6. Identify the impact of this change on other school factors.

7. Decide whether the move to the new position is important when weighed against the cost and impact on other aspects of the school.

8. Reevaluate the desired situation and confirm or alter the decision taken earlier.

    I believe that Jewish day schools interested in exploring the idea of integration and the issues it generates will find the matrix to be a useful tool. It serves to structure and focus a discussion that can help schools understand their current situation with regard to integration as well as plan for the future.

FROM BENNETT
ON CURRICULUM IMPLEMENTATION

CURRICULUM CHANGE

As we focused upon the creation of this new curriculum, the School Committee first reviewed the literature on educational change and accepted the fact that the innovations we desired would result from a process nurtured over time. We recognized the crucial role of the faculty in formulating specific objectives and materials within the general guidelines established by principal and School Committee and we allotted a number of years to meet our goals. This relieved the pressure which is usually placed upon principals and teachers to deliver a new product quickly. Keeping the School Committee in the project is a process which must be consistently addressed. While desiring excellence and favoring educational reform, lay people tend to focus upon fiscal rather than educational implications of the project. The principal must support the process by spending considerable time with School and Finance Committee members, in public and in private, to maintain lay leadership interest in the project. While this demands large blocks of time, it is, in the end, worthwhile since these lay leaders can become the champions of the cause.

Numerous staff days, meetings and discussions were dedicated to explicating the concept of integration in our school. I took an active role in providing reading material, leading workshops and encouraging fresh thought and original input from all members of the faculty. Understanding and consensus developed with each successive meeting. These meetings included all members of the staff: full and part-time teachers, general and Jewish studies teachers, content specialists and the psychologist. Everyone benefited from each other's input. These full meetings were an important statement of the unity and equality within the faculty with no discipline or individual assuming a position of greater importance. The task of creating an integrative curriculum was shared by all. Scheduling meetings which everyone could attend became an important administrative function of the principal which clearly reflected the school's commitment to this cause ...

Furthermore, the research has indicated that the ambience of the classroom and the school affects learning. It was necessary to create a school climate conducive to coordination among staff members and integrative thinking among the students. We attempted to eliminate artificial distinctions which existed within our school structure. Full-time jobs were created for teachers who could teach a number of disciplines and subjects. Efforts were made to attract teachers who were positive role models of Jewish identification and commitment. Middle school students' general and Jewish studies classes were scheduled throughout the day. New report cards were created which related each child's development in all language and conceptual areas, and parent/teacher conferences were scheduled with both general and Jewish studies teachers present at the same time.

Numerous new school wide activities were created which involved the entire faculty and cut across distinctions which had existed between staffs, children's perceptions of teachers' roles, and children[s perceptions of the school ...] Committees were formed with general and Jewish studies teachers (as well as parents) working together to create programs. Not only did the teachers grow and learn from one another but suddenly the children saw all their teachers involved in subjects which had previously been the exclusive domain of one or the other. This conveyed to the children that we were one school with many wonderful opportunities to learn and celebrate as Jews and as Americans ...

Throughout the process I have consistently offered instructional suggestions for specific integrative lessons and experiences. Without imposing a *specific* method which every teacher had to implement, I have insisted that all teachers attempt actualizing what they understood as the essence of our emerging school curriculum ...

My own persistence in reminding people to look constantly for ways to integrate might have become tiresome. It was known, however, that I was available to assist in the process of creating actual classroom methods and materials and that monetary support was available when needed. In this way the principal clearly served as a source of instructional leadership and maintained high expectations of faculty members.

There is some good news from recent studies of school improvement efforts within general education which makes us confident that we can successfully innovate within our day schools. A school must first determine its definition of integration and the importance of integration within its school community. An implementation strategy should then be developed, guided by the following recommendations gleaned from the last decade of curricular innovation:

1) Develop the teachers' commitment to the project either prior to the implementation itself, or during the process of using the new materials.

2) Create instructional materials which are well-developed, well-defined and determined to be effective by the teachers who are using them.

3) Train the entire staff by credible people who bring expertise in subject matter, child development and teaching methodology.

4) Assist and support teachers with a large array of individuals including other teachers, the principal, coordinators and outside experts.

5) Attend to factors contributing to the institutionalization of the new curriculum by creating line items on budgets, orienting new or reassigned staff members and writing the new programs into curriculum guidelines.

By pursuing these recommendations, efforts towards curriculum reform can gain a greater measure of success and help us accomplish our vital task as the transmitters of our rich heritage to the future generation of Jewish Americans.

Curriculum Innovation, pp. 14–21.

PROCESS

A summary of research on effective schools and successful curriculum innovation concludes that changing schools requires changing people—their behaviors and attitudes—as well as school organization and norms through strong leadership by principals. It assumes that consensus among the staff of a school is crucial for success. While specific tactics may vary, a general strategy should promote collaborative planning and collegial work in a school atmosphere conducive to experimentation and evaluation. In such settings, the improvement effort is directed toward incremental long-term cultural change. Mark Yudoff writes,

> The error of past research was to dwell too much on hardware and dollars and too little on school climate ... Government decisions made at the higher echelons are important only insofar as they create favorable conditions for or impede the quest for educational excellence in classrooms and schools.[1]

This is particularly relevant to efforts for curriculum reform within Jewish day schools in America.

Curriculum Innovation, p. 11.

---

1 Mark Yudoff, "Educational Policy Research and the New Consensus of the 1980's," *Phi Delta Kappan* 65, no. 7 (March 1984) p. 456.

KEDUSHAH AS AN INTEGRATIVE FOCUS

THE IMPLEMENTATION OF A VISION

Robert Abramson

This is the story of the first steps in the implementation of a vision of what I think the Conservative Solomon Schechter Day Schools should be attempting to do. I offer it as a case history, a contribution to the "clinical writing" on school change, as a reflective sharing of educational practice. At the May, 1986, colloquium of the Jerusalem Fellows, I delivered a paper, "Kedushah as a Generative Focus: An Example of A Way of Thinking About Schools." That paper forms the theoretical background for the work I describe here. This essay, told in the first person, is an effort to share my thinking, anxieties, and actions as I sought to implement the vision embodied in that paper.

I have chosen to offer this piece of "clinical writing" in this memorial volume dedicated to the memory of Bennett Solomon because the example which he offered of thinking hard and long about how to see the school as a whole and to render theory into practice is one of the many ways we are blessed by his memory.

Introduction

From 1975 to 1988, I served as headmaster of the Hillel Day School of Detroit. In 1985-86, I spent my sabbatical year in Israel as a Jerusalem Fellow and thus had the opportunity to think, study, and deliberate with a challenging group of colleagues. In August, 1986, I returned to the United States with new ideas about directions for Hillel and for the Solomon Schechter Day School movement in general. Much of my time in Jerusalem had been devoted to thinking about the vision that ought to inform our school and the way such a vision should be formulated.

In Israel I developed the concept, "Generative foci," which I believe contributes to the thinking and to the talking about the way values and ideas could give form and meaning to our schools. I had made the claim that the two specific generative foci of our schools should be, "the development in our students of the ability to sense and live with holiness, *kedushah*, and obligation, *hovah*."

In my presentation to the colloquium, I analyzed Heschel's understanding of *kedushah* and sought to show how *kedushah*, when understood from this perspective, could serve as a generative focus. Along with the paper which was presented to the weekly seminar of Jerusalem Fellows for critique and subsequently at its annual colloquium, I developed a short one page statement on the vision of our school for lay leadership and faculty. In it I attempted to distill in three paragraphs the vision I had elaborated at great length in my paper.

To provide a sense of what I was about, I quote part of that statement:

> Hillel must seek out ways to develop in the child a sense of the sacredness of others and through this a sense of his or her own sacredness. We must help the child develop as a thinking, feeling, valuing human being; one who can develop into an adult who can feel what he/she thinks, think what she/he feels, and have both passion and reason about values. We must nourish in our students a sense that their lives and deeds have meaning. We must help our students develop a sense of wonder, awe, and appreciation; a sense that their relationship to the world, others, and God is bound together by obligation. Such a human being has always been the ideal of Judaism.
>
> Ours can be no less. Our means are the total educational program, general and Jewish studies. Our Jewish heritage provides us with the means of Torah and sacred deeds. Our general studies are a source of knowledge, meaning, and understanding about people and the world. All our learning can become a way for our children to come to sense that they are precious to God.

Concomitantly with beginning to think through the direction our schools should take, I participated in a seminar on staff development. I was fortunate to have had Ayela Kamon assigned as a mentor. She was to play a key role in helping me think through the process for introducing this new direction to the faculty of Hillel Day School.

What follows is the story of the early stages of engaging a school's faculty in a vision. In telling this story I shall try to share with you, the reader, not the results but the process, what I thought, decided, and did.

Preliminary Thoughts and Decisions

In the seminar devoted to staff development we enumerated both negative and positive intrinsic and extrinsic motivations for change. The most telling critique of my work had been that, given our secular society, *kedushah* was an impossible generative focus. On the other hand, I was convinced that one could assume that many had a thirst for professional and personal meaning. Positing such a thirst as a positive, intrinsic motivating factor gave me reason to think that I could engage faculty in a process leading to awareness of *kedushah* in an alien secular societal setting such as ours. A staff development program, such as I had begun to think about, would not aim at improving instructional skills. It would deal with changing values and perspectives and in the enrichment of the teacher as a person.

Several assumptions about staff development had emerged in our seminar that would guide my thinking. One was that the focus has to remain on professional tasks even if speaking to the whole person. After all, the teacher becomes involved in a staff development program as a teacher. Another working assumption was that certain types of resistance would have to be eliminated or at least minimized. I could not expect teachers to put in extra time simply because I was returning with some new ideas. Further, I was aware that even for compensation some people are not interested in extra time commitments and work. Teachers have difficult teaching schedules, put in a lot of preparation time, and have a life after school with personal and family concerns and obligations. I wanted to avoid, at least at first, creating a conflict between my new agenda and the teachers' already existing personal agendas. Such conflict could obviate dialogue and long term development.

It was at my meetings with Ayela Kamon that I began to clarify what I wanted to do with the faculty. I would, in a sort of circular way, work from specific plans to general objectives and from objectives to plans. She would critique and require justification. I would make a proposal; she would ask me to focus on various members of the faculty to anticipate reactions. In addition, she also provided me the opportunity to talk out my anxieties. Over time a strategy developed.

As the sense of what I wanted to do began to emerge, the question of format loomed ever larger. Many factors had to be taken into consideration. The Hillel faculty was large and variegated. Hebrew and general studies teachers had different backgrounds and training. There were many veteran teachers but increasing numbers of new teachers. The teachers' contract obligated the faculty to attend monthly staff meetings. Like faculty meetings in many schools, ours were regarded as necessary and sometimes important but always a pain and an imposition. These obligatory meetings would not serve my purposes well. In addition, meeting with more than forty teachers would not permit the dynamic of engagement that I wished. However, there was a limit to the time I had for meeting with small groups. I had a great many duties besides staff training. This was a priority for me, but it could not supersede all my other duties that were required to keep a school of over five hundred students working properly. These reasons and the ability of some to undermine the enthusiasm of others mitigated against working with the whole faculty, either as a whole or in small groups.

I made the decision to start with a small group of teachers who would volunteer to participate. This was a framework that I could handle given the limitations on my time. Further, by beginning with volunteers I might be able to minimize resistance. I was also quite sure that I could convince the board to budget some compensation for the participants. Of course, this would be "creaming off the top" but it was a format that would permit me to get going, to probe and experiment. Such an approach clearly would not permit wide spread institutional change, but this could be an advantage disguised as a disadvantage. At this experimental stage, it might be better to keep things low keyed. Surely the promise of sweeping change can be threatening. It can also bring about premature demands for results or oppositional behavior. If there were no bandwagon, no one would have to expend energies in halting it. With these pros and cons in mind, I decided to go ahead and establish "Core Study Group I."

I returned to Hillel Day School with the following objectives for the study group:

1. Initiate participants into the language of wonder, awe, and *kedushah*. (NOTE: I assumed that these were not terms which teachers were comfortable with nor did they form a perspective on their work. An objective of the study group would be to initiate the teachers into a religious vocabulary and to make that vocabulary real for them in terms of their own experiences and their work.)
2. Explore the relationship of these terms to experience.
3. Explore what various areas of the curriculum could contribute to the generative focus of developing a sense of holiness.
4. Become capable and comfortable with "shuttling" back and forth between personal meaning and professional implications.

With the above objectives in mind and prepared with some tentative lesson plans, the theoretical paper, and the vision statement, I returned to the United States and Hillel Day School.

Rallying the Troops

Upon returning home, I shared my new sense of direction with both the board and the faculty. At my first meeting with the executive board they told me with a tinge of apology that they were not happy with the existing statement of the school's philosophy which I had written eight years before. With a smile, I responded, "No problem. I just happen to have a new statement which I wrote in Israel." The executive committee accepted the vision statement and allocated $3,000 for Core Study Group I. (To this day, I do not know whether it was endorsed because it sounded good and met a need or because it gave expression to their sense of what the school's purpose ought to be.)

The presentation to the teachers would be harder. I set aside a couple of hours during the two before-school professional days to discuss the vision statement and Core Study Group. Teachers consider this time as theirs for setting up their rooms and "getting ready" for students. They think of meetings as an intrusion. To make matters worse, the new facility we were building would not be completed on time. Fortunately, contract negotiations with the union had ended a few weeks before the start of school, and we were in an era of good feeling.

Seizing the fact that I had been away, I told the assembled faculty that I wanted to share with them a vision of the school which I had spent much time thinking about during my sabbatical. I read and adumbrated the statement. I explained my intention to form a study group to further explore its implications. The study group would be voluntary; there would be compensation, and, to permit real give and take, the number of participants would have to be limited to about ten. There were some questions, mostly requests for clarifications. I was thankful for each question and indication of interest. I had been afraid that my presentation would be met with silence and that everyone would want simply to get on with their personal work.

After a short discussion and further elaboration, I acknowledged the fact that we all had a lot to do. I turned my attention to the problems of moving into the new building, reiterating that we had a lot of extra help around to assist and sent everyone on their way. I knew that, so far as the teachers were concerned, theory was fine, but tomorrow the children were coming. A few weeks after school started, I sent a memo to the faculty inviting their participation in Core Study Group I. What follows is an attempt to chronicle the development of that group.

Overview: Themes and Topics

The opening session took place on Sunday, November 9, 1986. This was the only session that was not held after school and it was a long session, lasting three hours. It was to serve as an initiation into the meaning of wonder, awe, and holiness. We discussed experiences of holiness. We also studied Chapter I of Genesis and there was a brief introduction to Heschel's epistemological assumptions.

Session II consisted of a study of Genesis, Chapter II: 1-3, the Sabbath of Creation. We then changed our focus from the wonder of creation to the holiness of man. To do this, we revisited the story of man's creation as found in Chapter I of Genesis and analyzed Psalm 8.

In Session III, we reviewed a third grade social studies textbook to investigate what it said about the nature of man. The purpose of the analysis was to see the possibilities the textbook provided and the problems it created for conveying a sense of the holiness of man.

We dedicated Session IV to a review of some writings on wonder and awe and the planning of activities for the sixth grade Tamarack Trip, a two night stay at the Detroit Jewish community's camping facility. We looked at the trip as an opportunity to increase possibilities for students to experience wonder and awe.

Session V, in February, was a report on the Tamarack Trip and a discussion about trips as an example of structuring experience and seizing opportunity. At this session, I also handed out some material from Heschel's *Who Is Man*, which we read together as an introduction to session VI.

Session VI was an examination of the implications of the sacredness of man for teaching acts and materials. In this session we sought to relate classroom activities to what we had learned and valued. It was now the spring and we were coming to the end of our scheduled sessions.

Session VII was to be a summary and looking forward. We would try to delineate future directions for working together.

Close-up of Sessions I, II, IV, and VI
Session I

It is hard to describe the dynamics of a group; to trace the moment when an idea takes hold. It is even harder to pin point why words like "authentic" and "sharing" seem appropriate to some groups and have nothing to do with the life of others. The Core Study Group became a special experience for its leader and, I believe, its members.

While this was a developing process, the first session played a crucial role. Our first meeting would be the only extended session, from 1:00-4:00 on a Sunday. It was the closest we would come to a retreat. In my introduction I acknowledged that each of us came with our own backgrounds and expectations. Further, this was a new experience for all of us. I assured those that needed it that this was not a curriculum group nor was this an academic class with major reading obligations. The amount of beyond-session-time that would be required was of concern to several participants. Our group would try to relate Jewish thought to our school. We would be concerned with theory and practice. We would, I hoped, in the course of time become a fellowship where our work, experiences, and aspirations could be shared.

Based on Heschel's view that religious language points to dimensions that are gained by insight and are within the range of common human experience, I decided that it might be possible for the group to call up and acknowledge experiences of wonder, awe and even holiness in their own lives. After an internal debate with myself, I opted to begin by calling for a sharing of experience even though this meant risking resistance and its companions—silence and non-participation—for it was not within the participants' ordinary expectations of in-service programs.

I asked the participants to "Please write down some experience you have had which you associate with the word holiness—*kedushah*. Describe it." After we all put something down on paper, I asked each to share their response with the person next to them. This turned out to be an important move for it allowed for an intimacy of sharing.

I then asked the participants to describe their experience to the whole group. The responses were put up on the board—birth of a grandson, standing at the dig at the Temple Mount, birth of a child, watching a sparrow, marriage, the resolution of personal Jewish commitment that came at a son's Bar Mitzvah. There were others. We reflected on the common elements between them.

The members of the group sensed that they had experiences in life that were best referred to by religious language; that though the experiences were highly personal, many were overlapping. Most important of all, they had spoken to each other of having sensed wonder and holiness. At this point it was not important whether their experience belonged more to the former than the latter. I then went on to discuss Heschel's distinction between the "realm of response" and the "realm of conceptualization." The twenty minutes or so that we spent on Heschel had the effect of legitimizing their experiences as something more than being merely subjective and ephemeral.

We then moved to a study of Genesis I. I chose Everett Fox's translation because it was both literary and literal. Hebrew and English teachers worked together in groups of three. They were asked to read it out loud and to share their reactions as they listened to it as a poem. What did they sense as they heard it? The discussion that followed in the large group began with their responses. Only then did we look at form and meaning. After thirty minutes of literary analysis and insight,

I ended by suggesting that Genesis I might be thought of as a way to inform our responses to the world.

Session II

As we began Session II, I knew that Session I had caught the imagination of the participants from the responses to my question. "What homework assignment would you give on the completion of Genesis I to encourage a pre-conceptual response." If the small groups came back with typical assignments such as "list what was created on each day," I would have known that they had not grasped the implication of the first session.

But other types of ideas started to pour forth: They would ask students to record everything they saw when they woke up in the morning. They would ask the students to pretend they were very small, the size of a mouse, and describe the world around them. They would ask their students to look outside their window for a few minutes when they wake up. A third grade teacher explained that in her class they read "Kola's Hawaiian Donkey," a story about a donkey that likes to smell the roses and a boy who finds a companion in the donkey for he, too, likes to look around and savor the world. This caught our imagination and we offered ways that a Torah teacher might call on the story and how a third grade general studies teacher might use it to encourage students to look at the wonders around them. This story became a kind of code word for seeing possibilities in materials that are in the curriculum and using them to further the response of awe and wonder.

In Session III we had moved from a look at creation to a look at the place of man in creation through a study of Psalm 8. However, since my purpose is to give a sense of the Core Study Group and not a detailed review of each session, I shall now skip ahead to Session IV.

Session IV

Session IV did not go according to plan. I wanted to investigate with the group the images of man in general studies materials. I had chosen a third grade social studies book that had recently been replaced. They read the book before the session. I was surprised when there was virtually no response to my lead question, "What is the image of man in the book?"

As I probed with reformulations of the question, I began to realize that they did not grasp it. They were not sure what I was looking for. They did not know how to do the analysis and they certainly did not share my assumptions about conceptual structures. I assumed and continue to assume that cognitive problems impeded the discussion. However, it is possible that the silence was an avoidance mechanism and not an intellectual problem. After all, we were dealing with school work and a critique of it could imply a critique of themselves as teachers. However, only one of the teachers had ever used the textbook and most of the group did not teach social studies. Besides, they just did not seem to understand what I meant by "What are the images of man?"

I went into a far more directed teaching mode than in previous sessions. I demonstrated how the text assumed an economic definition of humankind: "Communities need another important resource—people. People are a source of work and skill for a community. They are called the human resources of a community."

It became evident that the teachers did not see this as a definition or as a conceptual framework but as a fact. Though they were uncomfortable with reducing man to an economic resource, they were prepared to accept a "fact as a fact." Only when we began to compare their understanding of "Jewish community" with the text's understanding of community did they begin to see that they were dealing with something more than facts. The definitions and concepts in the textbook were not the only possible ones and our images of man and community need not be solely that of the textbook. The textbook need not be allowed to render invisible the Jewish community or to reduce it to a group that merely shares some customs. Nor do we need to reduce our image of man to that of the textbook.[1]

I have since asked myself whether this session was of value. I do not ask this question because it was a break in the style of the study group but because it did not seem to take on a vital role in the logic of our discussions. And yet, I, at least, was able to use the expression "image of man" more easily with the group. Further, the group from this point on seemed to increasingly make a distinction between man as a means and as an end.

Session VI

I wanted to use this session to begin a process of "getting a grip on educational implications." At the end of the previous session I had distributed as a summary and discussion starter several sections from Heschel's, *Who Is Man?*, and asked the teachers to think about the educational implementation of any ideas that spoke to them. As we settled down to begin the session, S.F., a Judaics teacher originally from Israel said, "I enjoyed reading the Heschel material. I wish I had been brought up with this philosophy."

---

1   I am not suggesting that the social sciences are invalid ways of looking at man. For many purposes they are very valuable but they are by their nature incomplete. Should not an institution concerned with religious education also look at traditions of religious anthropology and personal insight as valid ways of thinking about the nature of persons and community?

To give you a flavor of where we had come as a group, I shall here quote extensively. What follows are excerpts taken from the transcript of Session VI that capture both the spirit and content of the thinking of the participants.

S.F. I was working with a vocabulary lesson (second grade Hebrew) and one of the students gave me a sentence "The boy of that sad woman is very important" and it triggered a whole thing. He put a kind of negative adjective. It sounded like, "Even that boy is important." If I didn't read that I probably would have gone on to another sentence and called on another hand. We just stopped and discussed it and the kids really added things. And I thought that if I had not read that article the discussion would not have happened.

F.F. What if somebody doesn't belong to somebody.

S.F. That's the fact that we have to bring. We belong to a society; we belong to a neighborhood; we belong to a family.

F.F. But they are no longer productive.

S.F. But they are still important.

F.F. I think they still have a value when they are no longer productive.

C.A. In the Jewish values class in the seventh grade we try to look at the events around the school or in the newspaper and relate them to values that we studied. Sometimes they bring something in. They know it is a value but are not quite sure what it is.

I don't know whether I mentioned this last time. I had someone come to me and say, "Guess what. I have been collecting all the articles about the hostages in Lebanon and they want to trade someone for 400 prisoners in Israel." Then we started to talk about that; and he knew it was a value but he did not know what the value was. We talked about *Pidyon Shvuyim*, (redemption of captives). "The value," he said, "that you learn from this is that every life is important."

Another student said that she came to talk about Liberace today. Of course, everyone giggled. After the giggles, she said, "It bothers me very much that after he died the coroner had to announce that it was AIDS. What bothers me a lot is that this was a man who probably tried to hide this all his life and that we have no respect."

S.C. I would like to say that I think I have a super opportunity. I have started a new book with the fifth grade called *Bridge to Tarabithia* and if this book doesn't correlate perfectly with our class, absolutely nothing does. It is about two youngsters who both feel that they are misfits ... They create a place which is referred to in the book as holy and sacred ...

I made pages and pages of notes of all the different values that are brought out in this book and different activities that we can do. Actually, almost to mimic this study group, when my class will get to the part that they find Tarabithia we can have the same discussion of what is holy [that we had here]. I am going to need some help. The author deals with death. He says, "Being means striving to go on." [That's] the preciousness of existence, the love of life. We can just go on and on in terms of values and what we are doing here.

R.I. Did you choose this book after taking this course?

S.C. No, it was very coincidental. If I hadn't taken this course ... If I hadn't had this background, I would not have seen any of it.

F.F. I have a child that really is a problem ... I said to the children that we are all here to learn the things that we need, and we are teaching her how to be friends with us. This is what she needs to learn now. But it is a very difficult thing because the parents come in complaining ... This only clarified in my mind something that I was doing all along, but I do it with a little more clarity now ... care of their bodies ... helping each other when they are hurt.

The sharing and conversation went on for over 45 minutes before I said anything. I reflected on the discussion and articulated what I considered to be our educational challenge: these are things that go on in the school but often in an isolated sort of way. How do we make sure that they add up so that they can make a difference? A colleague of mine, Annette Weinshank, after reading my original paper, had said that "generative foci" were a way to make articulate the hidden curriculum and plan for it.

How do we plan and build structures and how do we make sure that we seize the moments? How do we recontour what we have been teaching in the light of a generative focus such as *kedushah*, holiness?

Resistance to Planning: Is It a Personal Matter or in the Nature of Generative Foci?

Core Study Group I had coalesced. The group had clearly become important to its members. The members were comfortable sharing matters that they had never talked about previously as teachers.

Had they changed as people? Had they changed Jewishly? To say so, would probably overstate what had taken place. What can be said is that the members of Core Study Group I had developed a new vocabulary and a new way of looking at teaching at Hillel Day School. As to how deep and how permanent was the change, I am not yet in a position to say. There is not much in our societal context and little enough in our school context that can assure that holiness, *kedushah*, will enter into the very fabric of their lives as teachers and be generative. There is little to support and sustain that which members of the group had begun to internalize unless we create it.

By the end of the school year I was concerned with finding some means to concretize or, should I say, curricularize our work. How could we plan for the nourishment of the sense of wonder and the sacred? I had begun to look for a project that could be done together to develop examples of how our ideas could be translated into teaching acts. In the last session, I thought we had hit upon such a project when one of the group had suggested developing a "teachers' file" and the others responded positively. We had agreed to meet in August, and I looked forward to these meetings as a new stage. In preparation for the August meeting, I sent out a memo asking the teachers to think of ideas and material that might nourish the sense of wonder, awe, holiness, and the sacredness of others.

It was obvious that the participants had given thought to the memo for they came in with ideas. I thought that everyone was ready to work on the teachers' file. I was ready to break up into groups and spend the next morning and a half working out their various ideas so that they could be shared with other teachers. However, when I asked how we should proceed from here, everything stopped.

Finally, one of the teachers said: "What seems to have happened is that studying together we have come to see our work differently." Many of the participants then stated a strong feeling that others had to go through the same experience, otherwise their materials would not be understood and used properly. C.K. said: "We had an experience." That statement seemed to sum up where the group was.

As we continued to talk it became clear that they were telling me that there was no short cut; other teachers would need the Core Study Group experience before they could communicate with them. They also made clear that they expected and needed their group to continue. One of the teachers did suggest that each of them should keep a record of what they did so they could share it subsequently with others who had participated in a similar study group. All were prepared to do this.

Closing Thoughts

When we finished the session, I was of two minds. I had accomplished more than I had originally hoped for, but, in the specific area of curricular planning, I had not reached the point that I wished. The reason for not taking the next steps in planning might be psychological or in the nature of generative foci.

Were these members of the faculty resistant to the next step? Maybe it moved them into an activity that they were not ready for? Maybe they were not ready to go public? Maybe they liked what was happening to them and how it was working and did not want to produce for others? It was possible that there was resistance for one or more such psychological reasons.

It was also possible that wonder and holiness as generative foci were "curriculum resistant" even if all that was meant to result was a teachers' file. If "generative foci" was a conceptual tool for talking about the culture of the school or the hidden curriculum, perhaps written reports were not the right direction. Perhaps the curriculum could be recontoured and take on new tones and coloration only after the pool of participants in the Core Study Group had grown.

Perhaps Core Study Group I correctly sensed that there were no short cuts; that there needed to be Core Study Groups II and III and that only then would the faculty, having shared similar experiences, be different and be able to share work with one another about such matters. Maybe then we would be able to think and plan together about such matters as wonder and holiness and find ways to record that thinking and those plans.

FROM BENNETT

EXAMPLES OF INTEGRATION IN THE CLASSROOM

A very effective means of fostering integrative capabilities is the pursuit of large projects which involve all aspects of the educational program. A short account of a few such projects will be instructive:

Class Newspaper—a bi-lingual newspaper could be undertaken. The children could be divided into various staffs representative of a typical daily newspaper—International, National, Local, Economy, Living, Sports, Movies and Theater, Television and Radio, Classified, Editorials, Comics. Each child would be responsible for writing at least one article in both English and Hebrew. The content of the paper might reflect a community of the world just studied in Social Studies, i.e., a newspaper from Israel, South America, or even from Jerusalem in Biblical times. The content included and the critical language skills needed, e.g., proofreading, punctuation, capitalization, etc. would be melded into the very essence of this experience.

Simulated Trip—A trip to the Sinai desert might involve skills as diverse as a letter and journal writing; map and sundial reading; application of Jewish dietary laws to foods found in the desert. Information about the lives of the Jewish Patriarchs and the lives of the contemporary Bedouin would help the students prepare for the trip. Value clarification exercises could be included concerning the best way to "help" the nomadic Bedouin.

Communal Feast—A large communal feast in celebration of Thanksgiving could involve the comparative study of Thanksgiving customs and rituals of Jews, Pilgrims, contemporary Christian Americans and a primitive tribe like the Bushmen of the African Kalahari Desert. The study of the structure of prayer and the nature of worship, and the function of myth within holiday celebration could be molded together around this theme.

Dissertation, pp. 125-126.

Moral Education

All of the students are asked to respond to a hypothetical moral dilemma similar to those dilemmas published by Professor Kohlberg and associates. Each child is encouraged to assume the various roles within the story and consider his responses. He is also encouraged to clarify conflicting interests which make the situation problematic. Following extensive considerations of the various issues involved in the dilemma, and an opportunity to list which issues are most significant to each student, a relevant quotation from Jewish sources is read by the group. Everyone is encouraged to suggest why this saying is part of the Jewish ethical tradition—why was this particular statement made by the Rabbis or by the author of the Bible?

Then the group is asked if this value statement is relevant to the dilemma under discussion—what principles connect the ethical commandment to the story? The leader asks if this Jewish commandment would help resolve the problem were it accepted by the participants in the story. Throughout the process, the quotation (in Hebrew) is repeated for memorization. Additional sources are dealt with on the same topic, and then a new dilemma is described.

Through this procedure, students must articulate their values and consider alternative responses. This can lead to a development of more sophisticated moral reasoning—an assumption which we hope will lead to moral action as well. At the same time, Jewish ethics are seen as they relate to real life situations—as opposed to being mere words in a book or quotations from "the Rabbis." This program is more than values clarification. It is an opportunity to learn Jewish values while participating in a value clarifying type exercise.

Dissertation, pp. 127-128.

III. COMMUNITY

OBSTACLES TO THE DEVELOPMENT OF THE DAY SCHOOL AS THE NORMATIVE MODE OF JEWISH EDUCATION IN THE CONSERVATIVE MOVEMENT

Burton I. Cohen

A Goal to be Achieved

Near my home in Long Island, a wing of the local Orthodox synagogue is dedicated as the "Sarah Goldberg Memorial Hebrew School Building." Yet, for the past fifteen years, the building has served no students. In fact, the five Orthodox synagogues in the neighborhood together have enrolled fewer than 100 students in a combined afternoon Hebrew school program. Meanwhile, many hundreds of Orthodox children from the area are attending *yeshivot*. When this Young Israel synagogue building was built, about 25 years ago, it was not foreseen that a time would soon come when day school education would become normative for children of families affiliated with Orthodox synagogues in the metropolitan New York area.[1]

Reflecting upon the situation in the Orthodox community, the question arises whether the Conservative movement will ever experience a similar evolution of attitude. Various spokesmen for the Conservative movement have espoused the idea that the Solomon Schechter Day School is a potent instrument of Jewish education and a "guarantor" of the future of Conservative Judaism. But will the Conservative Jewish day school ever

[1] *Trends* (New York: Jewish Education Service of North America, No. 11, Spring 1986), p. 4.

become the *normative* mode of Jewish education for children of Conservative families affiliated with our synagogues both in New York and across North America?

When I think of the many pitfalls on the path of achieving a normative status for day schools in our movement, pitfalls that I have observed first hand as a day school parent, board member and consultant to Conservative day schools, I wonder whether this day will ever come to pass. In this paper, I will discuss four challenges to the day school's becoming normative in the Conservative movement: (1) the narrow enrollment base; and (2) the perception of Conservative Jewish parents that an intensive Jewish education will detract from their child's college and career preparatory experiences. Further, we need to look at making some improvements in day schooling itself: (3) creating a teaching profession and training Conservative personnel for it; and (4) designing and implementing a distinct Conservative curriculum. Until we solve these problems we cannot hope to achieve the goal of making the day school the normative pattern of education for Conservative families.

Parental Attitudes and the Need for a Broader Base

The first problem is, of course, whether we can make the idea of day schooling for the Jewish child acceptable to a broader base of Conservative Jews. It is often suggested by educators and lay leaders of day schools that it is because they fear that their children will become *too* Jewish that many parents are unwilling to enroll their children in a day school. Further, parents often receive much of the blame for the inability of the Conservative day school to imbue its students successfully with a love of Jewish learning and desire to observe the *mitzvot ma'asiyot*. From my long experience in the Ramah Camps, however, I am convinced that parents are usually ready to "take a chance" when it comes to Jewish education and will often willingly take to heart what their children learn and excitedly bring home. Parents also seem to respond supportively to what their children learn when the camp and school respond adeptly to the needs and criticisms of parents. It seems to me that there is a series of problems more basic than alleged parental indifference that impedes the growth of day school education.

Today, with all of its success, the Solomon Schechter Day School serves only one child in ten of those enrolled in an educational program under Conservative auspices. Historically, until the 1950's when the Conservative day school movement began, most American Jews felt that it was un-American and un-Jewish to withdraw Jewish children from the public schools and place them in parochial schools.[2] That this is no longer the case can be attributed to the increased popularity of non-public schools, the new legitimacy given to expressions of ethnicity, and a series of factors internal to the Jewish community which have mitigated the former broad antagonism toward all-day Jewish schooling. Even Reform Judaism, which feared that the opening of day schools and concomitant defection from the public schools might signal an abandonment of that movement's social justice orientation, has in the last decade officially embraced the idea of the day school.[3]

Today, it can be hypothesized, parents who would not consider enrolling their children in day schools are not simply people with a pro-public school commitment, but rather people who lack any deep interest and commitment to Jewish life. The majority of non-Orthodox families—those who send their children to the synagogue school primarily so that they can become Bnei/Bnot Mitzvah, and for whom Jewish concerns and activities are peripheral, will rarely send their children to day school.

It is arguable that the parents of the Orthodox Yeshivah student, with rare exception, are most likely also to be synagogue Jews and involved comprehensively in Jewish life. They make their decision regarding schooling as but one in a series of important "Jewish life choices" they confront regularly.

We cannot hope to make the day school the normative course of education for children of Conservative Jews, therefore, until we have succeeded in converting a much higher percentage of those only nominally affiliated with our synagogues into active and involved Jews. Where a family is involved in synagogue life and manifests a willingness to try out, if not fully commit themselves to Jewish observances, the rabbi or synagogue educator is often able to convince them to enroll their children in the day school. To complete this task the educator will have to rely on the efforts of the synagogue rabbi.

Careerist Orientation of Parents

A second set of problems relates to the college and career orientation of typical Jewish parents. They are extremely concerned that the elementary and secondary education which their children receive should prepare them for admission to a selective college which, in turn, will lead to a prestigious and remunerative career. This, apparently, is the chief reason

2 Eduardo Rauch, "The Jewish Day School in America: A Critical History and Contemporary Dilemmas", in James C. Carper and Thomas C. Hunt, eds., *Religious Schooling in America* (Birmingham: Religious Education, Press, 1984), pp. 130-165.
3 Michael Zeldin, "Establishing Reform Day Schools: A Revolutionary Move in Perspective", *The Pedagogic Reporter* (November 1987):12-14.

for the sharp decline in enrollment in the upper grades of the Solomon Schechter elementary schools and the difficulty in establishing and maintaining Solomon Schechter high schools.[4]

Even those parents who are committed to day school education are concerned that their children should have that kind of social life, breadth of curricular offerings, and extra-curricular activities which characterize the modern American comprehensive high school. Many parents may not even consider enrolling their child in an elementary day school because of their apprehension that its program does not prepare students for such a high school program.

It is the task of the day school educator (1) to develop and maintain general studies programs and extra-curricular activities in the day school which match the offerings of public schools and prestigious private schools and (2) to mount a vigorous public relations campaign to make the community aware of these aspects of the day school program.

Need to Train Appropriate Teachers

A third problem is the lack of a cadre of Judaic studies teachers who are not only Hebrew-speaking, but are knowledgeable as to the Conservative approach to Judaism and committed to the observance of mitzvot. Today there are approximately 80 Solomon Schechter Day Schools, each needing approximately ten Judaic studies teachers. There is only one institution that can train teachers who are *familiar with the Conservative approach*—The Jewish Theological Seminary of America and its west coast branch, the University of Judaism. As hard as the Seminary tries to recruit students for its day school teacher training programs, offering attractive programs and generous scholarship funding, in any one year the Seminary graduates an average of only 20 students majoring in Jewish education. At least one third of those graduating will go into some other field and another third will, either immediately or soon afterward, be invited to serve as a principal of a Jewish school. This means that the vast majority of Judaic studies teachers upon whom the schools must rely continue to be unqualified to teach in a manner that is informed by the ideas of Conservative Judaism. Many of the teachers currently teaching in Solomon Schechter Day Schools are Israelis who have either immi-

---

4 At the present time, the only Conservative day high schools which continue through twelfth grade in North America are the Solomon Schechter High School in W. Orange, N.J., and the Hyman Brand Hebrew Academy of Greater Kansas City. Two other non-Orthodox day high schools (through grade 12) which have an ideological affinity to the Conservative movement and a large enrollment from families affiliated with the Conservative movement are the Akiba Hebrew Academy in Philadelphia, PA and the Charles E. Smith Jewish Day School in Rockville, MD.

grated to the United States or whose spouses are studying at American universities. Unfortunately, most of them do not fit into any easy definition of a religious Jew. They have brought with them from Israel the secular Israeli approach which enshrines Jewish nationalism as their civil religion. Consequently, knowledgeable as they may be, they cannot exemplify a religious approach to Judaism.

The other large group of Jewish studies teachers in our schools are Orthodox Jews. Like the Israelis, they work in our schools not out of commitment to the basic objectives of the school, but for *parnasah* (to make a living). Even when their attitude towards the beliefs and practices of Conservative Judaism is not antagonistic, their very different religious approach and patterns of personal practice demonstrate to the students that these people do not have a high regard for the Conservative philosophy which undergirds the program of the school. What else is a student to think when, as often happens, such a teacher is contractually obligated to be present at the morning religious service yet does not personally *daven*? Worse yet is the Orthodox fundamentalist approach which is employed by many such teachers when they teach religious subjects, especially Torah.

I have become concerned that many Conservative day schools would begin to employ large numbers of *baalei teshuvah* from the *baal teshuvah yeshivot* in Israel in an attempt to relieve the serious shortage of Judaic studies teachers. I recall visiting a school on the east coast and sitting through a *Mishnah* lesson taught by a *baal teshuvah*. He was a brilliant Yale graduate who, after graduation, had gone to an Israeli institution catering to this population. He was teaching a passage from *Mishnah Shabbat* which was so obscure even to me that I was convinced it could not possibly have had any meaning to the students. Undoubtedly, the principal, relying on what he assumed was the teacher's rich background in Judaic texts, had left the choice of study materials up to him. Thus, there is a problem not only of locating teachers with an appropriate religious orientation for non-Orthodox day schools but also, when hiring teachers, of sacrificing teaching skill and competence for depth of Judaic background. It is clear that unless our teacher shortage is ameliorated from within the Conservative movement, our schools will continue to be forced to invite people to teach who are lacking in Judaic background, limited in pedagogic skills, or have a narrow religious approach.

A final aspect of the personnel problem lies in the fact that many of the schools have not yet accepted the urgency of establishing a salary scale for Judaic studies teachers which will make these positions truly desirable in the eyes of capable young college students and graduates. It is easy enough to call upon the Seminary to produce more teachers as do some lay leaders of the Solomon Schechter Day School Association; but apparently, it is significantly more difficult for these same lay people to commit themselves to raising and allocating the funds which are required to create a day school teaching profession which young people will want to enter. No one will "knock down the doors" of Jewish teacher training institutions unless there exists an attractive profession to draw students. The lack of such a profession, it seems to me, is largely why the Hebrew colleges have dwindled in number and in enrollment.

Lack of Curricular Materials

The final pitfall is the failure of the Conservative movement to develop and disseminate curricular materials which reflect the unique philosophical approaches and emphases of Conservative Judaism. Most Solomon Schechter Day Schools are located in metropolitan areas in which Orthodox day schools by and large have stable, experienced faculties and are well established financially. Surely there is no compelling reason for Conservative parents to enroll children in a Conservative day school which is probably struggling financially and has less experienced teachers if its curriculum closely resembles that of the neighboring Orthodox school. Conservative Jews will not embrace the day school as the normative mode of Jewish education for their children, until the curriculum of Conservative day schools speaks in a distinctive voice, reflective of the philosophy of Conservative Judaism.

At the present time, the extent to which the school's curriculum reflects a Conservative approach (and it varies greatly among the schools) is related not only to the extent to which that institution has a principal and teachers who were trained at the Seminary or the University of Judaism, but also to the extent to which that school can afford to allocate valuable teacher time and funding towards curriculum development. Undoubtedly, there are many skillful teachers working in Solomon Schechter Day Schools who do not contribute what they might to creating distinctly "Conservative classrooms," simply because they have not been given appropriate curricular materials.

The United Synagogue Commission on Jewish Education began work on a curriculum for the Conservative day school in 1975. Only recently has the first part of the curriculum been published. The appearance of this section, relating to the teaching of the *mitzvot*, is certainly an important development, as it represents the first piece of curricular material specifically prepared by the Conservative movement for use in the Solomon Schechter schools. Additional materials will, undoubtedly, be welcomed by teachers and their principals.

Yes, there will still be serious lacunae, not just because curricula in e other subject matter areas (which are both supportive and integral to the teaching of *mitzvot*) are not yet issued, but because even that *mitzvah* material will not be accompanied by the support system necessary to adapt it to each school, teacher and class. Will the Conservative movement be able to provide principals and teachers with the assistance they require to adapt and emend these new materials to meet the needs of each school? The Department of Education of the United Synagogue of America has never had sufficient professional employees dealing solely with the day schools.[5] Establishment of the day school as a normative mode of Jewish education will require the establishment of such a fully-staffed department.

It is clear that the Conservative movement has a significant way to go before it will have created the conditions which are essential to converting the Solomon Schechter Day School from an institution serving a minority of the children in the movement to one which becomes normative for Conservative families. To achieve this will require the following:

1. Synagogue rabbis will have to convince significantly more Conservative Jews of the legitimacy and need for day school education.

2. Schools will have to mount a better public relations program (and school program as well!) to convince upwardly mobile Jewish parents that a day school education will not harm opportunities for higher education and prestigious careers.

3. The availability of trained Conservative teachers will need to be increased by improving the offerings in Conservative teacher training programs and by assuring better salaries and working conditions to potential day school teachers.

4. The Department of Education of the United Synagogue must provide curricular materials designed to meet the unique philosophy and religious needs of the Solomon Schechter Day School, as well as adequate supervision to aid the schools in the use of these materials.

These are some of the challenges and the steps that need to be taken in order to meet them.

---

[5] My own observation, having visited a significant number of schools, is that the movement needs at least *three* full-time consultants to assist with the existing schools, especially with problems of curriculum and personnel.

CREATING A MODEL FOR SYNAGOGUE-DAY SCHOOL COOPERATION

Charles A. Klein

I began this article over 15 years ago at Brandeis University, when Bennett Solomon and I were seniors at Brandeis. He had decided to do graduate work in Jewish education preparing himself for a career in Jewish day schools. I decided to study at the Jewish Theological Seminary of America and to enter the rabbinate. During that year, we spoke of what might be accomplished in a community where the leadership of the day school and synagogue understood the strengths each institution could bring to the other. What we were envisioning in words then uncoined was a programmatic synergism of two institutions with a commonality of goals.

Years went on and Bennett and I continued to talk about the day when we would forge the model relationship between the synagogue and the non-Orthodox Hebrew day school. We never had that opportunity. However, there *are* communities where leaders have sought to actualize that which Bennett and I were only able to speculate about.

In the fall of 1988 I wrote to 50 members of the Rabbinical Assembly serving congregations in communities where there was a non-Orthodox day school. I asked about the nature of their personal relationship, as well as the relationship of their congregation to the community day school. Colleagues were asked to respond to six questions:
1) In what ways do you attempt to link day school students and their families to the ongoing work of your congregation?
2) In what ways does your congregation support the day school in your community?

3) What programs have you developed within your congregation to acknowledge your day school students?
4) Do day school students have a special role in the life of your congregation?
5) What is being done in your congregation to encourage enrollment in a day school?
6) What role do you play in the day school? What should be the rabbinic role in the day school?

Preliminary Impressions

I think of these first impressions from the survey as the beginning of a discussion on a topic critical to the future success of the non-Orthodox day school and synagogue. Without exception, the respondents felt strongly that the day school has a vital role to play in the future of our people. Yet, several colleagues felt compelled to recount with some pain the opposition they faced in either promoting or cooperating with the day school. Some rabbis, who played a significant role in establishing a day school as the preferred educational model in the community, faced opposition from those who believed that their efforts had a negative impact upon the stature of the congregation's Hebrew school. Many had attempted to convince their synagogue leadership that the day school students were the shared treasure of the Jewish community only to face, as one rabbi wrote, "the friction from the *baalei batim* who hear praise of the day school as degradation of our own Talmud Torah."

Another colleague, frustrated over the ongoing disputations within his congregation, said of the synagogue-day school relationship, "It has been only a source of tension between my education committee and me, so much so that when I spoke about Jewish education on Rosh Hashanah I had to spend a few minutes explaining that the day school students should not be seen as a threat to the synagogue. On the contrary, they should be seen as a boon to the synagogue."

This same colleague also faced hostility from those who protested that "the day school students monopolize the service." He went on to say that it became such an issue within his congregation that "I had to prohibit the day school students from taking part in services for several months. I had to tell these students, my own children included, that they could not lead the Shabbat Services until further notice." Nonetheless, and despite powerful political opposition, most responding rabbis hold the position of Rabbi Michael Katz of Long Island, namely that, "getting families to send their children to the day school should be a top priority for rabbis along with Shabbat and Kashrut."

There are, indeed, colleagues who have been able to inspire a congregation and develop a cooperative relationship based on the perception that the day school student is also a significant member of the congregational family. What follows are some examples of what has been done by rabbis on a personal basis and with their congregations institutionally as they have attempted to link these two front line institutions of the Jewish community. We will focus on four major areas of achievements in synagogue-day school cooperation: integration of day school families in the synagogue; congregational financial support for the day school; student recruitment efforts; and the personal roles rabbis can play in their local day school. Finally, I will speculate on some additional areas that need further attention.

Synagogue Integration

There is deep concern on the part of rabbis about finding strategies to integrate the day school student and his or her family into congregational life. Many colleagues have observed in the synagogue-affiliated day school family a pattern of minimal synagogue involvement which does not differ substantially from that of other congregational members. Although many day school students and their parents attend synagogue regularly, there are significant numbers of both students and parents for whom synagogue attendance and synagogue-based programs are not a priority. One colleague responded that, "day school attendance fulfills or takes the place of commitment to synagogue life and observance for some families." Common are the words of a parent reported by one colleague who said, "since my child attends day school he/she learns enough during the week and does not have to attend Shabbat Services."

Therefore, some rabbis and their congregations have developed strategies to bridge the gap separating the day school family and student from congregational life. One popular tradition sets aside one Shabbat a year when day school children lead the Shabbat Services including the reading of the Torah and offering a Dvar Torah. The motivation for this special Shabbat transcends showcasing the day school students. It signifies that the synagogue is the religious home of those students who receive their education in the day school.

Other strategies range from including the day school students in the consecration services of the afternoon Hebrew school students to holding programs which more formally link the two student bodies. Dr. Aaron Landes, rabbi of Beth Sholom Congregation in Elkins Park, Pennsylvania, wrote, "We have developed a very large children's choir of almost 70 voices made up of children from our afternoon religious school and from Solomon Schechter. Through our children's choir and our youth programming, we effectively integrate the day school student within the congregation." Rabbi Landes visits with the students at least once a year and schedules a special luncheon sponsored by the congregation for day school students. His concern and involvement is clear to the students.

At the Bethpage Jewish Community Center on Long Island, day school graduates participate fully in the religious school graduation. The completion of their studies in day school is not a private event. Their accomplishment is acknowledged by their rabbi and their congregation.

Congregation B'nai Israel of St. Petersburg and its rabbi, Jacob Luski, have developed several programs similarly intended to make the synagogue a home for its day school students. The congregation's youth program reaches out to both groups throughout their period of schooling. Two of my colleagues, Rabbi Samuel Kieffer of Congregation Agudat Achim in Schenectady, New York, and Rabbi Elliot Salo Schoenberg of Needham, Massachusetts, have a program which fully integrates the students of the day school with the Hebrew school as they prepare for Bar or Bat Mitzvah. They teach a special Bar/Bat Mitzvah class for all seventh grade students in the congregation. Day school students are required to participate in this class as well, alongside their Hebrew school peers.

The time of Bar or Bat Mitzvah is another opportunity for the rabbi to focus the attention of the congregation on day school education. But more than that, it is an occasion when the well-prepared day school student can become a full participant in the religious life of the synagogue. In one community, during the weeks preceding the Bar or Bat Mitzvah the rabbi joins with the child for a special service held at the day school. The rabbi offers a Dvar Torah at the school during Tefilot. The congregation presents the Bar or Bat Mitzvah with a gift on that occasion, as well as at the Shabbat Service which follows. This rabbi wrote, "The program instituted by my congregation became popular very quickly. When the other day school students saw what my congregation was doing they became somewhat jealous. Envious not of the gift we give, but of the interest my visit and my gift symbolizes."

Financial Support

When it comes to the ongoing need to encourage synagogues to provide some financial assistance for the day school, there are exemplary efforts being made by rabbis and congregations who obviously subscribe to the traditional maxim, "If there is no wheat—there is no Torah." Many congregations include the local day school among the Jewish institutions for which they schedule appeals. There are synagogues which provide direct financial assistance to the day school.

Rabbi Herbert Silberman of Beth El Congregation in Phoenix, Arizona, writes that his congregation houses the Solomon Schechter School, absorbing all utility and maintenance costs. A similar commitment to the day school is found at Congregation B'nai Israel of St. Petersburg with the Pinellas County Jewish Day School. The congregation has hosted the school for eight years. Rabbi Jacob Luski writes, "The synagogue leadership made a commitment eight years ago to do everything possible to allow the Solomon Schechter School to develop, even though the day school is responsible for only a minimal contribution to the congregation."

Beth Sholom Congregation of Elkins Park, Pennsylvania, which hosted the Forman Hebrew Day School for the first thirteen years of its existence, has maintained a substantial level of financial support for the school even after it moved into its own facility. According to Rabbi Aaron Landes, the congregation includes a request for voluntary contributions to the Solomon Schechter Day School in its annual dues statements. One colleague suggested another, albeit more modest, form of assistance which enables a congregation to provide support to the day school. His congregation provides its day school students with a subvention to cover the cost of their textbooks. These congregations and others have made a tangible commitment to Hebrew day school education in their community.

Yet not every congregation has similarly committed itself. In a Jewish community where institutions view themselves as competing for limited charitable dollars, there is a reluctance on the part of congregational leadership to participate in fundraising for the day school. Several colleagues described the opposition they met when confronted by some who were disinclined to place the congregation or its rabbi in the forefront of fundraising for the day school.

Student Recruitment

Almost every rabbi who responded to the survey expressed a strong commitment to encourage day school enrollment. Many used the pulpit and congregational publications to publicize day school programs. Others permitted the school to recruit from within the congregation and, more specifically, among the students of its nursery school program. Rabbis attended informal meetings for the purpose of familiarizing parents with the program of the day school. A small minority of rabbis arranged for individual meetings with parents in the belief that this personal contact could further day school recruitment. One rabbi stated, "One of the most important things I can do as a rabbi for a child in my congregation is try to convince that child's parents to choose the day school. It's a tough decision for them to make. If I can help them make that decision, then I have helped make a Jewish future for that family and that child—something that can be rich with meaning."

Personal Roles

The rabbi's personal role in support of the day school generally goes beyond assistance in fundraising or student recruitment. Most congregations view the rabbi's personal involvement with the day school positively. It is a role they wish their spiritual leader to play within the community. Every rabbi who responded to the survey serves on the governing board of the local day school, on either the educational committee or what is frequently called the rabbinical advisory committee. The rabbinical advisory committee assists the principal both to develop the Judaic studies curriculum and to guide the principal on matters of Jewish law or an overall religious approach in the school. In these areas, rabbis have had a significant influence on day schools. In addition, a number of colleagues serve as teachers of Tanakh and rabbinic literature in their community's day schools thus helping to alleviate the shortage of Judaic studies teachers.

Students of most day schools have grown familiar with the rabbis of their community through their voluntary teaching and special programs arranged by rabbis and school leadership working together. At our local Solomon Schechter Day School, a rabbi joins the students for Tefilot on each Rosh Hodesh, followed by breakfast and a class taught by the visiting rabbi. The success of this program led to similar teaching opportunities for rabbis especially on subjects not normally covered in the curriculum of Jewish studies.

Further Steps

What remains to be accomplished? There are many possibilities. But about a year before his death, Bennett Solomon and I discussed linking the day school and the synagogue in a cooperative effort to address the very important issue of parent education. Together, rabbis and day school educators should create a program within the synagogue integrating both formal and informal educational techniques. This program would teach families to experience the art of Jewish living and an appreciation for Jewish learning. It would find rabbis and day school educators working together to cultivate within the parent body a fuller understanding of the philosophical and theological foundations of the movement which sponsors the day school and to which the congregation and the rabbi are affiliated.

In fact, one of the unique roles that the day school could yet play in the life of the American Jewish community is to become a "greenhouse" in which the religious philosophy of the sponsoring movement can take root in the lives of both the students and their parents. According to Dr. Burton Cohen, the day school has the potential to become a living laboratory wherein the perspectives on law and life of a religious movement come to play a significant role in the daily life of the student body.

There is a clear and pressing need to create an educated laity for whom the religious guidance of the non-Orthodox movement is legitimized and actualized. Few better environments are available wherein children can be instructed in conformity with the ideology and philosophy of a movement. The day school should be the educational setting in which young children are guided along as they grow to become the kind of laity which will give validity to the religious approach of that school, of the movement and its congregations. This common goal alone should stimulate broadened cooperation between the day school, the rabbi and the synagogue. For together we seek to raise a generation of Jews who truly will become the builders of our future.

THE DAY SCHOOL PRINCIPAL AND REFLECTIVE PRACTICE

Alvin Mars

It was a beautiful fall morning in 1972, when I welcomed two young men to my office in an old mansion which served as the administrative headquarters of the Solomon Schechter Day Schools of Philadelphia. I was the headmaster of the school then, and my visitors were my former student and aspiring colleague, Bennett Solomon, and his friend, a young rabbinical student, Joshua Elkin.

I believe that Bennett was still at Brandeis, but he had already made up his mind that he wanted to be a Jewish educator, and that he wanted to run a day school, just as I was doing. I cannot pretend I was not flattered. We all want students and proteges who will follow in our footsteps. But I felt that Bennett was still young, that his career goals could yet take many unanticipated turns, and that his years at Harvard might take him in directions he could not yet imagine.

That meeting has remained with me throughout my career on a conscious level not only because of the engaging personalities of the two then fledgling educators with whom I met, spoke, and, hopefully, influenced; but especially, because of a question Bennett Solomon asked me most innocently. He wanted to know how I could have accepted a position as a day school educator at the Philadelphia Schechter school where my education committee was made up of people like Chaim Potok, Louis Newman, David Mogilner, Burton Caine and Daniel Elazar. "My God," Bennett exclaimed, "they know so much more than you. How can you even consider directing a school and offering it leadership, when there are so many scholars and renowned educators among the lay leaders of the school?"

The question struck at the core of my own feelings of inadequacy. Whether one is dealing with a talented, intelligent laity or any constellation of issues and concerns which face a day school educator on a daily basis, the responsibility of directing a day school is, at the very least, extremely difficult and challenging, and sometimes frustrating and unmanageable. I suspect I shared these feelings of inadequacy with many day school colleagues. I do not remember the exact response I gave Bennett and Joshua, but it was something close to the following: "These people may all know more in one field or another, but I am the only one who feels this endeavor is so important that I am prepared to devote my entire professional existence to it."

The question, however, has never left me. Perhaps this is because the answer I gave so many years ago was too glib (and inadequate). It did not address the deeper epistemological questions about knowledge and knowing which I believe Bennett was really asking about his future profession. What do you need to know to be a day school professional educator, and, in this context, what does knowing mean?

The entire area of training personnel for Jewish education is in a period of redefinition and adjustment. Certainly, the subspecialty of a Jewish day school educator has already emerged as a profession in its own right. That being the case, if we can develop a better understanding of the nature of the professional tasks which face the day school educator, we may begin to comprehend the epistemological questions which are implicit in them. Is there something unique about the knowledge which a day school principal must have? How similar or dissimilar is this knowledge to that of allied professions in the public arena, such as public school principals or private school headmasters? Is it different from the knowledge which a scholar of education or Judaica acquires, and if so, how so? How does being a religious educator impact on what one needs to know to be a day school principal? What are the implications of all this for those concerned with preparing a new generation of day school educators and strengthening those already in the field?

These questions are very broad in scope and worthy of intensive research and thought. I limit my intentions for this essay to setting an agenda for a future professional discourse about these crucial epistemological concerns.

To explore these questions and to frame the issues involved, I will enlist the help of a few guides whose thinking will inform our task of agenda setting. Morris, Crowson, Porter-Gehrie and Hurwitz[1] have outlined the conventional wisdom about the practice of the public school principalship. They have debunked some of that "wisdom" through their own ethnographic research and have shed helpful light on the requisite skills and knowledge required for the elementary and secondary

1 Van Cleve Morris, Robert L. Crowson, Cynthia Porter-Gehrie, Emanuel Hurwitz, Jr., *Principals in Action: The Reality of Managing Schools* (Columbus: Charles E. Merrill Publishing Co., 1984), pp. 13-18.

school principalship. Donald Schon's exploration of the relationship of theory and practice in professional education[2] raises important questions about the nature of professional knowledge which have implications for the field of education in general. Robert O'Gorman's thoughtful article on reflective practice and religious education[3] offers a good bridge to the epistemological concerns that confront Jewish religious educators.

Conventional Wisdom About the Public School Principal

Conventional wisdom about school leadership emerges from a shared understanding of what a principal should be doing along with a set of understandings about the nature of the professional field which has been developed and codified in theory. This theory informs the field and gives it structure.

In their book, *Principals in Action*, Morris, et al, summarize the conventional wisdom of six decades of educational scholarship on the role of the principal.[4] Their composite includes five headings: the principal as 1) instructional leader, 2) decision maker, 3) site manager, 4) mediator, and 5) creator of a learning environment. Each has implications for the question of what a principal needs to know to do the job.

While notions of educational leadership have changed significantly over the years from authoritarian to democratic, the concept of the principal as an instructional leader has held fast. Indeed, it is expected that the majority of a principal's time, as much as three-quarters of the day, should be devoted to enhancing classroom instruction and working on staff development.[5] According to Morris:

> ... conventional wisdom stipulates that building principals should assist each teacher in identifying learning goals, selecting activities, and assessing results. Observations should culminate in an end-of-the-year evaluation conference with each teacher to identify strengths and weaknesses ...[6]

Another descriptor of the building principal is that he should be the prime "... decision maker, problem solver, and agent of change at the school site."[7] As the decision maker and problem solver, the principal must be able to attend to the needs of individuals as well as to the institution's well being.

---

2 Donald A. Schon, *The Reflective Practitioner* (New York: Basic Books, Inc., 1983).
3 Robert T. O'Gorman, "The Search for a Usable Knowledge in Religious Education: Educating Reflective Practitioners," *Religious Education* LXXXIII:3 (Summer, 1988).
4 Morris, et. al., *op. cit.*, pp.13-18.
5 J. Lloyd Trump, *A School for Everyone*. (Reston, VA: National Association of Secondary School Principals, 1977), pp.66-71.
6 Morris, *op. cit.*, p.13.
7 *Ibid.*, p.14.

As a site manager, the principal assumes a burden which may, in fact, be dysfunctional when combined with the responsibilities of instructional leader. As instructional leader the principal attempts to be innovative in order to bring about change. As site manager stability is the watchword. There is an expectation that good management will be maintained "by avoiding conflict and engendering an ordered school environment."[8]

As manager, it is the principal's responsibility to monitor school facilities and finances; maintain a communication system; recruit, engage and assign faculty and support staff; oversee ancillary services, school programs and pupil assignments, student discipline and student activities.[9]

As mediator, the principal is forced to face in many directions at once to deal with the many constituencies involved in the school. The principal is responsible for developing a program of community relations with those interest groups within the neighborhood and greater community which may have an investment in some aspect of the school program.[10]

Finally, it is conventional wisdom that the principal plays an important role as the creator of a learning environment in the school, although this aspect has not received much attention from educational researchers. Administrative decisions, interactions with faculty, incentive systems all create an ethos for learning which flows from the principal. And most important, if any change is to come about in a school which will affect the learning environment, the principal will, indeed, play a significant role. As Sarason has said:

> We begin with the principal because any kind of system change puts him or her in the role of implementing the change in one's school. I have yet to see any proposal for system change that did not assume the presence of a principal in a school. I have yet to see in any of these proposals the slightest recognition of the possibility that the principal ... may not be a good implementor of change.[11]

When, however, one is dealing with a professional field like school administration which is based on the relationship of the professional to many different individuals, groups and changing circumstances, there is a dynamic which cannot be captured by or described within the boundaries of any one theory or even the overlap of more than one. Morris and his colleagues addressed this by using a reality-immersion ethnographic strategy based on the collection of a set of interaction pairings from the observation of twenty-six public school principals in Chicago.

---

8 Arthur Blumberg and William Greenfield, *The Effective Principal: Perspectives on School Leadership* (Boston: Allyn and Bacon, 1980), p. 21.
9 Morris, *op. cit.*, p.16.
10 *Ibid.* p.18.
11 Seymour B. Sarason, *The Culture of the School and the Problem of Change* (Boston: Allyn and Bacon, 1982), p. 140.

The following data are drawn from the study conducted by Morris, et al.[12] Their first instrument measured the variety of principal interactions over the course of a day. In other words, with whom did the school administrator spend her day? Their answer: The elementary principal spent 22% of the day interacting with students (range of 8-35% for all cases), while the statistics for the high school principal were significantly lower—15% in student interactions (range 8-24%). For the elementary principal, interactions with a faculty member filled 18% of the day (range 10-24%) on this. Elementary principals spent 7% of their time with parents (range 2-12%), and secondary principals just 2% of theirs (range 1-5%). Elementary principals interacted with their superintendent 7% of the day (range 1-10%) and secondary principals 5% of the day (range 1-14%).[13]

A second instrument measured who initiated the interchange activity between the principal and the categories of people with whom she interacted, including parents, faculty, and the superintendent. The elementary school principal initiated 70% of all her interactions over the course of a work day (range 51-76%), and the secondary school principal was not significantly behind with 68% of all interactions being principal initiated (range 51-79%).

One last set of statistics measures where the principal spends her time. The elementary principal is in the inner office 48% of the time (range 30-56%), off school grounds 11% of the day (range 0-22%), and in the outer office 8% of the time (range 2-15%). The secondary principal's experience is similar. He is in his inner office 45% of the time (range 28-58%), in his outer office 5% (range 1-10%), and off school grounds 12% of the time (range 0-36%).

The most interesting statistics in this category are that the elementary principal spends 11% of his day in the school corridors (range 4-17%) and only 9% of his work time in the classroom for all kinds of visits (range 3-12%). The secondary principal is in the corridors 9% of the time (range 3-12%), and in the classroom only 7% of the day (range 3-14%). Given these numbers, we may have to revise some of our conventional wisdom about the role of the principal as instructional leader, at least in the public school.

12 Morris, *op. cit.* pp. 31-41.
13 The categories which I have chosen to present at this time are selected from a much longer list of interaction pairings. Students, faculty and parents were obvious categories which relate to day school as well as public school principals. I selected the superintendent as another illustrative category because it most closely approximates the type of interactions which a day school principal might have with his board of directors, rabbi and/or president.

The Private School Principal

Jewish day school principals are private school principals first. They have additional sets of concerns, issues, beliefs and realities which are integrated into the nature of the tasks they must perform, but they do so within the arena of private education. Usually, their schools are independent of rigorous system-wide controls, even when funding comes from communal sources such as local federations or Boards of Jewish Education. The schools operate under the authority of their own boards of directors and education committees, or their governance is part of a synagogue body which delegates authority to a standing committee tied directly to the congregation. In either case, the scope of responsibility and authority delegated to the day school principal is more or less similar to that of colleagues in most private schools and is consequently much broader than that of the public school principal.

The private school principal has an opportunity to run his own show with few of the bureaucratic constraints which face his public colleagues. In fact, each independent school is actually a small, self-contained school system unto itself, with its principal or headmaster serving as the system head as well as the school director. Hence, the private school educator has a whole range of tasks to perform and decisions to make in addition to the normative tasks and roles spelled out for the public school building principal by professional conventions and research. This, then, changes the nature of the day school principalship as a profession and the knowledge and skills one must have to practice it in the private sector.

It would be informative to attempt to derive a new conventional wisdom about some of the special roles of the private school/day school principal which distinguishes her from her public school counterparts.

A first dimension would be *institutional leadership*. The private school head works directly with the board and its leadership and is involved and concerned with matters of institutional governance. The principal, not the superintendent, is the top professional in the institution and represents the school to the community. He is usually the prime spokesman for the school.

Budget and financial planning become responsibilities of more significance for the private school administrator than the public school principal. In the private school, the principal assumes a more central role in policy planning for the financial well-being of his institution. He has more latitude in budgetary decisions and more responsibility for income production.

Marketing management is another task expected of the private school head, not required of his public school counterpart. Without sufficient students there will not be a viable school, and it is the ultimate responsibility of the private school principal to direct successful programs of recruitment and retention.

Finally, the educational leader of an independent school is expected to be closely involved in *curriculum development*. Since there is usually no prescribed curriculum required by a central authority for a private institution, curriculum construction becomes an immediate, challenging and demanding task.

All of these tasks, of course, take time and add new sets of interactional pairings, and change the weighting of the ones typical for the public school principal. Were the interactions of the private school principal measured, one can only wonder about how different they might be from the public school principal's, all the more so for the day school principal.

We have heard from many sources that principals spend little time in classrooms. In the public school, one gets a picture of a principal who is on the move through the halls of his school and, thereby keeps track of the pulse of the school. Would a private school principal, with more global responsibilities for the operation of a micro-system, have the same opportunity to stay in day-to-day contact with the "corridor culture"?

To this point, conventional wisdom and ethnographic research have helped us examine some of the components of the principalship. It is a complex profession, even without the issues presented to the day school practitioner of Jewish religious education and Jewish communal reality.

The Reflective Practitioner

In Donald Schon's two books, *The Reflective Practitioner: How Professionals Think in Action* and *Educating the Reflective Practitioner: Toward a New Design for Teaching and Learning in the Professions*, he has offered new insights on educational administration, with a particular emphasis on the nature of the professions and of professional training. Most important, he has reintroduced and validated the concept of professional practice as art. In his own words:

> If it is true that there is an irreducible element of art in professional practice, it is also true that gifted engineers teachers, scientists, architects, and managers sometimes display artistry in the day-to-day practice. If the art is not invariant, known, and teachable, it appears nonetheless, at least for some individuals, to be learnable.[14]

Schon has become convinced that universities "are institutions committed, for the most part, to a *particular* epistemology, a view of knowledge that fosters selective inattention to practical competence and professional artistry."[15] He has called for an epistemology of practice

---

14 Schon, *op. cit.*, p.18.
15 *Ibid.*, p. vii.

which will attempt to define the intellectual rigor of professional practice.[16]

According to Schon, the dominant epistemology of practice is based on a model in which theory is more basic, more important than, and takes precedence over skill in the training curriculum. He calls this technical rationality. In this model, the work of the professional is reduced to "instrumental problem solving made rigorous by the application of scientific theory and technique."[17] When there is a problem there is also a clear definition of a desired end result, and theory can be applied to resolve a problem. For example,

> A conflict of ends cannot be resolved by the use of techniques derived from applied research. It is rather through the non-technical process of framing the problematic situation that we may organize and clarify both the ends to be achieved and the possible means of achieving them.[18]

While basic and applied sciences and academic research in general require convergent thinking to bring ideas together, *practice is divergent*. To be a practitioner one must be a divergent thinker.[19] And, according to Schon: "there is nothing strange about the idea that a kind of knowing is inherent in intelligent action."[20]

Schon believes that the everyday life of the professional depends on a tacit knowing-in-action. He must make many delicate decisions and judgments of quality which he senses are correct but for which he cannot state adequate criteria. He has pointed out that "writers on the epistemology of practice have been struck by the fact that skillful action often reveals a 'knowing more than we can say'".[21]

How many of us have made sensitive, delicate decisions affecting a student, class, teacher or administrative issue which we knew were correct, but for which we could not articulate the reasons or even the principles? As Schon has said: "Although we sometimes think before acting, it is also true that in much of the spontaneous behavior of skillful practice we reveal a kind of knowing which does not stem from a prior intellectual operation."[22] "It is this entire process of reflection-in-action," Schon states, "which is central to the 'art' by which practitioners sometimes deal well with situations of uncertainty, instability, uniqueness, and value conflict."[23]

---

16 *Ibid.*, p. viii.
17 *Ibid.*, p.17.
18 *Ibid.*, p.41.
19 *Ibid.*, pp.45–46.
20 *Ibid.*, p. 50.
21 *Ibid.*, p. 51.
22 *Ibid.*
23 *Ibid.*, p. 50.

We can all think of examples of what Schon has referred to as reflecting-in-action. He cites the example of a baseball pitcher finding his groove. How many of us have made on-the-spot adjustments while teaching a lesson or counseling a student. Consequently, it is easy enough for us to understand that "reflection tends to focus interactively on the outcomes of action, the action itself, and the intuitive knowing implicit in the action."[24]

"Reflection-in-practice ... is central to the art through which practitioners sometimes cope with the troublesome 'divergent' situations of practice."[25] Through reflection, the practitioner can criticize what she "knows" through repeated experience of practice. She is able to create a new frame of reference through which she may approach a problem. The practitioner can use reflection to make more sense of the unknown and unique, for problem setting rather than just problem solving. It becomes a matter of finding what Schon calls a "frame experiment," a new way of looking at the problem, to impose on the situation.[26]

The Reflective Practitioner and the Educational Bureaucracy

Organizations are "dynamically conservative." That is, they have a need to adapt to change, but they also place a premium on constancy and predictability. Principals must rely on the predictability of the behavior of their teachers in order to be free to manage the bureaucracy of their schools.

According to Schon, in an educational bureaucracy, a teacher who thinks and acts as a reflective practitioner and not as a technical expert "poses a potential threat to the dynamically conservative system in which she lives" by virtue of her reflection-in-action.[27] If such is the case for one teacher within a school, the implications of a principal's reflective practice of her profession have even more dramatic implications for the homeostasis of a school organization.

However, for the creative dynamic of reflective teaching to be present in a school without being the source of constant conflict and crisis, there must be an educational leader at the helm of the institution who practices reflectively herself. It is not just a matter of modeling or tone setting. It opens up the school environment to self criticism and fosters divergent thinking. It accepts that the creative contribution of all who reflect-in-action is a legitimate part of the professional dialogue which goes on within the school. In Schon's own words:

24 *Ibid.*, p. 56.
25 *Ibid.*, p. 62.
26 *Ibid.*
27 *Ibid.*, p. 332.

In a school supportive of reflective teaching, teachers would challenge the prevailing knowledge structure. Their on-the-spot experiments would affect not only the routines of teaching practice but the central values and principles of the institution. Conflicts and dilemmas would surface and move to center stage. In the organizational learning system with which we are most familiar, conflicts and dilemmas tend to be suppressed or result in polarization and political warfare. An institution congenial to reflective practice would require a learning system within which individuals could surface conflicts and dilemmas and subject them to productive public inquiry, a learning system conducive to the continual criticism and restructuring of organizational principles and values.[28]

This is a tall order for a principal to fill. But where could there possibly be a more fertile school environment for reflection-in-practice than within a relatively small, private day school setting?

The Day School Principal and Reflective Practice

Day school principals face unique issues regarding reflective practice. Unlike their public school colleagues, they do not work within the setting of a large bureaucratic organization, yet they do work within the structure of a religious tradition. He is more free to apply his own thinking-in-action, encourage the same within his faculty, and risk outcomes, than he would be in a more rigid bureaucracy. He also works within a religious tradition which values the uniqueness and contribution of the individual, calls for continuous *heshbon hanefesh* (self reflection and accounting), and is based on conflict resolution through reflective application of sacred texts, religious values and principles, and common experience.

It is the role of the reflective Jewish educator to know-this-tradition-in-action, to make it a part of his repertoire, as he would the other fields of thought which are applicable to his practice. He need not be a scholar of Judaica, just as he need not be a scholar of education or one of the allied social sciences. His profession is neither dependent solely upon their knowledge nor derived solely from their theories.

Robert T. O'Gorman interprets Schon with regard to religious education noting:

Educators learn to be effective not primarily through the study of theological research and educational skills but through long and varied practice in the analysis of educational problems, which build up a generic, essentially unanalyzable capacity for dealing with problems ... He or she has to become disabused of the self-image of

---

28 *Ibid.*, pp. 335-336.

being the expert to the lay person. If this view ... is not changed, the educator will not be free to reflect in action but will have to hide behind the "solid knowledge" that comes from the research theologians.[29]

But, to be an effective, reflective Jewish educational practitioner, to be able to be a problem setter and not just a problem solver, to be one who can artfully respond to the exigencies of the moment, the day school educator must have a rich background which is acquired in conjunction with the dynamic of action and practice.

On Becoming A Reflective Educator

There are day school educators today who have successfully prepared themselves for the profession and for reflective practice by seeking out internships and guided practical experiences which professional education programs still provide only minimally. This, in my opinion, is a result of serious gaps in the Jewish educational training establishment on our continent.

An august profession of day school educator has emerged because of the interplay of a series of sociological, educational and religious needs and forces. Yet, there are still only a few training programs specifically designed to meet the needs of the field by offering professional training which focuses on the acquisition of the "art" of professional day school leadership.

We must begin to ask ourselves the most basic questions about what one needs to know to be a day school educator and how one can acquire that knowledge. Obviously, it is not just a matter of studying Judaica in conjunction with a general education degree. What then does the thoughtful and reflective practice of the profession require? It requires graduate programs which incorporate significant components of coaching and mentoring to foster the development of a reflective day school practitioner. If knowing-in-action can only emerge from a significant practicum, are future day school educators to acquire this type of knowledge by happenstance or by curricular plan?

In Bennett Solomon we had one important model of a reflective practitioner. His ability to think simultaneously about curriculum, nurture a faculty, manage a budget, strengthen a board and construct a school facility, and to do it all in an intelligent and humane way, is a paradigm for us of a day school principal who was a reflective practitioner.

How he actually trained himself to become a reflective day school head cannot be adequately recounted through a simple review of his academic and professional experiences. Bennett's resume would not capture the essence of his personal and professional maturation and

29 O'Gorman, *op. cit.*, p. 334.

development. Only he could have provided us with some insight into the internal path he pursued.

True, some of that "essence" is now gone forever. But we can begin to construct a path or program for others that might lead to a better training process for Jewish day school principals. As a first step, we need research which will provide us with the same thick description of the tasks and complexities of the profession of day school principaling that we already have for the public school principal.

There is much interest nowadays in the training of senior personnel for the field of Jewish education. Among the most senior of the positions in the field, in my opinion, is the day school principal. Through the artful practice of this profession, the dynamism of our people can be maintained, and the knowing-in-theory which, I believe, could be deadly for a living religious tradition can be transformed into a knowing-in-action. This is the power of reflective practice, and this is the depth of the perceptive question Bennett Solomon asked me so many years ago.

This essay was delivered as the Bennett Solomon Memorial Lecture and keynote address at the Solomon Schechter Day School Conference at the Jewish Theological Seminary of America on December 11, 1988. This essay is dedicated to the memory of my dear friend, student and colleague, Dr. Bennett Solomon. He made me more proud to be a Jewish educator.

FROM BENNETT

ON EFFECTIVE PRINCIPALS

A related major topic of recent research within general education has been "Effective Schools" ...

Most of the emphasis of this literature has focused upon the role of the principal as the school's instructional leader. The effective principal is recognized as the key educator in the building, setting the agenda for instruction and creating high expectations of student and teacher accomplishments. Instructional leadership is broadly interpreted as those actions that a principal takes or delegates to others to promote growth in student learning.

But as Theodore Sizer has noted, while "it is hard for teachers to carry a school with a weak principal, a strong principal doesn't make a good school." Wynn DeBevoise, in "Synthesis of Research on the Principal as Instructional Leader"[1] notes further that there is agreement about the functions of effective instructional leadership. These include: communicating a vision of the school's purpose and standards; monitoring student and teacher performance; recognizing and regarding good work; and providing effective staff development programs. However, it is noted that the principal alone need not perform all these tasks ...

This important caveat to the effective school literature is crucial for understanding the ingredients of successful school improvement. It is rare to find a principal who has the ability to accomplish all of these objectives, especially within a Jewish school setting. Effective delegation of these responsibilities is a crucial task of the effective principal. There are also many intangibles concerning the principal's personality, which are difficult to identify when speaking of successful leadership. To simply apply the specifics above to an educational context without consideration of the personalities involved will be a poor implementation of the research findings.

Curriculum Innovation, pp. 9–11.

---

[1] Wynn DeBevoise, "Synthesis of Research on the Principal as Instructional Leader," *Educational Leadership* XL:5 (February, 1984) pp.17ff.

LAY-PROFESSIONAL RELATIONS IN THE JEWISH DAY SCHOOL

Joshua Elkin

A recently completed study of Jewish educators revealed that relations with lay leaders are one of the major sources of frustration and job dissatisfaction for senior personnel in Jewish education.[1] This finding comes as no surprise to those familiar with Jewish educational settings. Ongoing lay-professional interaction is indispensable to the effective functioning of these institutions. When these working relationships are progressing smoothly, a calm, productive atmosphere prevails. When there is evidence of friction or disharmony, however, the entire institution and all the individuals associated with it suffer.

These remarks are particularly germane to the non-Orthodox day school world. Many of these day schools have experienced remarkable growth during the last two decades. Such extensive expansion necessitates active lay-professional collaboration; furthermore, such a continuing, successful collaboration is vital to the future organizational and educational health of these institutions.

This paper represents a contribution toward improved lay-professional relations in day schools. After reviewing the place of lay-professional relations within the Jewish educational world, we will make the case for the vital importance of placing such relations squarely in the center of the day school community's agenda. We will then provide some concrete suggestions for how one goes about giving lay-professional relationships their deserved attention. Finally, we will furnish some specific proposals for consideration, followed by a selected bibliography.

1 Steven M. Cohen and Susan Wall, "Recruiting and Retaining Senior Personnel in Jewish Education: A Focus Group Study in North America" (Jerusalem, Israel: The Jewish Education Committee of the Jewish Agency, October, 1987).

Current State of Affairs

Generally speaking, we can say that the working relationships between lay and professional leaders in day schools and, for that matter, in all of Jewish education, have attracted relatively little attention. For the most part, professionals meet their lay counterparts within a context marked by a severe lack of reflection. When a productive working relationship does seem to exist, energy rarely exists to think systematically about the components contributing to that positive collaboration. Few, if any, case records exist which document successful working relationships such that someone could analyze them in the future and derive some useful guidelines for others. If, on the other hand, a day school is experiencing "difficulties" on the lay-professional front, many of the parties involved are quick to ascribe blame to others for the trouble.

Professionals sometimes characterize their volunteer leaders as meddling, or lacking an understanding of the limits of their involvement in the day-to-day operations of the school. Lay leaders have, on the other hand, occasionally bristled in the face of a rhetorical, judgmental model of leadership, which some Jewish educators practice.[2] Such a stance on the part of the professional does little to inspire a sense of partnership and mutual respect.

In contrast to Jewish education, the world of Jewish communal service has paid considerably greater attention to the vital lay-professional link in its many agencies, organizations, and institutions. Though of interest, speculating on the reasons for this pronounced difference is beyond the scope of this paper.

The Importance of Lay-Professional Relations for the Day School Community

The research on senior personnel in Jewish education provides us with one compelling set of reasons for giving lay-professional relations a more prominent position in our thinking and discourse. An area that is the source of such substantial job dissatisfaction can certainly serve as a key catalyst in propelling talented professionals to leave their current positions, or, even more disturbing, to leave the field of Jewish education altogether. Given the current state of affairs in the day school and Jewish educational world as a whole, we cannot afford to remain passive. The shortage of qualified administrative personnel is well-documented.[3] To

---

[2] Samuel Schafler, "Voluntary and Professional Leadership: Partners for More Effective Jewish Education," *Journal of Jewish Communal Service,* LXIV:2 (Winter, 1987), pp. 137–140.

[3] Jacob B. Ukeles, "Senior Educator: A Career Option for Jewish Studies Students." (Jerusalem: The Jewish Education Committee of the Jewish Agency, 1987).

lose competent Jewish educators because of weak skills and training in forging the lay-professional bond is simply not acceptable.

Agencies have expanded to become large, complex organizations with diverse functions, many levels and types of staff, and large operating budgets. The composition of boards of directors has been modified to reflect the changing profile of the leadership of the American Jewish community. Today's boards are dominated by the third and fourth generation American Jews, many of whom are well-educated professionals and managers. This is in contrast to the earlier era's first and second generation board members who typically were merchants or businessmen.

It would seem that a strong case could be made that the more sophisticated educational and vocational background of the new board members would be an asset in view of the managerial challenges posed by the growth of the Jewish social agencies.[4]

While these observations are based primarily on the world of agencies not involved in delivering Jewish education, their value for the day school community cannot be overestimated. The expansion of non-Orthodox day schools during the last two decades has been remarkable.[5] The operating complexities and costs have become astonishing, when compared to the 1960's or even the 1970's. The day school world needs sophisticated lay leadership if it is to continue to flourish over time. Without professionals who are attuned to this need and to the strategies for creating and sustaining successful lay-professional collaboration, the recruitment and retention of top-quality board members will be significantly hampered, if not rendered altogether impossible.

Finally, we must note the trends emerging within the organized Jewish community as a whole where Jewish education is at the top of the agenda. The worlds of the federations and Jewish Centers are buzzing with interest and activity focusing on Jewish education. Such a favorable climate is unlikely to reappear for some time to come. Given the widespread recognition that successful day schools are among the most powerful vehicles for transmitting Jewish knowledge and identity, we must capitalize to the fullest extent on the current positive climate. High-calibre lay leaders are more likely than ever before to be enticed into Jewish education, and we must be prepared to receive and involve them effectively. With the energies of the lay and professional leadership working synergistically, the day school can achieve new heights in the short run, and ensure for itself strength and continuity for decades to come.

---

4 Bernard Reisman, "An Alternative Scenario for Tzedakah," *Sh'ma* 16/304 (December 27, 1985), p. 28.
5 Alvin Schiff, *The Jewish Day School in America* (New York: Jewish Education Committee Press, 1966).

Lay-Professional Collaboration: Some Manageable Strategies For Private Schools

Of particular note is the experience of the private school world. Though there are differences between the Jewish day school and the many more established and prestigious private schools in North America, the similarities in their governing structures and in the challenges of forging effective board-head relations are quite pronounced. The cumulative experiences of the many independent schools convey the kind of thoughtfulness and guidance which is so critically needed in the Jewish day schools. In the most recent edition of the *Trustee Handbook* which presents for lay leaders "generally accepted principles of sound practice for the governance and administration of independent schools," the school head is urged to be

> equally concerned with the responsibilities ... for the educational leadership and management of the school and with the quality of the working relationship between the board and head, upon which the success of the school depends.
>
> The key importance of this relationship—ideally, a partnership of mutual endeavor and trust—has been the central theme of the *Trustee Handbook* since it was first published in 1964. It deserves even greater emphasis in today's climate ...[6]

One of the most useful insights that emerges both from the independent school literature, as well as from the literature on school change, is the importance of the individual school as the locus for change. We cannot hope to have any meaningful impact on lay-professional relations on a macro level without a solid foundation of hard work, discussion, and reflection within each school.

The Key Relationship: The Bond between the Lay Head and the Professional Head

The relationship between the lay head and the professional head of the individual school is the key to building a stronger sense of lay-professional collaboration within the institution. Of critical importance is the need to set regular face-to-face meeting time on at least a once-a-month basis. Such a meeting can cover a wide range of topics, including, but not limited to: establishing and monitoring goals for a given year; setting

---

6 Eric W. Johnson, *Trustee Handbook* (Boston: National Association of Independent Schools, 1984), p. vii.

the agendas for executive committee and board meetings; creating mechanisms for performance evaluation of both the professional and of the board as a governing entity; taking stock of the operative division of responsibility between the lay and the professional leadership; and providing adequate orientation to the board at the start of a school year and on an ongoing basis. This fundamental relationship should be characterized by mutual respect and trust; however, the friendship pitfall must be avoided. An honest and candid sharing of perspectives is in the best interests of the day school. Howard B. Rosenblatt, a day school head, has described the relationship as rigorous, but not adversarial.

We will now explore a number of areas in greater detail in an effort to understand the critical nature of the collaboration between the lay and professional heads.

Setting Goals and Agendas

The lay and professional heads of a day school need time together to exchange opinions concerning the overall performance and direction of the school. A useful strategy to build a collaborative vision for a given academic year is to target the summer for a marathon meeting of the lay and professional heads to review the previous year and to target specific goals for the new year, including a tentative outline of proposed agenda items for the full board and for its committees.[7] As this shared vision for the year gets communicated to the full lay leadership and professional staff, changes can be made to respond to other perspectives, as well as to the realities of the given school year as it unfolds. Ultimately, the process of developing and refining the school's goals and agendas should become an ongoing task. By regularly tracking the progress made in each area of priority, the school's leadership ensures efficient performance and honest accountability to all constituencies. Such ongoing reflection and dialogue between lay and professional is a mark of a dynamic and healthy Jewish day school.

Evaluating the Professional and the Board

In order for the lay-professional bond to mature, this reflection must extend to individual performance evaluation as well. Day school professionals devote a great deal of time to the task of staff development and evaluation; however, rare is the institution that takes time to review the performance of the principal, the board chair, and the board as a whole. The two leaders of a day school would do well to make this topic a

---

7 The author is indebted to Bernard Pucker, President of the Solomon Schechter Day School of Greater Boston from 1978-1980, for first introducing him to this annual strategy.

centerpiece of their collaborative work. In most cases, it falls to the professional to provide the necessary initiative and inspiration to tackle these sensitive, yet critical areas of evaluation.[8]

The most important guideline for such evaluation is that it be regular; waiting for a crisis or a communications breakdown is the worst strategy to adopt in approaching performance reviews. The professional should insist on an agreed-upon mechanism for annual feedback on his/her performance. One valuable framework for evaluation can emerge organically during the scheduled meetings of the lay head and professional head. Out of that relationship can grow an acceptable format to ensure wider feedback.

A challenge for professional leaders of day schools is to instill within the lay head and the board as a whole the value of periodically taking stock of their own performance as lay leaders. The pressure to address an urgent issue facing a school somehow always manages to take precedence over a seemingly leisurely evaluation; however, such introspection by a board may indeed be the most urgent item for the group to consider.

Assessments can assume a variety of shapes and formats; the key is to tailor it to the realities of the particular day school. The publication, *Evaluating the Performance of Trustees and School Heads*, contains a host of forms and strategies that have worked for specific independent schools.[9] They are worthy of serious consideration as potentially useful starting points. The catalyst to progress in this area must be the principal who should provide the required leadership and inspiration to think through a board performance review in a manner suitable to the vision of the specific school.

Division of Responsibilities: Policy Development and Implementation

One of the most sensitive areas associated with lay-professional relations in day schools is the division of responsibility for aspects of the school's functioning. The commonly-held understanding is that lay boards are in charge of setting policy, while the principal and his/her administrative staff have the job of implementing the policies. (Once again, the key setting for monitoring these roles is the regular meeting between the lay and professional head.) This seemingly neat delineation of roles masks,

---

8   A convincing presentation of the professional as catalyst and inspirer can be found in Gerald Bubis and Jack Dauber, "The Delicate Balance—Board-Staff Relations," *Journal of Jewish Communal Service* LXIII:4 (Summer 1987), p. 189. See also *Trustee Handbook*, p. 46.
9   Eric W. Johnson, *Evaluating the Performance of Trustees and School Heads* (Boston: National Association of Independent Schools, 1986), pp. 39-69.

however, the complexities which lie underneath, for the day school director should be positioned not only to implement policies, but also to make policy recommendations to the board, as well as to educate the lay leadership with what is needed for sound policy decision-making. Achieving and nurturing this delicate partnership requires some thoughtful use of proper channels.

> We have stated that the board makes policy, but we have also stated that heads should be leaders. In that role, it is their responsibility to propose policies, but through proper channels. Experience has shown that the proper avenue of approach to the board with new policies is through the appropriate committee of the board ... By taking this approach, the head immediately acquires several informed trustees who understand the problem and who can help support the plan, perhaps with revisions jointly arrived at. If the committee turns down the proposal, the head probably will not bring the matter to the board.[10]

Orienting the Board

Finally, if they aspire to foster authentic involvement by the full board, the lay and professional heads must allocate time to think through two vital tasks: educating the entire board to the issues and challenges to be tackled in a given year, and orienting the new board members to the overall workings of the school and to its history. A well-informed board is more able to engage in the necessary policy development, and the school becomes the direct beneficiary of sound policy decision-making.

The complexity of the Jewish day school, with its dual curriculum and the accompanying unique features, makes board orientation all the more essential. Once again, the full agendas of many day school board meetings pose an obstacle to finding the required time to do any in-depth orientation. The school principal and the president or board chair must seek out the appropriate settings to ensure adequate opportunities. Some schools have used a special Sunday "marathon" meeting at the start of the year, while others have adopted the tradition of an annual board retreat.

In addition to an orientation time, some schools have found it valuable to produce a policy handbook for all board members—a book which is constantly updated to reflect the emerging realities of the school. Schools have also seen fit to establish a board-level committee to deal exclusively with board education.[11] When the lay head and the professional head decide on such a committee, they are making an important

---

10 *Trustee Handbook, op. cit.,* p. 47.
11 The Charles E. Smith Jewish Day School in the Greater Washington, D.C. area is one example of a day school with both a loose-leaf policy notebook and a board education committee.

statement to the entire board, as well as ensuring that the priority of keeping the board properly informed does not get lost in the crunch of immediate issues.

Inter-School Sharing and Learning

Though the individual school is unquestionably the central arena for forging the lay-professional bond, there is great value in collegial support and inter-school sharing. Day school directors must be able to talk openly with professional peers from other schools about the workings and challenges of lay-professional work. This topic should be a standard agenda item at professional conferences, and individuals should encourage each other to speak and share candidly in the interest of seeking guidance and documenting what works. These sharings could form the basis of badly-needed case study materials.

Creating networks among board members from different day schools is an equally important goal. While the non-Jewish independent school world has been fostering trustee-to-trustee dialogue across schools for decades, the Jewish day school world is still groping for direction on this issue. The various organizational structures that connect day schools are the most likely umbrellas under which such a dialogue could be fostered.[12] Workshops for board members from a variety of schools help to place individual school problems in perspective. Younger day schools can learn from the experiences of more mature institutions. The successful policy deliberations of one school can be shared with others, thereby encouraging the circulation of good ideas and improving the overall health of many day schools at the same time.

We must stress, however, that the day school professionals once again need to assume the role of catalyst in bringing about not only their own network, but also the network of lay leaders. By making the lay-professional bond a fundamental priority, the professionals can energize themselves and their lay counterparts to speak regularly on the intricacies of creating and sustaining successful collaboration.

Proposals for the Future

We have pointed to a few attainable steps that could help to overcome the lack of attention to a vital aspect of day school functioning. To achieve more permanent improvement, however, the Jewish day school community will need to rally collectively behind a number of concrete

---

[12] The Reform, Conservative, Torah U'Mesorah and Community day school networks already have annually scheduled times for convening the professional leaders from member schools. Some of those also include opportunities for lay leaders to meet.

proposals for the future. The following three ideas are meant to serve as examples of the necessary efforts that might be attempted.

1. **Training programs for the school heads**—Built into the few such programs that exist, there must be at least one solid module on the lay-professional bond. To do this effectively will require the commissioning of case study literature which can serve as the raw material for the training sessions themselves. Supervised internships, which include an opportunity for lay committee work, should also be a component of such a training program.[13]

2. **Lay leadership recruitment and development**—The high priority being accorded to Jewish education makes this an opportune time to embark on systematic and long-term programs to ensure quality lay leadership for the future. Though there is a definite place for a national lay constituency, such as found within JESNA, the emphasis must still be on the single institution. Schools should be sharing with each other current efforts to recruit and nurture new lay leadership, and together they should be seeking more effective strategies. The experiences of many federations in leadership development can serve as models for the kind of structures that need to be put in place. A school's nominating committee, working together with a coordinator of human resources and the school head (who collectively pool their familiarity with the parent body and the community-at-large), could develop over time the outlines of a full-blown program to identify, tap, try out, and ultimately involve quality lay leadership for the future. One independent school head has noted that his nominating committee works twelve months of the year in an effort to make sure that the very best talent and minds are harnessed in the service of the day school's mission and operation. This endeavor requires a great deal of hard work and honesty.[14]

3. **A network of the Jewish communal agency world**—Most, if not all, day schools are located in metropolitan areas where other Jewish communal agencies exist. Regular communication among professionals and among lay heads can serve to bring those involved in Jewish education into close contact with the successes and failures in other Jewish agencies. The agency world has benefitted at least from more systematic reflection and from the supervision received by professionals in their training for Jewish communal work.

---

13 A useful training resource, already commercially available, is Gerald Bubis, *Building for the Nineties: New Dimensions in Lay-Staff Relations* (Los Angeles: Hebrew Union College, 1985).
14 Robert Hurlbut, Headmaster of the Park School, Brookline, MA, unpublished paper.

Conclusion

The reader will recognize that we have resisted the temptation to present a recipe for successful lay-professional collaboration. No two settings are the same, and in many instances, there probably exist more than one potentially successful course of action. The Jewish day school world in particular is highly diverse in both ideology and organizational structure. Our focus has been instead on making a strong appeal to the entire day school community to take this vital area of functioning much more seriously and to engage in regular reflection about its workings. More visibility and discussions of the lay-professional bond will go a long way toward improving these relations, thereby enhancing the functioning of individual schools.

In concluding, however, we feel that some pointers for avoiding friction may be in order, with one proviso that each reader views this advice through his/her personal and individual school lenses.

- From the professional's point of view, it is vital to avoid dropping surprises at board meetings; a regular flow of information in a candid manner keeps the laity up-to-date and engaged in the dilemmas and challenges confronting the school.
- The principal must prepare well for all board and committee meetings, and must be ready to provide details on the specifics of policy implementation. The board has the right and the obligation to know what is going on if it is to be in a position to be supportive and to fulfill the duties of institutional trusteeship. The withholding of unpleasant information or the whitewashing of difficulties will only undermine the sense of collaboration and ultimately damage the school.
- Finally, the principal needs to be receptive to advice and attentive to the climate of public opinion within the school's constituencies.[15]

From the point of view of the lay leadership, each board member must be able to examine issues with some detachment and objectivity. Some sensitive issues require the keeping of confidences. When a board member becomes aware of a potential problem, the best course of action is to bring the matter to the immediate attention of either the school's principal or the chairperson of the appropriate committee, and not to the board as a whole. Finally, each board member needs to recognize that no individual lay leader has the authority to give orders or directions to any member of the professional staff. Such authority rests only with the principal or board as a whole.[16]

The Jewish day school world has witnessed unprecedented expansion during the last two decades. In order to realize its full potential in

15 *Trustee Handbook, op. cit.*, pp. 27, 52, 54.
16 *Ibid.*, pp. 24, 46–47.

the years ahead, the school-based collaboration between lay and professional leadership must improve. Our Jewish educational institutions belong to the lay community. The professionals must rise to the task of inspiring a dedicated laity to confront the challenges facing the Jewish day school in the years ahead: rising tuitions, inadequate facilities, faculty salaries, shortages of qualified personnel, long-range planning and vision, as well as ongoing curricular decisions. It behooves each day school to develop an "individual tradition" of lay-professional partnership that works, and to take the necessary steps to ensure its continuity and refinement over time.[17]

For Further Reading

This listing includes some additional thoughtful pieces on lay-professional collaboration which have emerged in recent years from within the Jewish communal agency orbit.

Berenbaum, Michael, "Effectiveness and Professional Responsibilities." *Sh'ma* 18/346 (Jan. 22, 1988), pp. 41-42.

Brownstein, Solomon M., "Tzedakah Confronts the Corporate Mind." *Sh'ma* 16/304 (Dec. 27, 1985), p. 25-27.

Ellenoff, Theodore. "The Excellence Good Lay Leaders Prompt." *Sh'ma* 18/346 (Jan. 22, 1988), p. 43.

Frost, Shimon, "JESNA: The Catalyst for Lay Leadership in Jewish Education." *Pedagogic Reporter.* p. 10.

Huberman, Steven. "Making Jewish Leaders." *JJCS* 64:1(Fall, 1987), pp. 32-41.

Kahn, William, "On Working with the Agency Board: A Sometimes Neglected Skill." *Journal of Jewish Communal Service.* 54:3 (Summer 1978) pp. 309-313.

Menitoff, Paul. "Diverse Expectations in Congregational-Rabbinic Relations." *Journal of Reform Judaism.* (Fall 1987), pp. 1-7.

Paul, Joel H. "Strong Staff Needs Engaged Volunteer." *Sh'ma* 18/346 (Jan. 22, 1988).

Solander, Sanford. "We Need Partnership Not Dominance." *Sh'ma* (Jan. 22, 1988), 18/346 pp. 45-47.

Sorin, Samuel I. "Our Agencies, Then, Now and Tomorrow." *Sh'ma* 16/304 (Dec. 27, 1985), pp. 29-31.

Wolf, Larry M. "Observations on Lay-Professional Relationships." *Pedagogic Reporter* pp. 15-16.

---

17 The notion of an individual school tradition came from a personal communication with Dr. Robert Abramson, now Director of the Department of Education of the United Synagogue of Conservative Judaism.

THE LEADER OF THE TEAM

Walter Ackerman

Bennett and I first met when we worked together at Camp Ramah in Canada in the early 1970's. Our contact had actually begun months before in correspondence around plans for the summer. I remember even now the imagination and enthusiasm of his ideas. The two months we spent together were the beginning of a conversation which, despite geography, went on uninterruptedly for some ten years. Even after a year or more of not seeing one another, we never had any trouble picking up the threads; sometimes it seemed that we had never really stopped talking. We talked about many things; but no matter the beginning, we inevitably got around to kids and schools, the Celtics and the Red Sox, and the Phillies. Kids, schools, the Celtics and the Red Sox we shared in common; despite all his efforts, Bennett never really sold me on the Phillies.

During our last time together Bennett made an observation which brought together the two worlds of our passions—schools and sports. As had been the case many times before, we were talking about the role of the school principal. Bennett's perception of that function was open-ended; I don't remember a time that he did not add some new dimension to his understanding of what was required of him as the head of a school.

On this occasion he noted that he had come to think of himself as the manager of a team. In selecting staff and distributing assignments, the principal, like the manager, had to consider all the different tasks, aside from direct classroom work, which the school setting creates and demands. He had to think carefully about who was asked to do what. For all the encouragement of individual effort which self-contained classrooms necessarily require, the total workings of a school cannot be effective without group effort. The principal must, of course, permit teachers the freedom of personal expression; he must also meld the different personalities and styles of members of the staff into a harmonious and cooperating whole. In the language of our metaphor: winning depends on teamwork.

I was struck by Bennett's remarks; so much so that when I got home I wrote him suggesting that we try our hands at a paper which would expand on his idea. That paper never was written; what follows is my effort to do singly what cruel circumstance prevented us from doing together.

The literature of Jewish education teaches at least two things: (1) children in supplementary schools, the setting which engages the majority of children in Jewish schools, learn very little; (2) Jewish schools of all kinds, day and supplementary alike, do not attract and hold youngsters beyond the elementary school level. The recent study conducted by the Board of Jewish Education of Greater New York reports that "... [supplementary] schools do a poor job in increasing Jewish knowledge in all subject areas. They show no success in guiding children towards increased Jewish involvement. And they demonstrate an inability to influence positive growth in Jewish attitudes."[1] That statement is at one with the findings of earlier research.[2] Repeated studies of Jewish school enrollment consistently demonstrate that the enterprise of Jewish education in the United States, as in most Jewish communities around the world, mainly serves children of elementary school age. The overwhelming majority of pupils who enter and complete elementary school do not continue on to a secondary school.[3]

In attempting to understand and explain these seemingly intractable phenomena, Jewish educators generally cite factors outside of the school. The low level of achievement and the high drop-out rate are attributed to the limited amount of time available for Jewish schooling, the competing demands of the public school (particularly of the college oriented secondary school), the pull of leisure time activities, the indifference of parents and community to Jewish learning, and the anti-intellectualism of American society which places little value on learning for its own sake. Only rarely does one hear or read that the school itself might be responsible, in some measure, for the problems highlighted here. Little attention is paid to a study, unfortunately never replicated, which demonstrates that the major reason for "dropping-out" was not

---

1 *Jewish Supplementary Schooling: An Educational System in Need of Change* (Executive Summary), (New York: Board of Jewish Education of Greater New York, 1987), p. 9.
2 A. Dushkin and U. Engleman, *Jewish Education in the United States*, (New York: American Association for Jewish Education, 1959).
3 H. S. Himmelfarb and S. Della Pergola, *Enrollment in Jewish Schools in the Diaspora, Late 1970's*. (Jerusalem: Institute for Contemporary Jewry, Hebrew University, 1982).

insufficient parental interest and support but rather "dissatisfaction with the program of the elementary school."[4]

The tone and character of the explanations offered by Jewish educators as justification of the school's inadequacies are remarkably akin to those employed by public school personnel in schools which have been less than successful in dealing with disadvantaged and culturally deprived children. Principals and teachers alike in these schools rarely hold themselves accountable for pupil failure. The fault, in their view, lies in the child her/himself, the family from which he/she comes, and the impoverished environment which failed to provide the skills and to inculcate the attitudes required for successful coping with the demands of schooling. The very terms *disadvantaged* and *culturally deprived*, with all their negative resonance, lend credence to their position. The rhetoric of excuse, however, does not honestly confront the fact that some "inner city" schools, both in the United States and Europe, succeed in bringing their pupils to respectable, and even higher levels of achievement.[5]

A large and growing body of research helps us to understand why some schools have a greater impact on their students than others. The "effective" school is distinguished by certain defining characteristics absent, in part or altogether, in less successful institutions. Schools which significantly advance the academic progress of their pupils, no matter native capacity or environmental circumstance, are guided by clearly stated goals, a belief in the child's ability to learn, the assumption of responsibility for pupil failure or lack of progress, consistent and systematic monitoring of pupil's work, cooperation and teamwork among teachers and strong instructional leadership. While we do not know the relative influence of each of these aspects of school climate,[6] there is general agreement that instructional leadership, provided by the principal and other administrators, is an absolutely necessary condition.

A portrait of the principal as instructional leader, drawn from the findings of innumerable studies, reveals a distinctive pattern of performance.

1. *Goals and Production Emphasis.* Effective principals are actively involved in setting instructional goals, developing performance standards for students, and expressing the belief that all students can achieve.

2. *Power and Decision Making.* Effective principals are more powerful than their colleagues, especially in the areas of curriculum and instruction. They are also seen as leaders in their districts and are

---

4 E. Jacoby, *A Study of School Continuation and Dropout Following Bar Mitzvah*, (Los Angeles: Institute for Jewish Social Research, University of Judaism and Bureau of Jewish Education, 1969).

5 M. Rutter, et al., *Fifteen Thousand Hours*, (Cambridge: Harvard University Press, 1979).

6 C. S. Anderson, "The Search for School Climate: A Review of the Research," *Review of Educational Research*, 52:3 (Fall, 1982), pp. 368-420.

effective in maintaining the support of parents and the local community.

3. *Management.* Principals in effective schools devote more time to the coordination and management of instruction and are more skilled in instructional matters. They observe their teachers at work, discuss instructional problems, support teachers' efforts to improve, and develop evaluation procedures that assess teacher and student performance. An important part of their leadership role is setting standards, clarifying program and curricular objectives, and sustaining school wide improvement efforts.

4. *Human Relations.* Effective principals recognize the unique styles and needs of teachers and help teachers achieve their own performance goals. They instill a sense of pride in the school among teachers, students, and parents.[7]

The excerpt above stands in sharp, if not dismaying, contrast to information provided by two recent studies in Jewish education. The report of the Board of Jewish Education of Greater New York cited earlier notes that "... the majority of [supplemental school principals] lack the necessary Judaic knowledge, pedagogic expertise, supervisory know-how and the needed time for instructional leadership and staff development."[8]

That datum can be joined to the comments about their work offered by principals, of both day and supplementary schools, who participated in a series of focus groups organized in various cities throughout the country. They felt that

... much of the time they do spend as principals is devoted to necessary but petty administrative details ... they feel overburdened by paper work and seemingly excessive catering to the needs of board members. The net result of the excessive time demands is a mounting frustration with the discrepancy between the time available for serious educational work—such as curriculum planning or teacher supervision and training—and the time necessary to make a significant educational contribution.[9]

There certainly is no reason to quarrel with this description of their work provided by the participating principals. Another section of this same study, however, adds a dimension which is equally important.

Neither the boards which hired them nor, in many instances, the educators themselves were clear about the prerequisites for successful functioning as senior Jewish educators. The lack of standards implied

---

7 S. T. Bossert, "Effective Elementary Schools" in *Reaching for Excellence: An Effective Schools Handbook*, (Washington, D.C.: National Institute of Education, 1985), p. 40.
8 *Jewish Supplementary Schooling, op. cit.*, pp. 7-8.
9 S. M. Cohen and Susan Wall, *Recruiting and Retaining Senior Personnel in Jewish Education: A Focus Group Study in North America*, (Jerusalem: Jewish Education Committee of the Jewish Agency, 1987), p. 22.

the absence of a genuine profession. And the lack of a professional conceptualization of their field had adverse consequences for their self-image and for their relationship with lay leaders.[10]

With this in mind, and even with the danger of sounding cynical, it may not be out of order to question whether, even if given the time, many principals would know how to use it efficiently and effectively.

It would, of course, be foolish to deny that what goes on outside of the Jewish school and in the society which it serves does not affect its ability to function properly. Despite a recent increase in support and a welcome rise in interest, Jewish education still does not enjoy the level of communal backing which is essential to high quality education. Objective circumstance prevents many principals from functioning as they should; declining enrollment and the resultant small schools prevent the creation of conditions conducive to attracting qualified personnel; the still low status of the Jewish educator deters young people from careers in the field. At the same time, understanding the critical role that the principal plays in relation to school effectiveness and holding power has important implications for policy.

There is no question that Jewish education today is marked by a range of activity and level of sophistication which is well beyond anything we have known before. Curricula, textbooks and other teaching aids, teachers centers and in-service training programs are now on a plane thought unattainable not too long ago. These advances, remarkable in many ways, have not, however, been accompanied by a carefully developed strategy for the recruitment, training and retention of principals and other senior personnel. The evidence brought here suggests that failing such a strategy the full potential of much that is innovative and imaginative in Jewish education may never be realized.

---

10 *Ibid*, p. 18.

IV. BENNETT I. SOLOMON: REFLECTIONS & WRITINGS

FROM BENNETT

PERSONAL BELIEFS

My educational objectives are not merely human growth, development and certain universal humanistic values (a la Kohlberg). A sense of Jewish identity, manifested by activity and participation in Jewish experiences (either within the local Jewish community or with Israel), and a concomitant desire for the continuity and preservation of Judaism are my educational goals, as I begin my efforts in Jewish education.

But I am convinced that I will make a significant contribution to this field only if I remember always that these principles must be blended with an educational approach which is primarily concerned with the desires, needs and interests of the children I teach. The challenge is to somehow unite these two philosophical predispositions without compromising either one of them. That is the problem with the Jewish educational system, as I suffered through it and teach within it even today.

The component of the child's interests, desires and enjoyment has been "sold out" in an atmosphere of religious indoctrination. Memorized facts and mechanical skills have become the essence of the elementary Hebrew school experience with little or no cognitive challenge or emotional stimulation. Thus, Hebrew school has become an unpleasant experience, or worse, which has effectively succeeded in turning off the majority of children and parents who come into contact with it.

In relationship to this, the outstanding trait of Conservative educational practice, with which I am most familiar, is its propensity for evading fundamental issues. Whether concerning supernatural revelation versus reason; reason versus emotion; laws and beliefs; God; or the Messiah, the educational process and content do not present a consistent or desirable pattern to the child. And rather than present these issues as open to discussion, question and personal interpretation, the Hebrew school typically presents them as fixed and final convictions which must be accepted as taught.

I maintain that the Hebrew school program, if altered radically in its philosophical rationale, content and practice, can not only excite and motivate young children toward a positive Jewish identity and value system but also serve as the bridge to their parents.

The Cruel Paradox

Clearly, the problems of Jewish education and Jewish life in America today are far too complex to be solved solely through the curriculum of a Hebrew school. Even if a child comes home turned on to Jewish values, ritual and commitment, parents have been known to berate the Hebrew school for making their child too Jewish! All they wanted was preparation for the Bar Mitzvah. Too often, the real success of the Hebrew school has been measured by its lack of success. This cruel paradox—that too much success in school may lead to a *drop* in enrollment or synagogue membership—is the heart of the problem of Judaism in America. And confronting this issue must become the priority of Jewish religious and educational leaders alike.

But until some rationale or perspective, some broader institutional changes or restructuring, can be formulated which will offer both middle aged and young American Jews access to a sense of joy and commitment to the particular moral, religious and educational norms and values of Judaism, we must depend on the Hebrew school to fulfill its potential and meet the challenges facing it. It *can* still make a far more significant contribution than it is doing today.

Winning the Student

The Hebrew school must realize that, realistically, it is an institution which must *win* the favor of its students. Most students come from homes which do not adhere to Jewish law, and very few are exposed to traditional rituals (such as maintaining a Kosher home, observing Jewish holidays and the Sabbath). I am, however, convinced that if the school encourages participation in family rituals or programs communal celebrations it will enhance a sense of belonging and lead to further curiosity about Judaism, as well as fostering moral development and positive feelings towards Judaism.

We can no longer afford the luxury of having Jewish educational practice lag behind general educational theory. We must begin a thorough appraisal of that educational theory and its relevance to the present condition and needs of the American Jewish community. Such an appraisal would lead, I believe, to the creation of an elementary Hebrew school program full of active projects, songs, dances, field trips and general *fun* activities. The only way young children will be motivated to continue their attendance is through pleasant, exciting, informative reinforcing experiences! It is time to change the situation and at least give the child, and Judaism, a fair chance within America!

Reflections II, pp. 4-6, 10, 15-17.

A COLLEAGUE REFLECTS

Joshua Elkin

Today marks the first Yahrzeit of my friend and colleague Bennett Solomon, z"l. This past December when the principals last convened, Bennett was losing his courageous battle against cancer—a battle that he waged for over half a decade.

These are a few of my own recollections of Bennett. I first met him over twenty years ago, but from a distance—at Camp Ramah in the Poconos. Sue Ettinger was also in camp that summer, and they were subsequently married. Bennett was a model product of our movement. His parents gave him a strong orientation to Yiddishkeit and certainly laid the foundation for his career in Jewish education which rapidly unfolded.

About twelve years after that summer in Poconos Ramah, I became director of the Solomon Schechter Day School in Newton, Massachusetts, where Bennett had been a faculty member up to the year prior to my arrival. I just missed his tenure as the Grade 4 General Studies Teacher, but I certainly heard about his work. Even today, there are parents, whose children have long since graduated, who point to Bennett as a decisive influence on their children. He had that gift of the art of teaching. He was positively charismatic. He was profoundly respected.

During those teaching years, he completed his doctorate at Harvard, and he pioneered in the classroom many of his ideas on curriculum integration which represent a permanent legacy to our entire field and to the non-orthodox day school movement in particular. He blended the theoretical and the practical with grace.

While teaching at Schechter, he coordinated much of the development of the first personnel code, doing much to raise the status of the teaching profession, both within that one school and beyond.

His accomplishments at the Cohen-Hillel Academy were even more impressive, and, considering that for most of his tenure he was battling cancer, his performance there was nothing short of remarkable. He took a struggling school and put it permanently on the map. He did so much in such a short period of time—and against so many odds.

Some highlights:
- he attracted an enviable faculty and retained them for many years;
- he took the concepts and the practice of curriculum integration to new heights;
- he (together with his wife Sue's invaluable contribution) developed a model language arts program for the Jewish Day School; and
- he was instrumental in raising funding to establish the Ramat El Curriculum Center dedicated to the development, publishing and dissemination of teacher-created curriculum materials for the Jewish Day School—an enormous undertaking conceived through the profound vision that he possessed.

Finally, and possibly the most grand of all, he envisioned a permanent home for Cohen-Hillel. Between bouts with severe illness, he spearheaded a capital drive for well over two-million dollars that culminated in a new home for Cohen-Hillel, and what a beautiful home it is!

Throughout all of his hard work and his numerous hospital stays because of the cancer, Bennett managed to be a devoted husband and a caring and nurturing father. I have vivid memories of Bennett's exuberance as he talked about Jordan's and Noah's accomplishments in sports. Sports were a passion for Bennett and he made herculean efforts to the very end to "be there" for his two boys as they were developing their physical skills.

I must also recall what a devoted colleague Bennett was. He believed in working collaboratively; he drew his Massachusetts and Rhode Island fellow principals into the Ramat El venture. But even before that, he pushed us to meet together on a regular basis—to share, to support each other, to complain, to find strength in creating and sustaining a network. In many ways, I see our Principals' Council as an outgrowth of Bennett's earlier efforts to achieve a regional network.

Sue Solomon asked that we remember Bennett as someone who believed in making schools exciting for kids. Kids have to be actively involved in projects! He strived to make of his school a "Camp Hillel"—where the best of formal and informal education could be blended together. His ideas on integration were organic to this whole way of thinking.

Sue also told me that Bennett would want to be remembered to his colleagues primarily as someone who was proud to be a Jewish educator. He loved every minute of it. He felt good about this type of work. And he felt that it takes special individuals to be successful in it.

His contribution, his ideas, and his memory—may they be a continuing inspiration for all of us to strive to achieve new heights in all of our Jewish educational endeavors.

I would like to conclude with a story taken from the Midrash recorded both in *Shir Ha-Shirim Rabbah* and *Kohelet Rabbah*.

The Laborers in the Vineyard

When Rabbi Bun, the young son of Rabbi Hiyya, died, Rabbi Zera delivered a eulogy. He took as his text Ecclesiastes 5:11; "A worker's sleep is sweet, whether he has much or little to eat."

I will tell you to whom Rabbi Bun can be compared.

A king had a vineyard. He hired laborers to tend it. Now, there was among the laborers one who worked better than all the others. When the king saw how diligently this laborer worked, he took him by the hand and began to stroll with him up and down.

But when, in the evening, the laborers came to receive their wages, the king paid that man as much as he paid the others. When the other laborers saw this, they complained and said: "Your majesty, while we have labored the whole day long, this man has only worked for two or three hours. Is it right that he should receive the same wages we do?"

But the king replied: "Why are you angry? This man has done as much work in two or three hours as the rest of you have done in a whole day."

Thus, too, Rabbi Bun has accomplished more in the realm of the Torah during his twenty-eight years than a diligent student could ordinarily accomplish in a hundred years [*Shir Ha Shirim Rabbah* 6:2].

So, too, Reb Binyamin ... who accomplished more in the realm of Torah and education in his 36 years than can ordinarily be accomplished in 100.

This talk was delivered December 1, 1988, at the Solomon Schechter Day School Association Biannual Conference. The opening plenum was called the Bennett Solomon Memorial Lecture.

BENNETT I. SOLOMON

OUR MENTOR, OUR COLLEAGUE, OUR FRIEND

Pearl Brenman Greenspan, Laura German Samuels
Marcie Greenfield Simons, Leah Pearl Summers

What I love most here is that my professional life and my person are so mingled. I watch, I teach, I lead, I play ... I am immersed in Hillel. I am blessed by being here.

Dr. Bennett I. Solomon
Principal, Cohen Hillel Academy
1979-1987

We, too, have been blessed. We were blessed because we were touched by the magic of Bennett Solomon, z"l. For eight years, the spirit and energy of this brilliant educator permeated the halls of Cohen Hillel Academy in Marblehead, Massachusetts. We, as faculty members, were privileged to participate in Bennett's vision: the creation of a school where students, parents, and faculty could learn and grow together as committed American Jews.

Working with Bennett was an experience that enriched us not only professionally but personally as well. In his role of principal, Bennett wore many hats. As our mentor, he facilitated our growth by modeling what an exceptional teacher could be and by motivating us to strive beyond our limits. As our colleague, he respected us as peers and worked with us in implementing his dreams for the school. As our friend, he nurtured us and made us smile.

Bennett: Our Mentor

Bennett was our mentor, our wise teacher whom we trusted implicitly. As the school's principal, he set standards of excellence which often seemed impossible to reach. Yet, because Bennett demanded so much of himself, we were continually inspired to make the extra effort, to persevere in spite of fatigue, disillusionment, or burn-out. We strove to emulate him.

Bennett was an intense, exciting and passionate teacher. He transmitted this excitement and passion to us and we, in turn, passed it on to our students. The last faculty meeting which Bennett conducted was a few days before a Reagan-Gorbachev Summit. No one knew it was to be Bennett's last faculty meeting, but he was clearly not feeling well. In spite of his weakness, our meeting was conducted with as much professionalism as any meeting Bennett facilitated. He began by addressing the importance of the upcoming summit. He wanted teachers of all grades and all subjects to discuss it with their students. Pedantic teaching was not Bennett's style. So, instead of mandating this and moving on to the next agenda item, Bennett demonstrated one way to integrate the significance of the summit in our school curriculum.

Bennett taught us a midrash about that week's Torah portion, *Vayishlah*. In this *parashah*, Jacob and Esau, who had been enemies were reunited after twenty years. Jacob was overcome with fear of the unknown. How would his brother greet him? "And Esau ran to meet him, and embraced him, and fell on his neck, and kissed him, and they wept." (Genesis 33:4) Bennett explained the Rabbis' interpretation that God had turned Esau's hate to love. Though each brother continued on his own path, they were, for a moment in time, able to embrace with love.

Bennett questioned, "Might this be possible for the world's two superpowers? The ways of the United States and the Soviet Union are indeed different, but a world of difference need not be void of love." As faculty, excited by our own learning, we were inspired to bring this excitement into our classrooms.

He valued the notion of teacher as facilitator and cherished the idea of students learning through their own discovery. He exemplified this in all of his dealings with the faculty, as a true mentor would. A favorite scholarly pursuit of Bennett's was moral education. He believed so strongly in its importance that he once devoted an entire staff day to it. At that time, Bennett presented us with this scenario based on materials he had studied with Lawrence Kohlberg at Harvard:

> There were two brothers. One was dealing drugs to children. Charges were brought up against him and his brother was called as a witness. The second brother was faced with a dilemma. Should he testify and

be responsible for sending his brother to prison? Or should he lie on the stand knowing that if his brother was acquitted, children would suffer the consequences of drug use and abuse.

Obviously, as the faculty discussed this problem, Bennett knew we would not arrive at a unanimous decision. But that was not his objective. His aim was to stimulate our thinking, to send us to the depths of our souls to confront our most basic human values, and to experience the struggle our students would experience when faced with a moral dilemma. Being a master educator, Bennett achieved these aims.

Bennett played the role of mentor in other ways as well. He never asked his faculty to do anything he was not willing to do himself. As part of a faculty in-service training workshop on report card writing, Bennett joined us in an exercise designed to sharpen our observation and recording skills. He invested us in the process by calling upon two teachers to role-play a situation that could occur in school. He asked them to interact while constructing a puzzle together. The rest of us, including Bennett, recorded our observations and interpretations. We then shared our writing and analyzed the validity, objectivity, and impact these reports might have. Bennett guided us through our discussion, but he was also one of us, learning from his "students" as he hoped we would learn from ours.

We were also Bennett's proteges in an area of great passion for him: the commitment to curricular integration in the Day School. While this permeated everything Bennett touched, two of us wondered if we could possibly bring integration to a new level at Cohen Hillel Academy. We approached Bennett with the idea of a completely integrated second grade, team taught by a general studies and Jewish studies teacher. Bennett had taught in such a program earlier in his career (at the Solomon Schechter Day School of Greater Boston), but it had not yet been done at Cohen Hillel Academy.

Bennett was initially thrilled with the suggestion. Yet he knew this was a major project requiring great commitment on the part of the teachers as well as himself. He was the "integration expert" and could easily have executed all the steps necessary for such an integrated program to succeed. Instead, he wanted this to be an experience which would contribute significantly to our professional development. First, he handed us every journal article he could find about integration in the day school. We had to read and study the research, then return to Bennett for a discussion in which he challenged, stimulated and exhausted us. Once he was convinced that we truly understood the philosophy of integration and its relationship to developmental psychology, we were sent back to work.

We had to prepare a presentation to "sell" our integrated classroom to the school board. Again, it is important to realize that Bennett, who was beloved by the board, could easily have convinced them of the value of this innovative program by himself. But in order that his teachers grow professionally from this experience, he insisted that we present the proposal and the research supporting it. Several meetings followed and outlines were drafted and re-drafted. When the board meeting finally took place, and they unanimously and excitedly accepted the proposal, Bennett was as exhilarated as we were.

However, the process had only just begun. In order for our learning to continue, Bennett set up bimonthly meetings so we could discuss the integrated program. Together we "brainstormed" and hypothesized, we explored and analyzed, and we reached to the depths of our teaching souls to create for the students an exceptional educational experience. For us, too, it was truly the highlight of our professional careers. Not only had we developed an integrated setting worthy of the vision of our principal, but we had also been "led" to that accomplishment though Bennett's mentoring process and the skills he demonstrated.

Bennett: Our Colleague

Bennett was our "boss." In implementing his visions, however, we were colleagues, equals, who together were experimenting with an educational dream. One of the many ways in which Bennett treated his faculty as colleagues was to involve us in the decision-making process. He believed in "process" and seldom handed down decisions without including those involved. Bennett gave his staff the opportunity to exercise control. He did not come to meetings armed with all the answers. He delighted when someone had an idea different from his own. We felt that our opinions mattered.

Bennett was an avid sports fan. To Bennett, the school was a team, and that concept permeated every level of the school. By eagerly sharing decision-making, Bennett created a multi-tiered model of teamwork throughout the school. He met with teachers as an entire faculty and also by subject matter and grade level. Just as he met with faculty, he insisted that faculty members meet with each other. He also encouraged faculty to meet with their students to help them learn to deal with decision-making in their lives. The outcome of this complex process was that faculty members were deeply involved in the life of the school and that children saw adults working together as a team, a model which they learned to emulate.

There were other opportunities when Bennett made sure that his faculty was involved in making decisions. Moving to a new building was a time of great excitement as well as a chance to begin again in a new setting. New space required new routines which, in turn, required new discipline codes. When we first moved to the new building, Bennett conducted several faculty meetings for the sole purpose of defining lunchroom policies, playground rules, and general school behavior. During these meetings, Bennett shared his concerns about discipline and elicited from the faculty their concerns as well. Not only was he was very interested in learning about other schools' established policies, but he valued teacher input from his own faculty in every decision. For example, we asked ourselves: Should children bring their coats with them to lunch? How should milk be served? How should we dispose of trash? After listening to the teachers' concerns and suggestions, he drafted a rough copy of school rules. He then submitted this list to the faculty for final approval before they were written as school policy.

Once the policies were finished, it became the responsibility of each teacher to review the rules with the children. Just as Bennett discussed the issues with the staff, the staff was to discuss the rules with the students. He wanted students to be included in creating the best working and learning environment possible. He believed that if students understood the rationale behind rules, and if teachers constantly took the extra time to get students to think about their behavior, the students would ultimately become responsible for their own behavior and another goal of the school would be met.

Curriculum development was near and dear to Bennett's heart. He saw it as the center of a vibrant, dynamic school. Yet, Bennett did not simply hand down curriculum to teachers. He involved them in its development from beginning to end. He co-founded the Ramat El Jewish Curriculum Center, whose sole purpose was to publish teacher-made materials. Bennett valued teachers' involvement in curriculum development with a special emphasis on their functioning as a team. He always said that a kindergarten teacher had a great deal to offer a junior-high teacher and vice-versa.

One curriculum project that highlighted all of Bennett's philosophies about curriculum development was the school-wide curriculum created on Jerusalem. On the 20th anniversary of the Reunification of Jerusalem, the city was "rebuilt" at school. Bennett made the dream a reality beginning with a faculty "walking tour" through Jerusalem via slides, commentaries and personal experiences. The faculty was involved in every facet of the project and after his innovative and creative introduction, we then brainstormed and shared ideas as to how to rebuild the city.

With every new thought Bennett's enthusiasm grew, and, as was often true, his excitement had a contagious quality and we began developing the curriculum. While group decision making is often a lengthy process, Bennett allowed the faculty, whom he believed were the experts, to discuss, plan and decide the how's, where's and why's together. The Temple was rebuilt, the *shuk* recreated, a "wall" as a place for *tefillot* erected, all in an atmosphere that was dynamic, educational and fun.

Including teachers in so much decision-making as Bennett did and treating them as colleagues required his recognizing and utilizing the strengths of each teacher. Bennett always tried to find a way to "show-off" the faculty. He was proud of our accomplishments. When a faculty member received an award, Bennett was the first one there to take a picture. If someone was asked to lead a workshop at a conference or join a committee in the community, Bennett's response was, "This school is lucky to have you."

He was always searching for a way to develop teachers' talents. For example, if he felt someone had leadership abilities but was afraid to speak publicly, he provided ample opportunities for that person to engage in public speaking helping that person overcome the insecurity and transform a weakness into a strength. If he thought someone would be a good coordinator, he would create a position that tapped that person's organizational skills, once again recognizing the uniqueness of each faculty member.

To Bennett we were colleagues; colleagues for whom he had tremendous respect. Teachers were the professionals. He had great faith that he could trust his faculty to carry out his dreams. He believed in the maxim, "The teachers make the school." He spoke beautifully at the dedication of the new school about the building being only a building, "but it's the teachers who make the school."

Bennett was our leader and we were always proud of that fact. We constantly asked ourselves and continue to ask today, "What would Bennett do in this situation?" What made Hillel such an exciting, dynamic educational institution was not just his extraordinary leadership skills, but the fact that he created an environment where we always felt that we were a team of professional educators. We were always striving to do and to be more than we ever thought possible. We were a team who together experimented with a vision of what education could be.

Bennett: Our Friend

Bennett was not only our leader and partner in pedagogic pursuits, but he was also our friend. There was always a sweet smile, a pat on the back, and a sincere, honest "how are you doing" to start each day. Bennett possessed the wise understanding that our personal and professional lives were inextricably intertwined. He knew only too well how each impacted on the other and he worked hard to help us weave them together positively, efficiently, and meaningfully. He worried about us much like a father worries about his children. He listened to us much like a best buddy listens to his pal's concerns. He advised us much like a counselor guides a client.

We remember so well how much we felt cared for and heard. He always made us feel that our personal concerns were of paramount importance and required immediate attention. When one of our cars "died" on the way to school, he spent much time during that day making contacts trying to find a good honest deal for a new car. When another one of us was grappling with some very difficult life choices, Bennett was there to be a sounding board and support. When that teacher was struggling with the question of making a career change, Bennett verbalized more than once that he would unequivocally support her personal choice if she honestly believed it was the right decision. In his desire to protect us from hurt and disappointment, Bennett would share with us his own growing understanding about financial planning and options for savings. He worried about us. If a teacher was sick, Bennett practiced the mitzvah of *Bikur Holim* and called to offer his get well wishes. On snowy days, when driving was rough, we always received phone calls to see if we arrived home safely.

Bennett was not just our friend; Bennett was everyone's friend. Whether it was the nurse on the hospital ward, the school custodian, or the laborers who constructed our new school building, Bennett was a friend to them all. He showed a genuine interest in who they were as people and not just how they could serve his needs.

During his hospitalization, he worried that his primary care nurse might be working too late and would be overtaxed and overtired. When the custodian had so much to finish to ensure the tidy appearance of the school, Bennett himself would grab a vacuum cleaner and tend to the carpets in the school office. The construction workers who spent months and months at our new school site looked forward to Bennett's bantering as he arrived each day to survey the work. They all liked and respected him because he in turn demonstrated his respect, appreciation, and understanding of them. Once, some of the Black workers at the sight encountered some racial prejudice in the local area. Bennett, irate at the unfairness and injustice of the occurrence, personally telephoned the Chief of Police to register a complaint and demand an apology.

Pirkei Avot, Sayings of our Fathers, was one of Bennett's favorite Judaica sources, because it so closely reflected his moral and ethical standards. Upon meeting Bennett, each of us was able to fulfill one of the *mishnayot* in this wonderful text.

עשה לך רב וקנה לך חבר.

Make for yourself a teacher and acquire for yourself a friend (1:6).

In working with Bennett, we not only acquired a superb mentor, but we also found for ourselves the best of friends.

FROM BENNETT

ON TEACHERS

As the goal of integration has been so clearly emphasized in the Conservative day school, the employment and training of teachers capable of working within a program which integrates the Judaic and the general studies is crucial. Considering the amount of preparation time necessary, it might be too much to expect one teacher to teach both the Judaic and general studies curricula. However, given two teachers—one general education specialist with a strong Jewish background and one Judaic studies specialist who is well versed in reading and language arts, social studies and science—a partnership could be established. The children will appreciate each teacher's expertise, but they will also recognize the interests and abilities the teachers bring to the other subjects dealt with in school.

Dissertation, pp. 112–113.

The availability of full-time teachers for each class of students offers the best opportunity to coordinate instruction and create integrative experiences. The coordinated instruction allows for the mutual reinforcement of basic skills. Major projects such as a bi-lingual class newspaper can be undertaken with the entire class working together throughout the day with both teachers. Trips, plays, cantatas or creative writing sharing sessions could be attended by both teachers. There will also be time for the teachers to plan and carry out integrative experiences throughout the entire curriculum. Even if the teachers do little team-teaching, their presence for the entire day will permit them to interact with one another in front of the students, become familiar with all aspects of the curriculum, and relate to the children in a wide variety of settings.

Dissertation, p. 114.

School-wide faculty meetings and departmental meetings can be devoted to discussion and planning of integrative ideas. Holiday celebrations can be undertaken with all teachers present by scheduling them to overlap the teaching times on both sides of the lunch period. Pursuit of this vital aim of the day school might demand changes in contractual arrangements with the teachers but they must be made so the school can pursue this goal.

Dissertation, p. 116.

ON STUDENTS

For Jewish education, therefore, a well educated or knowledgeable young Jew would not necessarily be the child with the best ability in Hebrew or the most vast accumulation of Jewish historical or Biblical facts, but rather that child who possesses the fundamental means for eventually actualizing what he will learn within his own life.

Interest and enjoyment are basic and legitimate criteria of such an education, but it is the long term value of that experience as it relates to development which is most crucial. An experience is worthwhile only if it contributes to the developmental growth of the child.

Reflections I, p. 15.

The student taught to think as an autonomous individual, to seek evidence for conclusions and to ponder alternatives to actions, will use this capability and tendency in all aspects of life—cognitive, moral, social, religious and aesthetic. But these skills must not be seen as existing alone. Rather, they are crucial to understanding, appreciating and participating in all general and Jewish/religious knowledge and experiences. They must be developed as they are applied to substantive knowledge and authentic and challenging information. This is especially so given the rich Jewish religious tradition which we impart to students within our day school. The achievements of our people and of all human culture will be preserved and advanced only if these processes and this knowledge are embodied in growing minds. Our school, therefore, committed itself to a dynamic idea of educational processes and to a broad conception of educational content.

Curriculum Innovation, pp. 13-14.

ON THE HOME

Yes, the home is vital to the success of Jewish education. But as Dr. Alvin Mars, Educational Director, has been attempting at Beth Shalom, Philadelphia, the school can also successfully create Jewish life experiences. It must if American Judaism is to survive. Children are now going to have to influence their parents towards greater Jewish identification and participation. And even if they don't change their parents, today's Jewish youth must be so influenced by their schools that they will maintain their commitment, even in spite of their parents ...

Judaism must be taught as the "answer to the ultimate personal problems of human existence, and not merely as a way of handling experiences" as Professor Heschel writes. We must begin teaching the Judaism that Rabbi Akiva and Maimonides *knew and lived*, rather than merely the *things* Rabbi Akiva and Maimonides *did or wrote!* ... [A] child should use his Hebrew to extract the finest meaning from our literary heritage, and feel a part of the pulsating Jewish reality that is Israel ... It is up to the American Jewish community to re-order its priorities so that educational matters take precedence over sisterhood fashion shows and Men's Club New Year's dances.

Goals and Objectives, pp. 34-35.

THE COOKIE JAR

Susan Solomon Stibel

The jar sat on a diagonal on the right hand corner of the desk. It was always filled with Sunshine Vienna Finger cookies or chocolate chip cookies and, sometimes, lollipops. Children who came to see its owner were always welcome to take a cookie. Teachers who came into the office knew that they, too, were allowed to share the goodies. The cookie jar belonged to the principal of the school. The principal was Bennett Solomon.

The cookie jar wasn't just any cookie jar. It was an Ernie (of *Sesame Street* fame) cookie jar. It was given to Bennett by his sister, Vicki.

The cookie jar symbolized Bennett's being—his openness, creative energy, sense of humor, philosophy, love of learning and innocent childlike nature.

The Cookie Jar—Ernie ...

In June of 1971 Bennett discovered that his *edah* (unit) counselling assignment at Camp Ramah in the Poconos was to be in the second youngest division called *Sollelim* ("pavers"). The division leader was a graduate student at Temple University in Philadelphia in early childhood education. She felt that the *Sesame Street* characters and program format could be a theme and positive vehicle for teaching campers during the summer. Bennett had never seen *Sesame Street*. However, in the weeks prior to going to camp Bennett began watching the show.

Ernie, Bert, and Grover became his friends. He began to reenact their skits. He fell in love with Ernie, the inquisitive muppet, who always had the silly punch line. Bennett even perfected an imitation of Ernie and began to work on how he could use Ernie educationally at camp. Bennett's sensational imitation became known around camp and suddenly "Ernie" was in demand as MC of camp talent shows, night bunk activities and teaching sessions.

The love affair with Ernie did not diminish. In his senior year of college Bennett bought his first car, a red Volvo. He named it Ernie. Proudly displayed on the dashboard next to the radio was an Ernie finger puppet which was a gift from a student.

As Bennett began his teaching career he used Ernie to teach language, Judaica and social studies. Some of his students even called him Ernie.

When Bennett became principal of Cohen Hillel Academy the first additions to his office were a Muppet poster, a Cookie Monster poster and a little Ernie doll that a friend gave him. Then came the cookie jar.

The Ernie cookie jar. It has an orange face with a broad red grin and a red bulb nose. Ears stick out on each side and big, innocent-looking, egg-shaped eyes with black pupils stare at you. Above them sits a black tuft of hair. The body consists of a blue and red striped jersey with a yellow ribbed collar and cuff. Ernie's folded fingers rest on his belly.

Like Ernie, Bennett possessed the perspective of a child curious with the universe. He was filled with a sense of wonderment. He always advocated for the child. He listened to his students. He took their praise, comments and criticisms seriously and responded honestly and sincerely to them. He often walked through the halls kibitzing with the students and would excuse himself from meetings in order to be with them each morning when they came to school. At faculty meetings he consistently pushed teachers to adapt their teaching to the needs of the student.

He would also model the importance he placed on education. He could be seen sitting on the floor in a kindergarten math class or participating in a junior high Judaica class that was comparing the Declarations of Independence of America and Israel.

The Cookie Jar—Bennett and Kids ...

Parents who came to speak with Bennett were incredulous that the focal points in his office were not his Brandeis and Harvard diplomas, but the Ernie cookie jar and little magnetic game that exemplified the child-based philosophy that Bennett modeled. He demonstrated a childish joy that was easy to observe. He could reach the children where they were, not an easy task for a man six foot two inches tall. He could talk sports or about the space shuttle. He proudly displayed pictures or stories given to him by students.

Bennett made it a priority to meet each prospective student and the student's family. Part of his interview was a private moment with the child. Laughter would be heard coming from the office. A look inside would reveal Bennett in his Ernie character playing the jester with the child trying to straighten him out.

Bennett learned a lot about the child from these few minutes together. He knew that "Ernie" allowed the child to feel relaxed and interact naturally. Of course the child always was allowed a hand in the cookie jar.

His love for children and their growth helped to shape his commitment to integrated learning in a day school education. He felt that a child had to be taught as a whole being, not a fragmented compartmentalized one.

On *Sesame Street*, Ernie always asked Bert, his pal, questions. Like Ernie, Bennett always sought to ask questions rather than supply an answer. He pushed people—children *and adults*—to think. He made people substantiate their ideas and actions. He taught. He modeled.

When Bennett first came to Cohen Hillel Academy as principal his enthusiasm to "put into practice" his philosophy was overwhelming. However, he gently nudged rather than pushed his faculty to understand the type of educational, child-centered, integrated program that he wanted in the school. He did this by modeling particular programs for the teachers such as school-wide song festivals and social studies units. He included faculty in the process of developing every aspect of the curriculum. He helped to mold his faculty by building upon the strengths of each person and encouraging people to share ideas.

The Cookie Jar—Ernie's Sheepish Grin ...

Bennett also possessed a keen sense of humor. He could relieve a tense moment with just the right touch of humor. Several days after many of the parents had assembled desks for the new school and dusted cubbies *ad nauseam*, the school held its opening *Hamishpacha* (PTA) gathering. The multi-purpose room where the people assembled was nowhere near finished. Bennett dealt with the awkwardness of the situation by taking a vote on people's preferences for the interior decor, "How many people prefer these flickering lights to no lights at all?"

And among the students his humor was appreciated. The dress rehearsal for the annual Hanukkah song festival always generated anxiety. On one occasion the rehearsal was particularly long. The students had been standing for a long time. To relieve the tension Bennett sneaked up behind the music teacher and began to conduct wildly a la Danny Kaye. The students could not control their laughter. Every time the music teacher would turn around Bennett would assume a serious posture. However, as soon as the teacher would return to the rehearsal, Bennett would resume his antics. When the teacher realized what was happening, she laughed too.

The Cookie Jar—Always There ...

The cookie jar was constantly being replenished, just as Bennett was always there with new energy for his family, friends, students, faculty, lay people and colleagues. Whenever you went to Bennett for help, he'd find the time to offer an enormous number of suggestions and you'd think he had exhausted his resources. Soon afterwards, however, Bennett would come back to you with even more ideas, more advice and more support.

People rallied around Bennett because he made you feel good about yourself. He made things happen: a new school building for the community, a community *Yom Ha'Atzma'ut* celebration, the Ramat El Curriculum Center, Friends of the Hillel Library, SSDS Principals Conference in Boston. One Jewish educator recently remarked, "I didn't really know Bennett Solomon, but I do know that everything he touched was a success."

There was always access to the cookie jar. There was always access to Bennett. His office door was always open. Phone calls were always returned. His home was open to everyone.

When teachers would come into Bennett's office for a discussion or to shmooze, they were greeted by the atmosphere that the cookie jar helped create. It was actually fun to be in the principal's office. It was a refuge for children and teachers as well, where a tense situation could be relieved by Bennett's humor, you could shoot a basket into the hoop on his door or get a cookie from the cookie jar.

The cookie jar is no longer in the office. It is at home on the counter in the kitchen. Last week the cookie jar broke. It can be mended, fortunately. Perhaps the fine cracks and the chip on the tip of Ernie's head that will remain are appropriate. But the spirit of the cookie jar will continue to flourish—intact and unbroken—among those who shared its contents and its owner.

December, 1989

FROM BENNETT

EPILOGUE

THE TASK IS NOT FINISHED

Rather than seek to communicate a predetermined, fixed view of the world, the day school might attempt to develop individuals able to seek unity for themselves. An "integrat*ed* person" might already have his/her ideas fixed into static positions, albeit they are harmoniously interrelated. New knowledge or novel situations might be perceived as threats to the existing unity.

On the other hand, the "integrat*ing* individual" might perceive each new experience and fact as a challenge to be assimilated into an ever expanding yet unified picture of reality. This integrating process would always remain an unfinished task!

Critical Review, p. 15.